Queen and Country

By the same author

The Royal Jewels
The Windsor Style

Queen and Country

Suzy Menkes

HarperCollins*Publishers*

For my mother, who brought us up in the country

HarperCollins*Publishers*,
77–85 Fulham Palace Road,
Hammersmith, London W6 8JB

Published by HarperCollins*Publishers* 1992
9 8 7 6 5 4 3 2 1

Copyright © Suzy Menkes 1992

A catalogue record for this book
is available from the British Library

ISBN 0 246 13676 6

Set in Linotron Bembo by
Rowland Phototypesetting Ltd,
Bury St Edmunds, Suffolk

Printed and bound in Hong Kong

CONTENTS

PREFACE

THE SEED corn of this book was a newspaper headline: The Queen Goes Green. The story was about the conversion of the royal fleet of limousines to unleaded petrol. The concept – that the Queen is a luxurious urban creature who had suddenly discovered an interest in ecology – is far-fetched to the point of absurdity.

For the Queen *is* green. Her instincts, her interests, her pleasures, her pastimes, her homes and her heart are in the country. She has what one landowner described to me as 'that animal imperviousness to the elements you find in country people'. She also has a farmer's brisk, practical attitude to animals – even if she sets sentimental store by her herd of Jerseys at Windsor in her father's memory. She has a real understanding of stock breeding, and the patience and discipline required to train animals. Watching the Queen working her gun dogs, with absolute concentration and quiet affection, is revealing – not least because only her closed circle know how much time and energy she spends with the labradors, as well as with her brood mares, foals and yearlings.

The Queen is a conservationist in the traditional way that landowners have always preserved their heritage. Prince Philip describes it as 'the stewardship which I believe all responsible landowners feel for their estates'. He is in charge of the private royal farms and as Ranger of Windsor Great Park sets policy at Windsor. 'The urge to improve and to develop the estates is as strong in me as in any of my predecessors,' he says, and his hands-on, mud-on-the-boots interest has enabled him to turn the 20,000 acre (8,000 hectare) estate at Sandringham from what the Duke of Windsor called a 'voracious white elephant' into profit.

Prince Philip was 'green' before the term was invented. He has spent a lifetime working for the environment, and although father and son do not always see eye to eye, Philip's trenchant views must have been a seminal influence on Charles.

The public image of Prince Charles as an ivory-tower intellectual converted to ecology is misleading. In the early stages of my research, I was with the Prince of Wales in France when he was visiting a dairy farm. His pertinent, precise and probing questions about milk yields and EEC quotas made me realize that 'going organic' at Highgrove is not a 'drop-out option for superannuated hippies', as he once described it with self-deprecating irony. As Duke of Cornwall, he may derive 'two-thirds of his income from the udder of a cow' – but he also knows how to handle an automated herringbone milk parlour. I traced the royal Wellington bootsteps through the Council Chamber of the florid Duchy of Cornwall building close by Buckingham Palace, through to Butterleigh folded in the Devon hills to see organic farming put in practice. It is largely, as Highgrove's farm manager David Wilson put it, 'just a return to the ways used fifty years ago, which owed more to husbandry than to chemicals'.

Charles has brought the so-called 'green issues' out of the countryside and into the public arena, talking about bottle banks, aerosols, pollution and conservation, and debating global problems: the destruction of rain forests and of the ozone layer. His practical contribution is rooted in farming, and in the lead away from intensive farming he gives to the agricultural community.

This book is intended as a panorama of royal family life in the country – told as much as possible in their own words. It is about private lives seen inside the

The Queen hacking out at Sandringham during the 1990 New Year holiday. She has 'an animal imperviousness to weather'.

vii

estate perimeters, over the garden walls and through the screens of trees.

If there are revelations, they include the amount of time Prince Charles has spent in the hunting saddle, and what an addiction speed and danger are for him, although neither press nor public seems to appreciate how great is the risk of serious accident. There is a clear parallel with the former Prince of Wales, who became Edward VIII and Duke of Windsor, and who also used jumping and steeplechasing as a wild escape from the straitjacket of protocol. 'If I didn't get the exercise – or have something to take my mind off things – I would go potty,' says Prince Charles of his release through polo-playing – the more acceptable part of his skill on horseback.

Because of the increasing controversy about bloodsports, the hunting fraternity is tight-lipped about the royal enthusiast who has been out with over forty hunts across the country and, as a member of his favourite (the Quorn in Leicestershire), says, 'goes like a bomb'. Hunting is still a traditional part of country life, and I believe Charles when he says that 'even when nothing much happens, I still just love being out.'

When he justifies hunting with vague claims about conserving 'coverts, little woodlands, hedges and similar features', Prince Charles is probably concealing from himself the adrenalin of excitement he feels, the fearful danger he runs, the sexual charge that comes from those wild seven-mile points over the oxers and exhilarating dashes through the Vale of Belvoir. It is the same thrill he gets from ski-ing, and it was interesting to read almost exactly the same pontification about the dangers Prince Charles runs in the mountains as were made about the then Prince of Wales's point-to-point racing and steeplechasing in the 1920s.

I had expected the story to contain more about horses, which figure so large in the public mythology of the country life of the Queen and her family. As Prince Philip once succinctly put it: 'If it doesn't fart or chew grass, she's not interested.' The Queen hacks out a great deal for relaxation, and can often be seen riding with Prince Edward – one of the bonds between royal mother and her youngest son. Yet Andrew, indisputably the Queen's favourite son (her private rooms are peppered with pictures of him), is allergic to horses – physically because they exacerbate his hay fever, psychologically because, like his father, he is a man of the open sea. One of the poignant images is of Prince Philip gazing out to sea across the Wash, from the shepherd's hut he has built on the edge of the Norfolk marshes. As Princess Anne, so much her father's daughter, says of his giving up a naval career to play first mate and second fiddle: 'There has got to be a problem, hasn't there?'

Philip likes his horses all ship-shape and under his control for the four-in-hand carriage driving that he has promoted internationally since, at the age of 50, he gave up polo. He has come to terms with his wife's passion for horses, which started more or less in the cradle. The royal governess Marion Crawford, whom Princess Margaret calls 'that snake' for publishing her observations of royal family life, first met Princess Elizabeth sitting up in bed in her rosebud patterned nightie, 'driving her team' by the cords of her dressing gown.

It is intriguing to see how Queen Mary's arcane interest in genealogy – she could trace all her most obscure European royal relations – has come out in her granddaughter's extensive knowledge of breeding. Although 'HM really doesn't like gossip', she insists on getting her weekly copy of *Horse and Hound*. I watched the Queen, animated, involved, fascinated, as the public never normally sees her, on a film about her racehorses made by Lord Mountbatten's son-in-law, Lord Brabourne, at her own behest. It proved what her racing friends in France had already told me: that the Queen could have made a career as a stud manager. It also showed that, however much British racing circles may criticize 'spivvy' Porchester (her racing manager Lord Carnarvon), the dissappointments on the racecourse, as well as the triumphs, have really been the Queen's own responsibility.

In the paddock, as in so much of the rest of her life, the Queen has been a dutiful daughter, following guidelines on breeding set down by George VI. She has also inherited his deep and abiding love of the country and his desire to escape the trappings of royalty to 'put off the King'.

But I do not underrate the influence of the sturdy, Scottish Strathmore stock of the Queen Mother, which comes out too in Princess Margaret, although she is urban by inclination.

I witnessed the warmth and joy shared by the Queen and her mother when the Queen Mother won the Grand Military Gold Cup at Sandown Park with The Argonaut in 1989 – and her daughter presented her with the cup. I understand much more about the steely character underneath the Queen Mother's marshmallow exterior when I see her at 'the sticks' – Kempton Park or Sandown – checking out the form in the paddock, her face puckered against a cruel wind.

But to know the Queen Mother, you have to go to Scotland – and especially to that impossibly inaccessible Castle of Mey, balanced on the edge of the cliffs, looking out over the Pentland Firth to the shadow of the Orkney islands. Her more sophisticated friends, forced indoors by the 'bracing' winds, say politely that they find Mey 'a teeny bit boring' when 'Queen Elizabeth spends five hours out on the Thurso, fishing in that funny hat with a feather'. Privately, the family say that the castle is an indulgence and, when the time comes, will 'be the first thing to go'. Prince Charles, who prefers the Queen Mother's Birkhall on the Balmoral estate to staying with his parents at the Castle, calls each of his grandmother's homes 'a unique haven of cosiness and character'. They share, among many things, a love of fishing in the whisky-brown waters of the Muick at the bottom of Birkhall's sloping garden.

This book started out to show the links between the monarchy and the land – a tradition that has continued a century after the industrial revolution swept most of Her Majesty's subjects into the cities. 'Many people are now four or more generations removed from anyone who actually worked on the land – and it shows in their attitudes,' says Prince Charles. It is a theme he constantly repeats in his crusade to get people to understand about modern farming, and its organic alternative that follows nature's traditional pace.

Charles is one of a line of royal agriculturalists, starting with 'Farmer George', George III ('He wasn't so mad,' Charles will claim of his ancestor), who did everything right on the royal farms – except to make them pay. From the Duchy of Cornwall archives, I learned how much visionary work Prince Albert did on the royal lands. I also discovered that this man whom I had judged fussy, pedantic and Teutonic, interested only in scientific and agricultural progress, also had an emotional attachment to the countryside: Balmoral's scenery was a reminder of the enchanted forest around the Rosenau hunting lodge of his childhood. His romantic streak – appealing to Victoria – comes out in the magnificent royal dairy at Windsor, which he designed, the last word in both Victorian technology and fancy decor, with its exotic tiles and baroque fountain. Milk still flows from Windsor into milk bottles stamped with EIIR and a crown, although the flow may soon be stemmed by royal money-saving cuts.

For Albert and Victoria, the countryside also stood for something else: the great escape. The historian Elizabeth Longford pointed out to me that the first royal visit to Balmoral was in the Year of Revolutions, 1848, when throughout Europe thrones were tottering and toppling. There is perhaps still, deep down in the subconscious, a desire for a royal bolthole which draws the Queen and her eldest son to Balmoral as it did her father before her. His unconventional brother – the future Duke of Windsor – disliked Balmoral, as did Edward VII, who called it 'a Highland barn of a thousand draughts'. Diana, Princess of Wales, would probably agree.

Because I was determined to create a picture of royal country life – by talking to people, by reading and from my own research and observations – the principal characters imposed themselves on the book as in a novel. I found the Queen and Prince Philip, the Queen Mother and Prince Charles taking centre stage, with other family members playing minor parts. In fact I may not have done justice to the Princess Royal's country lifestyle, partly because her estranged husband Mark Phillips was the farmer at Gatcombe Park, and partly because her story of royal horses and riding has already been written in her own words. Richard, Duke of Gloucester is still struggling to farm the family land and has a strong feeling for ecology; Prince and Princess Michael of Kent run an elegant country home at Nether Lypiatt Manor in Gloucester-shire and ride to hounds in the grand equestrian tradition.

But the shadow play of characters tells its own story. Diana, the most visible royal princess in history, hardly figures. Although, like her hunting-mad sister Sarah and the rest of the Spencers, she was brought up in the country, her adult exercise rituals feature the recreations of urban life: swimming and tennis. (A Highgrove neighbour says that she has never seen Diana in the garden at Highgrove, except with her children or on the way to the swimming pool. The distance between Charles and Diana stems root and branch from the fact that she does not care for the country pursuits which he and his close friends share.

It is to Diana's credit as a mother that, although nervous about riding herself, she has encouraged her children in the saddle, supported them at local gymkhanas, taken them to the Badminton Horse Trials and to watch the Beaufort hounds. She will even take them out at Sandringham to watch their father and grandfather 'bang away', as the Duke of Windsor called the shooting that rained a barrage of cartridges – each with a tiny red crown – on to the royal estates. In spite of a public myth that Diana abhors shooting, she enjoys bumping along in the beaters' wagons.

There are many contradictions in this love affair with the countryside. Prince Charles is both an efficient, modern farmer and a convinced old-fashioned gardener. The deep ties of affection between Charles and his grandmother are confirmed by the walled garden he created at Highgrove. It is almost a carbon copy of the Queen Mother's horticultural style at the Castle of Mey. She mixes flowers and vegetables, growing runner beans and papery sweet peas; he grows a bean tunnel with a carpet of nasturtiums underneath; she asks for coloured cabbages, and he speaks out for them too. She adores old-fashioned fruit trees; he goes into battle to defend the national apple collection.

Yet these family inclinations, and the public pronouncements about conservation, do not prevent 'progress' on the royal estates. A gardening expert called it 'a bloody disgrace' that, in the name of economy, an orchard of Cox's Orange Pippins has been grubbed up at Windsor and peaches and nectarines torn off walls. At Sandringham, the majestic teak glasshouses (built by Edward VII with the proceeds of his Derby winner Persimmon), have recently been demolished and replaced with aluminium-framed greenhouses for commercially-grown carnations.

The royal family is poised between a desire for efficiency and self-sufficiency on the estates, and the need to maintain the heritage. Vast wealth is tied up in the royal lands. The 50,000 acres (20,235 hectares) of the Duchy of

Lancaster are let out to tenant farmers. Their rents and that earned by prime town sites such as the Savoy in London provide much of the Queen's substantial private income. Such assets seem to contradict any need for royal penny pinching and cries of poverty, yet Sandringham's mighty acres require manpower and machinery to harvest them, and Balmoral's tracts of moor and forest demand the fleet of Land-Rovers lined up outside the estate offices.

But what about the royal family at play in the country – not just hunting and fishing but also shooting? I found the chapter about Sandringham the hardest to write, although I was repeatedly told that the pheasants shot there are no longer reared, but wild, and that shooting today is nothing like the big set-piece *battues* of the past, those army manoeuvres of beaters and guns introduced by Prince Albert and elaborated by Edward VII.

Yet it seems almost easier to accept the full-blown Edwardian shooting party than its modern counterpart: the picturesque quality of gnarled tweeds among russet foliage; the social hierarchy as the guns dined grandly in the luncheon tent while the beaters sheltered in the lee of a hayrick with a sandwich; the idea of the private battle expressed as much in the fancy bowler-hatted uniform of the head keeper as in his sergeant-major approach to the terrain.

The truth about royal shooting is that nothing much has changed in recent years, except that lunch is now a simpler affair, moved from a local village hall to the new purpose-built lodge. Sandringham is an anachronism: heavily keepered throughout the year to produce a big bag of game in a brief season, but not, for security reasons, syndicated out to bring in money. Prince Philip shoots regularly, as does Charles and, more surprisingly, Prince Edward. The Queen likes to pick up with her gun dogs, as did her father and grandfather – both excellent shots – before her, and Anne, the Princess Royal, will no doubt continue to do after her. And so it is with the next generation, all of them brought up in an atmosphere of shooting. Anne's son Peter Phillips already goes wildfowling with Prince Philip; William and Harry watch their father and grandfather. Although Diana has no interest in shooting (like Queen Mary and the Duchess of Windsor), her father and grandfather used to shoot with George VI and she goes along with the idea that William and Harry will be brought up to down birds.

How do Prince Philip and Prince Charles, conservationists by conviction, justify the slaughter? The official line is that shooting controls the 'crop', thus restoring the balance of nature, which, as Philip says, is 'a great deal more complex than a simple one-to-one relationship between predator and prey'; and it protects and improves the habitat.

For Balmoral this is a perfectly acceptable, even convincing, argument. Grouse survive only on well-kept heather, and shooting both conserves their habitat and controls a healthy population. Down the road from Balmoral, I witnessed the desert of destruction caused by marauding deer at Mar Lodge – owned, but not wisely maintained, by an American tycoon. To keep the balance the deer must be culled, and every summer the Queen, who is a fine shot, takes her rifle out 'on the hill'. I saw also another side to royal conservation in the nature reserve set up by the Duke of Edinburgh at Loch Muick – the glassy lake with its crofters' cottages which Victoria and Albert made a rural idyll – and where the Queen still calls in to make a cuppa for herself today. In the chapter on 'Balmoral's Outside Days', I have tried to convey the sense of fresh air, freedom and escape from the straitjacket of royal protocol that the Scottish holiday provides.

But shooting at Sandringham? Is there much difference today, except in number, in the 'bright limp carcasses', laid out in rows of 100 in Edwardian times? I have followed the work of the Game Conservancy Trust, and the debates in the *Shooting Times* and *The Field* between estate owners of Prince Charles's generation: the Dukes of Westminster and Roxburghe, and Lord Romsey at Broadlands. These are all friends of the Prince of Wales who talk about being stewards of the land, and who enjoy shooting for its own sake. My conclusion is that Philip especially, but also Charles, enjoy shooting for complex reasons of social background, *bonhomie* among male friends, pleasure in marksmanship and a desire to excel.

Out on the Norfolk marshes where sky and sea blur, I understood better that sense of personal achievement so poetically expounded by Aubrey Buxton, the sportsman naturalist who wrote about George VI as *The King in His Country*. A royal one-to-one with bird and gun is in the same position as Princess Anne on horseback, when, she said, 'The horse is the only one who doesn't know I am royal.'

For the royal family today, the country is an agreeable way of life, as it has always been for the great landowners, and part of their heritage. Compared to the past, royal farmers today set a fine example – but they have effectively reduced the kingdom for which they are directly responsible to a few manageable acres. For Prince Charles, responding to 'the melancholy of February and the thrill of spring' is more natural than putting on a show of pomp; the country and its sports offer him both tranquillity and freedom. For the Queen, the country is neither an idyll nor an escape. It is her real, royal world.

ACKNOWLEDGEMENTS

HM the Queen, for permission to reproduce material from her private collection at Sandringham. HRH Prince Charles, for permission to publish Duchy of Cornwall material. Buckingham Palace: Charles Anson, LVO; John Haslam, LVO; Dickie Arbiter; Kiloran McGrigor. Balmoral Castle: Captain J. R. Wilson. Clarence House: Lt. Col. Sir Martin Gilliat, GCVO MBE. St James's Palace, The Royal Collection: Marcus Bishop. The Estate Office, Sandringham: John Major, FRICS, Land Agent. Windsor Castle, The Royal Library: The Hon. Jane Roberts; Gwyneth Campling. The Duchy of Cornwall: David Landale, Secretary and Keeper of the Records; Kevin Knott, Deputy Secretary; Dr Graham Haslam, formerly Librarian and Archivist; Sir Nicholas Henderson, GCMG, formerly Lord Warden of the Stannaries. The Earl of Carnarvon, KCVO KBE, Her Majesty's Racing Manager. *Farmer's Weekly*. The Game Conservancy Trust. *Horse and Hound*: Michael Clayton, Editor; Caroline Standing. The Duchy of Lancaster. Master of Foxhounds Association: Brian Toon. *The Times*: Simon Jenkins, Editor, for permission to research the archives. Duke and Duchess of Windsor's House, Paris: Mohamed Al-Fayed.

With gratitude to those in England and Scotland, France, Italy and the USA who have helped me anonymously. I respect their privacy and their trust. And warmest thanks to: Hardy Amies; Rosemary and John Berry; Sadie Christie; Michael Cole; Nicholas Coleridge; Duke and Duchess of Devonshire; Roberto Devorik; Jessica Douglas-Home; Marchesa Fiamma di San Giuliano Ferragamo; Fulvia Ferragamo Visconti; Lady Fretwell; Nicholas Haslam; Max Hastings; Barbara and Patrick Hayes; Jean-Louis Dumas-Hermes; Christopher R. Hill; Betty Kenward; Countess of Longford; Jean Muir; Comtesse de Ribes; Baronne Guy de Rothschild; Tony Scase; Sir Roy Strong; Christopher Simon Sykes; Hugo Vickers; Lady Weinberg; Duke of Westminster; Colin Woodhead.

My most grateful thanks to all at HarperCollins, especially to Richard Johnson for his enthusiasm and his patience; to Janice Robertson for fine editing; to Robert Lacey; to Katherine Everett, picture editor, for her unstinting support; to Rosamund Saunders and to Sue Costen; to Maggie Usiskin; to my agent Mike Shaw at Curtis Brown. And, most of all, a debt of gratitude to my family – my husband David and our three sons Gideon, Joshua and Samson – for putting up with so many months mired in the royal mud.

HUNTING

*Prince Charles follows the thrill of the
chase in the hoofprints of
his royal ancestors*

ABOVE: *Prince Charles with Lieutenant-Colonel Sir John Miller, former Crown Equerry, who introduced the Prince to hunting in 1975 when Charles was 26.*

RIGHT: *The picture-postcard English meet at Althorp, Northamptonshire, where the Pytchley hunt was established in 1756 by the first Earl Spencer, an ancestor of Diana, Princess of Wales.*

PRECEDING PAGES: *The Prince of Wales out with the Cheshire. On the far left is Sir John Miller and second left Anna Wallace, a former flame of Prince Charles who 'is as mad about hunting as he is'.*

CHAPTER 1

A-Hunting We Will Go

There is only one cure
For all maladies sure,
That reaches the heart to its core;
'Tis the sound of the horn
On a fine hunting morn,
And where is the heart wishing more?

From 'The Hunting Day', traditional
North Warwickshire hunting song by WILLIAM WILLIAMS

THE BEDROOM window frames the Leicestershire landscape at first light. A pallid chill rises from the dark soil. Bony blackthorn twigs are X-rayed against the filmy background. On the horizon, winter trees and criss-cross timber fences shift into focus. Inside, wisps of warm breath hang in the air, even though, in deference to the heir to the throne, his hosts have set the old central heating boiler into unaccustomed early morning action.

'It was ironic that people were always very grateful when the Prince and his retinue were guests at a country house party in winter,' said Prince Charles's former valet Stephen Barry. 'The host would put the heating on full blast for his arrival. And the only person who didn't appreciate the warmth was the Prince himself . . . He can't abide heat.' Barry noted Charles's increasing enthusiasm for hunting in his unauthorized memoirs.

Prince Charles shares a passion for hunting and a dislike of stuffy rooms with his great-uncle – a former Prince of Wales, then Edward VIII and later Duke of Windsor. 'It was my impulse, whenever I found myself alone, to remove my coat, rip off my tie, loosen my collar and roll up my sleeves – the Duchess likes to describe this process as my "striptease act",' the Duke wrote.

Back in the 1920s, he kept a 'string of hunters' down the road at Melton Mowbray. Charles mostly gets by on horses from the royal stables or by borrowing a mount from his hosts on his frequent days out around the country, 'Since the beginning I have ridden a whole succession of different horses – and I think that has been the best possible thing for my riding,' he says. 'Of course, it can be quite anxious work, to say the least, getting up on a strange horse at the start of the day and not knowing what the hell he is going to be like.'

Melton Mowbray is the focal point of three famous hunts: the Quorn, the Cottesmore and the Belvoir. 'Pronounced "Beaver",' said the Duke of Windsor. 'In the Vale of Belvoir one could gallop for twenty minutes at a stretch without drawing rein.'

'The magic in Leicestershire is still there,' says his great-nephew, for whom the springy turf of the Shires holds a special attraction. Over the last decade, hunting has become a potent, if secret, addiction. During the 1989 season – the

3

Hunting is a potent addiction for Charles who has ridden with more than 40 of the 143 packs of foxhounds in the United Kingdom. 'I always had this longing to try. It seemed such a romantic thing,' he says.

winter months from 1 November until March or April – Charles was hunting for three, four, even five days a week: with the Beaufort or Berkeley near Highgrove; up in the Shires for a Saturday or Wednesday with the Belvoir; Mondays and Fridays with the Quorn.

When he broke his arm at polo the following summer, Charles suffered acute withdrawal symptoms from the saddle. As he lay in hospital at the Queen's Medical Centre in Nottingham recovering from a bone graft operation, Michael Farrin, huntsman with the Quorn since 1969, was summoned to his hospital bedside to talk about the Prince's 'dominant passion'.

Charles was introduced to hunting by Lieutenant-Colonel Sir John Miller, Crown Equerry from 1961 to 1987, the Queen's good friend and a passionate horseman who selected, procured and provided suitable mounts for all the family during his long service at the Royal Mews. He first took Charles – then aged 26 – out to hounds with the Beaufort from Badminton on a drizzling

February day in 1975. The Duke of Beaufort – 'Master' as he was affectionately known throughout the sporting world until his death in 1984 – received a telephone call from the Prince on Sunday, 9 February and arranged a small field of 30 local tenants and farmers for the Monday week.

Afterwards the Duke wrote a jubilant hunting report for *Horse and Hound*, filled with the excitement of the chase as the fox was holloaed across the plough, the hounds found again in kale and ran hard over the brook and along the valley, the hunt ending when both fox and hounds went to earth in an underground cave.

'His Royal Highness rode extremely well, jumping everything that came in the way and was always in the first flight,' said the Duke of Beaufort. 'He rode back to Badminton soaked to the skin.

'He had a hot bath and a good tea, and, driving his own car, set out at 4.30 P.M. for Buckingham Palace . . . I telephoned the next morning to inquire if he was stiff, and was not surprised to hear that he did not wish to be disturbed.'

Prince Charles's creditable performance was a tribute to Princess Anne, who had found her brother a suitable horse and coached him in the riding school at Windsor. Then, said Beaufort, Prince Charles, 'with Princess Anne in command, went out jumping horse fences and hunt jumps with great success in the Dauntsey Valley' (in Wiltshire).

'Princess Anne is a very good judge of horse character and suggested this horse Pinkers which belonged to her mother-in-law,' explains Charles. 'It was a marvellous, sensible old thing, and jumped like anything.' He wrote to Mrs Phillips describing the 'unexpected delight and excitement' of his first day following the hounds.

Hunting was part of country life for Captain Mark Phillips, Anne's now divorced husband, and for his family. It is their hunt-to-ride philosophy which Prince Charles has followed, rather than just joining the social round in Beaufort country where Prince and Princess Michael of Kent cut fine figures.

'I really like hunting for the view, for riding in different places and meeting different people in the field, learning a bit about the countryside,' says Anne, who could be speaking for her brother. 'Curiously enough, I don't go out much now,' she says. 'It wasn't so much a conscious decision to stop, but the fact that I never really had the right horses around at the right time.'

The days are long gone since hunting in the Shires meant an army of servants leading out the second horses, and when social life too was taken at a gallop in country houses stuffed with servants and furnished with luxurious white carpets and tigerskin rugs.

When the Duke of Windsor was an eligible young Prince of Wales, fancy dress parties were held at Craven Lodge, the rambling, red-brick hunting lodge at Melton Mowbray. It was rented out, and there bright young things would swing from the chandeliers. The hunting season in the Shires attracted three royal princes, Harry Duke of Gloucester, his brother George the Duke of Kent and the heir to the throne.

'Intermixed with the local landed gentry . . . was a lively sample of dashing figures,' said the Duke of Windsor. 'Noblemen and noblewomen; wealthy people who had discovered that the stable door was a quick if expensive short cut into society; . . . ladies whose pursuit of the fox was only a phase of an even more intense pursuit of romance.'

Ulrica Murray Smith, who was Joint Master of the Quorn for 26 years, remembers days when the future Edward VIII used to hunt in Leicestershire, staying with his latest flame, Lady Furness. 'Craven Lodge had been madly gay with the smart set all flocking there in the winter,' she said. 'The Princes started the fashion by having a suite there. Parties were apparently given every

Although Diana's sister Lady Sarah McCorquodale is 'as keen as mustard' on hunting, Diana 'doesn't like horses, nor a lot of the people associated with them,' according to Charles's former valet. Recently she has started riding again with her children.

night, and poker played for fabulously high stakes, while gentlemen ran off only too frequently with other gentlemen's wives.'

Hunting then had the glamorous, louche, raffish image that hangs round the polo field today. 'The night air over Melton Mowbray is alive with the sighs of adulterous love,' was the local boast.

Prince Charles is quite alone as he goes through the ritual of dressing for the hunt in front of the bevelled mirror on the door of the massive mahogany wardrobe. Diana may have been the Greek goddess of the Chase, but his eponymous wife does not share his enthusiasm for hunting.

'You don't think it will interfere with his hunting, do you?' asked Captain Ronnie Wallace, Chairman of the Masters of Foxhounds Association and the country's foremost foxhunter, when Prince Charles announced his engagement in 1981.

Diana, brought up to the country life at Park House on the Sandringham estate, broke her arm in a riding accident at the age of eight. Two years later, her pony Romany caught his hoof in a rabbit hole, just as, a century earlier, Edward VII, the squire of Sandringham, had injured his leg tripping over a rabbit hole. Diana came off her stumbling pony, and stayed off. She has hardly been tempted back into the saddle, even to ride with the Queen.

'She doesn't like horses, nor a lot of the people associated with them,' said Stephen Barry. 'One Monday at Highgrove, they'd just sat down to lunch and the Beaufort hunt came through the garden . . . In a flash, the Prince was out of his chair and through the front door to watch them . . . The Princess had come through the kitchen to ask for the food to be kept warm and she seemed very irritated.'

Diana was once persuaded out with the Belvoir, in 1984. She followed the chase not on horseback, but in a Range-Rover, sharing a stirrup cup with other followers, while staying in Leicestershire with her sister Lady Sarah McCorquodale, who keeps up the Spencer family's hunting tradition.

'Sarah's as keen as mustard,' says a fellow hunting enthusiast. 'When it comes to horses, Diana is "the one who got away" in the Spencer family just like Prince Andrew in the royal family.'

Andrew – who has the excuse that horses exacerbate his hay fever – expressed his irritation with the horsey world when a group of friends at Cowes insisted on discussing hunters rather than sailing. 'Horses, horses! I'm sick of hearing about them,' he said. 'Can't you talk about anything else?'

Prince Charles has had memorable rides to hounds with Sarah McCorquodale, out with the Meynell and South Staffs, over the vales below Ashbourne and the stone wall and grass country at the southern end of the Peak District, towards Derbyshire where the Devonshires' estate at Chatsworth is one of his safe havens.

'Derbyshire is wonderful because it has everything from here to the high Meynell country,' the Duchess says.

Now Charles puts on his white cord breeches, the mud splatters from the previous weekend's hunting impeccably brushed and scrubbed away.

'In the early days when he was trying it out, he would ride in jeans and a pair of boots,' said Barry. 'It amused me to think how he had once been so disinterested [sic] in hunting.'

Impeccable clothing was once a hallmark of hunting in the Shires.

'Gentlemen wore scarlet swallow-tail coats with white leather breeches, which they kept from getting a speck of dirt on by wearing a silk apron until they actually mounted their horses,' says Ulrica Murray Smith of the 'faultless' turn-out of the 1920s.

A dashing young Prince Albert, just back from the chase in scarlet hunting boots and velvet jacket, with Queen Victoria in Windsor Castle in 'Modern Times' by Sir Edwin Landseer (1842). Albert is stroking his greyhound Eos and is surrounded by sporting spoils.

Today's followers mostly wear easy-care riding breeches made of modern synthetic fabrics which have revolutionized both maintenance and fit. 'Nowadays there are new materials on the market which are extremely serviceable . . . stretching to mould the contours of the body,' said the Duke of Beaufort. 'These look very smart, always providing the shape underneath is suitable!'

The Duke's heir, his cousin David Somerset – now driven from the saddle by a bad back – wore riding boots with pale pink tops, a tradition with the distinctive Beaufort uniform of blue coat with buff lapels.

'Princess Anne was the first member of the present Royal Family to wear the blue and buff,' the Duke of Beaufort said. The Prince of Wales also wears the Beaufort colours when he hunts from Badminton, as a compliment to his host, and Princess Michael (whose country home is in 'Beaufortshire') has also been granted the right to hunt in the blue and buff. 'She adores hunting even more than her husband and she does look marvellous in her riding clothes,' says a member of the Beaufort. 'When you see her in the saddle, you see why she was nicknamed "the Valkyrie".'

Prince Albert, husband of Queen Victoria, wore a different kind of hunting uniform. His young bride described as 'very picturesque' Albert's scarlet leather boots with a black velvet jacket – the hunt dress of his native Coburg. The English aristocracy sniggered at Albert for looking 'like some foreign tenor' until they saw him get up and go on the hunting field, 'riding like an old hand' as Lord Melbourne's nephew said with surprise.

The riding boots that Charles is pulling on today (secured with the traditional white garter straps) are conventional black with mahogany tops, a

A former Prince of Wales, the future Edward VIII and Duke of Windsor, painted in traditional red hunting coat and silk topper on his hunter Forest Witch by Sir Alfred Munnings.

boot introduced by the Regency dandy Beau Brummell, who would gloss up the leather with boot blacking mixed with peaches and champagne – something that Charles's valet has yet to try.

'My riding boots with "mahogany tops" were not so very different from those of my Georgian forebears,' said the Duke of Windsor. 'Moreover, my hunting coat was very similar in cut to the coat that a gentleman wore in the street in the early nineteenth century.' For hunt balls, the Duke wore the red coat with 'the light blue watered-silk facings of the Quorn'.

Sir John Miller will be wearing out with the Quorn this morning a traditional red coat with hunting buttons. ('Please, not "pink" though scarlet is acceptable,' said the Duke of Beaufort.) But for Prince Charles, the former Crown Equerry created something special: a dark blue hunting coat with crimson collar and cuffs, smart but more discreet than the red coat for a sport that is increasingly controversial. It is based on the Windsor Uniform adopted by the Hanoverian King George III and his court. 'There are paintings of the King, hunting with the Buck Hounds in the Great Park, dressed in this blue coat with red collar and cuffs,' the Duke of Windsor said.

Charles's coat has his Prince of Wales crest on the buttons, rather than George III's Garter Star. As Prince Philip explained to his son, these solve the problem of how to respond courteously to gifts of buttons on each visit to a new hunt: better to wear none than make an invidious choice. It is not a new problem. In the Duke of Windsor's old home in Paris, there are drawers filled with sets of buttons from the Quorn and the Cottesmore, alongside other delicately detailed crests from more obscure hunts.

'I selected some of my old regimental and hunt buttons, which I had sewn onto my sports jackets,' said the Duke, who also broke with convention by having a sleeveless sweater knitted up in yellow 'to take the place of the thick buttoned waistcoat that I never found comfortable for hunting'.

Clothes are a crucial part of the hunting code, a badge of office, sometimes a mark of personal eccentricity or distinction. For his first day out with the Beaufort, Charles was obliged to wear an ordinary hacking jacket. 'He has no hunting clothes, so wore his polo boots, brown breeches, tweed jacket and a bowler hat,' said the Duke of Beaufort. 'He looked very smart, with a well tied hunting tie and a gold pin.'

The tweed jacket has a place and a name of its own in hunting circles. It is worn for cub-hunting, before the season proper starts at the beginning of November and is universally known as 'rat catcher' garb.

'Hello, been rat-catching?' the punctilious George V asked a friend dressed in casual tweeds in the country, and the name has stuck. Even Prince William and his brother Harry, brought up in bomber jackets and sweatshirts like other children, revert to horsey type in tweed jackets when joining the pony club meets or watching the hounds at Badminton.

Why does riding to hounds have such a mystique of dress?

'Clothes are part of the ritual of hunting,' says a lady who hunts in royal Gloucestershire. 'Everything is laid out the night before. There is the tension in the morning to get everything exactly so. Then, when you come back, everything from the hunting tie downwards is spattered with mud or with green from the leaves or marked by bark where you bump into the trees.'

Round his neck, Charles wraps his pristine white hunting tie fastened with a crested gold hunting pin. On his head is a deep-crowned ink-blue velvet cap. A cap? Not the dashing top hat he wore in the field at first? Not the especially reinforced hunting hat, with layers of calico cloth dipped in shellac and a hard-hat skull cap inside, made by Patey's at Elephant and Castle in South London in order to protect the royal head?

Pictures prove that the royal family has always worn a top hat in the saddle, from the archive photographs of Princess Alexandra in tip-tilted topper above an elegant riding habit, to the Munnings portrait of the Duke of Windsor as Prince of Wales, in scarlet swallow-tailed coat and liquorice black hat, painted

Prince Charles in his hunting coat adapted from the Windsor Uniform of George III: dark blue coat with crimson collar and cuffs and Prince of Wales crest buttons. For safety reasons he wears a domed velvet cap reinforced on the crown.

in profile on his hunter Forest Witch. 'The Prince of Wales always wore his top hat at quite an angle on the side of his head,' says Mrs Murray Smith of his turn-out in the 1920s.

Sir John Miller will still be riding out this morning in his traditional silk topper above the white moustache. But his protégé Prince Charles has decided to take wise precautions, and even fastens his cap with a flesh-coloured chin-strap, dismissed with contempt in the Shires as 'pure Pony Club'.

'If I wear a chinstrap playing polo why on earth should I abandon it in the hunting field where I jump fences?' Charles asks.

'Prince Charles was not only demonstrating that his responsibilities in life made it necessary for him to adopt a commonsense attitude to headgear, he was also giving a valuable lead in an area where the medical profession was still endeavouring to persuade people to behave sensibly in protecting their heads whilst riding horses,' said Michael Clayton, Editor of *Horse and Hound*. ('My paper,' says the Queen of the weekly magazine that she awaits eagerly each Thursday.) 'Prince Charles was among the first to show a sensible regard for head safety by wearing a chinstrap with a modern riding cap in the hunting field,' said Clayton, who believes this in no way demonstrates 'a "cissy" approach'.

In general, however, and despite breaking his arm in action at the age of 40, Charles dismisses the dangers of both polo and the hunting field. 'In any case, what is dangerous?' asks his father, who has been risking his neck at four-in-hand carriage driving for more than twenty years. 'There are some people who are not to be trusted with a bicycle.'

This velvet dome now strapped onto the royal head was inspired by the helmet of the Pytchley, the Northamptonshire hunt established in 1756 by Diana's ancestor, the first Earl Spencer. A tip over the oxers – the thorn-and-rail cattle fences – has unseated fine horsemen, including Prince Charles, who had two falls when he came out with the Pytchley following a meet at Ashby St Legers in December 1977.

The Pytchley country also unseated the future King George VI in December 1929, when Bertie was Duke of York. 'He won't hurt himself here. It's all plough,' said the Prince of Wales, who had introduced Bertie to hunting but soon found that his brother was a natural rider and had a much finer seat on a horse than he himself.

Both had been brought up to ride to hounds in the family tradition. 'We were all taught to ride at an early age; and as soon as we could jump fences without falling off, my father sent us out hunting with the West Norfolk Hounds,' the Duke of Windsor said.

While his brother went on to chase foxes and ladies in Leicestershire, the Duke of York hunted enthusiastically with the Pytchley. He took the Old House at Guilsborough in Northamptonshire for the 1923 winter hunting season, after his marriage to Lady Elizabeth Bowes Lyon. 'She rides and goes well to hounds, although she has not hunted as much as she would have liked,' claimed a contemporary of the Scottish earl's daughter who was destined to become Queen Mother.

But the natural succession from one royal generation to another was broken when the future George VI was forced to sell his hunters in the Depression of the 1930s. 'I must tell you the tragic news that I am going to sell all my horses at Leicester on October 31st. It is very sad for me as I really do enjoy my hunting,' he told the dealer Bert Drage in 1931.

The future Queen Elizabeth II had her first encounter with hunting as a follower in 1931, when her parents had taken Naseby Hall in Pytchley country. 'The Princess Elizabeth, with her mother holding the pony, was in the corner of Broughton covert, when the fox . . . passed right under the nose of the Princess's pony and jumped onto a wall,' said Captain George Drummond, who had taught Bertie and his older brother to ride to hounds.

'Hounds had not been long in the covert before they spoke, and a minute or two later a fox jumped onto the wall not twenty yards from her Royal Highness,' said Guy Paget of that April day. 'He gave her a good look over, and then crossed the field, so she was able to see the whole thing, fox, hounds, and horsemen, for several fields.'

Although his parents never hunted themselves, Charles too was introduced to the sport as a child. A royal hunting tradition had been established at Sandringham in the grand style by the future Edward VII, who would even serve the hunt breakfast in Sandringham's dining room. In 1863, the royal squire drove to Snettisham to ride to hounds with the West Norfolk and found the entire village decked out and filled with spectators to see him and his new bride Princess Alexandra.

'A characteristic reception was given them by the country gentry and peasantry, huntsmen gathering in their scarlet uniforms, while some 200 school children, strewing flowers and bearing flags, appeared to hail the Princess,' said Louise Cresswell, a tenant of Sandringham's Appleton Farm.

'I hoped the poor fox would get away,' admitted the soft-hearted Princess Alexandra.

Nearly a century later, Prince Charles attended a meet of the same West Norfolk hounds with his mother and grandmother, at Harpley Dams, near Sandringham, in January 1955. The Queen and the Queen Mother watched the six-year-old Prince Charles sit astride the Master's hunter. It was a seminal experience for Charles.

'I was taken to a meet there, or several, and I remember the extraordinary effect that it had when I heard the hounds and the horn,' he says. 'I have never forgotten the effect it had on me, so I always had this longing to try. It seemed such a romantic thing.'

Why then did it take him 20 years?

'I dare say that if my parents had been particularly keen on hunting, I would have gone into it from a much earlier age,' he says. Charles encouraged his own children, William and Harry, to go out with the junior Beaufort in the autumn of 1990 during their half term holiday.

After William's head was injured in an accident at school, he has been discouraged from taking risks in the saddle, but Prince Charles took out his younger son hunting during the Sandringham holiday in January 1992.

'Harry's the one who is a devil in the saddle,' says a Gloucestershire local. 'He's ready to jump anything. He'll be out to hounds with no stopping him.'

Charles picks up his whip – a cutting whip rather than the conventional hunting whip with a lash – and inspects himself in the mirror from the top of his velvet cap to his boots' shiny toes.

He may well be pleased with what he sees. But he may also remember the words of R. E. Egerton Warburton, who published *Hunting Songs* in 1883.

Prince Charles at a Quorn cross-country event wearing his white hunting tie. The Prince of Wales feathers are engraved on his crook.

> T'aint the red coat makes the rider
> Leathers, boots nor yet the cap.
> They who come their coats to show, they
> Better were at home in bed;
> What of hounds and hunting know they?
> Nothing else but 'go ahead'.

The castanet clatter of hoofs on the road reverberates through Old Dalby as the Quorn's followers edge past the flintstone church, up the hill and left to the turkey farm, where the hunt can expect a good send-off – sausage rolls laid out on a trestle table and, on a silver tray, thimble-sized glasses of sherry.

ABOVE: *Prince Charles, his grandmother and Princess Anne with the West Norfolk hounds at Harpley Dams, near Sandringham, in January 1955. 'I remember the extraordinary effect that it had when I heard the hounds and the horn,' he says.*

ABOVE RIGHT: *The Queen and the Queen Mother, with Prince Edward and his cousin Lady Sarah Armstrong-Jones, among the Beaufort hounds.*

Before hunting, the future Edward VIII was said to 'like a stirrup cup'. Charles is not much of a drinker, but a tot of Sir John Miller's whisky once had a dramatic effect, when he was hunting in the Duke of Buccleuch's country, up the wild Scottish hills near Hawick and over the craggy dykes. In a fit of bravado, the Prince took a gate on the Buccleuch estate – and demolished it. (Its replacement has been named 'The Prince of Wales gate'.) He was introduced by the Duke of Northumberland to a 'Percy special', 'an invigorating cocktail of cherry brandy and whisky', when following the Percy in 1976. And today the Prince sometimes carries in his hip flask a fortifying brew of gin and cherry brandy – a little liquid warmth to stave off winter.

This morning the narrow country roads in Leicestershire are already lined with cars, metal glinting through the sparse hedgerows in the sudden watery sunshine. This press of sightseers is nothing new. When Princess Alexandra was in the saddle at Sandringham, 'two hundred carriages and five hundred horsemen blocked the roads, with such crowds afoot that the sport was unrewarding'.

The Quorn, with its smart Shire reputation, attracts a large field, especially for the Monday and Friday country packed with fences to jump, but also for the wilder Tuesday terrain and for the Saturday country with its fences,

Prince William with his brother Harry at Badminton House near Bath with the Beaufort hounds in May 1991. On the right is Lady Gabriella Windsor, daughter of Prince and Princess Michael of Kent who hunt with the Beaufort.

woods and scattering of plough. Between the ranks of supporting vehicles today will come 120 mounted followers, hacking to the meet.

'I have met more farmers, and more ordinary British blokes than in any other exercise or sport that I have ever done,' says Charles, who has charted the English countryside on horseback since he took up hunting in 1975. He has ridden with more than 40 of the 193 packs of foxhounds in the United Kingdom, from the black and tan, booming-voiced foxhounds in Dumfriesshire to the huge fences of the Pytchley and the rolling grassland of Sir Watkin Williams-Wynn's country on the Welsh borders.

'He has a friendly word for everyone, whether they are on horse or on foot,' says Ulrica Murray Smith.

Through hunting, including meets on his own Duchy of Cornwall land in Cornwall, Devonshire and Wiltshire, Charles has forged friendships and made uncontrived contact with ordinary people, just as his great-uncle did before him. 'Because my official life was already ridden with formality, I instinctively sought relaxation in company where, though there was no lack of respect for my position, there was no tedious standing on ceremony,' said the future Duke of Windsor.

In the 1920s, when protocol was as rigid as the caked furrows this winter morning, that former Prince of Wales made a fast friend of Major 'Fruity' Metcalfe, who behaved 'not as though I were a prince, but as though I were a ordinary human being like himself'. 'Once, riding beside me in the hunting field, needing to light a cigarette . . . he light-heartedly struck a match on the sole of my boot – an impulsive and characteristic gesture which amused and delighted me,' said England's future King.

Prince Charles's close hunting friend is Brigadier Andrew Parker Bowles, a career officer in the Household Cavalry, formerly commander of Knightsbridge Barracks, and now in charge of the Army's horses and sniffer dogs – his nickname is 'chief barker'. He lives near Badminton with his wife Camilla who is Charles's soul mate, confidante and best friend, and shares the Prince's passion for country pursuits.

'Like most of the Prince's friends they lead a low profile horsey life,' said Stephen Barry of the Parker Bowleses.

Friends made in the hunting field include James Teacher, a former Joint Master of the Quorn, and his wife Chloe; the Quorn's huntsman Michael Farrin; Jim Webster, whom Charles met when he was hunting the Belvoir; and Brian Gupwell, huntsman of the Beaufort until the old Duke's death.

The Quorn meet this morning makes a merry splash of colour, the red coats of Joint Master and of whipper-in standing out against the dung brown furrows that unroll to a grassy horizon – the turf that is the joy of hunting in Leicestershire.

'I can still hear Harold Nutting's voice of incredulous horror asking "No – Where?" when I remarked that I had seen a ploughed field in the Quorn Friday country,' says Ulrica Murray Smith. Nutting was Master of the Quorn between 1930 and 1940.

'Those apparently carefree and wirefree years between the two wars,' says Charles. He believes that hunting helps conservation, preserving the traditional broken-up British landscape that might otherwise be uniformly ploughed and turned into a vast agricultural prairie.

Here is Lady Margaret Fortescue, still riding side-saddle, as Ulrica Murray Smith remembers the ladies in the 1920s 'with beautifully cut habits, top hats, or occasionally bowlers, all with veils'. Princess Alexandra was the acme of Edwardian elegance in a velvet riding habit gathered to the right, because rheumatic fever had stiffened her right knee, obliging her to have her pommel moved to the 'offside'. The royal family album shows Lady Elizabeth Bowes Lyon, the future Queen Mother, riding side-saddle on her Shetland pony Bobs at the age of nine.

Clustering round Michael Farrin are the hounds – a pack bred for the scent and the chase. They quiver with taut energy, straining forward slightly on straight forelegs. Among the foxhunters who feel for the horse, the ride and the jumping, there are hound men who enjoy the rapport with the highly trained hounds, brought to a peak of fitness during the autumn cub-hunting season and now capable of running on a scent for miles at a stretch.

Prince Charles, brought up to see his mother meticulously training her gun dogs, respects the disciplined energy of the Quorn pack. 'No one seems happier out with hounds than Prince Charles,' says Ulrica Murray Smith. 'He enjoys watching hounds work.'

Sporting dogs are part of royal family life. For the young Queen Victoria, among her earliest memories of Albert was his arrival from Coburg with his silver-streaked black greyhound Eos. 'How many recollections are linked with her! She was my companion from the fourteenth to my twenty-fifth year, a symbol therefore of the best and fairest section of my life,' Prince Albert said to his grandmother after the dog's death.

Princess Anne made one of the distinctive black and tan Dumfriesshire foxhounds – a bitch called Pleasure – part of the household at Gatcombe Park, her Gloucestershire home. 'One of the most intelligent dogs I've ever had the misfortune to meet,' said Anne's former husband Mark Phillips. 'Her low cunning was almost unbelievable. At Gatcombe, she became a great visitor . . . We'd try to stop her going off, but she'd wander out of the house as if she was only going to spend a penny . . . then she'd get to the corner – and be gone like a lamplighter.' When Pleasure died, Princess Anne was given another hound, Random, by the Dumfriesshire hunt.

Charles is greeting the terrier man, whose Jack Russell – a breed named after the nineteenth-century West Country hunting parson John Russell – may be called on to bolt the fox if it goes to earth. This procedure caused nationwide controversy in November 1991, when the Quorn's terriermen were accused of digging and despatching foxes during cub-hunting – allegedly breaking the Masters of Foxhounds Association's rules.

The Prince's own Jack Russell terrier, Tigger, given to him in 1986 by his gardening friend Lady Salisbury, has been left at home. Sarah, Duchess of York had another of the same breed called Bendicks (after the chocolate mints) which was a gift from her now estranged husband when she was expecting their first daughter Beatrice, and Andrew was off to sea.

During the summer months the hound puppies are physically strengthened by being taken out to walk and trained by cub-hunting. At that stage the pack, as the Duke of Beaufort said, is 'made or marred'. So far Prince Charles has contributed by judging form at a puppy show each hunt holds annually, but Mrs Murray Smith thinks back nostalgically to the 1930s, when the Quorn's kennel records show the royal family playing a more active role. 'The late Duke of Gloucester walked puppies that year,' she says. 'And before that both he and the Prince of Wales (the late Duke of Windsor) had walked them. An idea comes to my mind – but perhaps not!' The redoubtable huntswoman would be delighted if Prince Charles offered to 'board out' a hound puppy at Highgrove.

The field is silent, tense, waiting for the hounds to find as they are put into the covert for the first draw. 'It really thrilled me as a child: the sound of a horn or hearing the hounds sent tingles up and down my spine. I just knew I would have to do it one day,' says Charles.

And here is the sweet cry of the hounds, as one speaks and others crash round the covert taking up the yelping chorus. A fox bolts from Grimston Gorse in a russet streak, marked by a holloa from a foot follower and the twang of the horn. Huntsman Farrin and 21 half couple – hounds are traditionally leashed together and always counted in pairs – swing away on the line through Saxelby Wood and by the road leading to the Welby Osier Beds. The field stampedes forward; twigs explode under trampling hoofs; a thudding, rhythmic gallop like gunfire shakes the hard ground.

'When you first visit the Quorn you can't help feeling, while being trampled in the rush, that the majority of the field are still in training for one of Wellington's campaigns!' Prince Charles has commented. He once admitted to Lady Longford that he would like to have taken part in a cavalry charge.

One distinguished rider will meet her Waterloo now as the thrusters push towards a narrow gap in the hedge in a confusion of chestnut, bay and grey. 'The only difficulty being to keep your head while others in the vicinity tend to be losing theirs!' says Charles.

Hounds are running hard and two riders are together taking a fly fence, the kind that can be cleared from a gallop. Four erect ears and two neatly plaited manes are silhouetted like shadow pictures against feathery clouds.

'I have been one of six riders taking the same fence abreast – a wonderful

Prince Charles prefers riding his own hunters, but he often borrows mounts. 'It can be quite anxious work . . . getting up on a strange horse at the start of the day and not knowing what the hell he is going to be like,' he says.

feeling,' the Duke of Windsor wrote of the soaring rhythm of the chase.

'It is like the start of the Grand National,' says Charles. 'I had never seen anything like it, everyone pushing and shoving. It was terrifying to start with . . . going for a fence you get knocked over. Now I know nearly everyone I know how to cope.'

'Push on, Sir, push on,' cry eager voices, knowing that the Prince of Wales should be up front now that they have hit the grass and the hounds are singing to the scent.

'Ah well,' said a rueful Prince Charles when he was out with the Belvoir and trying to jostle into position at a jump, 'I just wasn't brought up to barge.'

For Charles – under private pressure from family and advisors to be 'sensible', and under public scrutiny if he falls – it seems wisest to hold back and avoid a 'nasty'. 'My view is that there is always an opportunity for "dash and fire", if you have a reasonable horse, once you have got going,' he says. 'But displaying it in the gateway can be somewhat hazardous to all!'

Now they are sweeping past the Broughton Lodges, up and over the Nottingham turnpike to the Smite and into Belvoir country. It is time to fight for position, to gallop flat out across the grass, soar over the fences and join the first flight. But keeping up with the professionals has caused Charles a few tumbles over the years. 'Trying to follow that Ian Farquhar, for instance,' says Charles of the former Joint Master of the Bicester and now Joint Master of the Beaufort. 'That fellow will jump *anything*.'

Staying near hounds with the Quorn today, up here at the sharp end of the hunt, beside whipper-in Charles Watts, requires a high degree of skill, a strong nerve – and a good horse. Prince Charles is riding Reflection, the compact strawberry roan hunter mare he acquired from the Guards' Saddle Club at Melton Mowbray. Together they take fences in perfect stride: hold, kick and over a thorn hedge; first and fast over the iron gate; slipping reins at a drop fence 'like a real Meltonian', as they say in these parts. He has a secure seat and does not, like his royal forebear, 'point' his horse at a fence and sit back.

'Why doesn't my son ride like a gentleman?' George V asked 'Fruity' Metcalfe.

'Because he does not have Your Majesty's hands,' was Major Metcalfe's reply. Anne's hands make her a better natural rider than her brother Charles. 'Strong workmanlike hands – equally good for driving or riding,' says Anne's good friend Jackie Stewart, the former Grand Prix racing driver.

Hunting gossips inquire why Prince Charles – better placed financially than most these days to invest in really good horses – should further risk his neck with a make-do policy of borrowing. It has taken all Sir John Miller's ingenuity, powers of persuasion and military training to marshal the horses that will get Prince Charles to the front rank in so many disparate hunts.

'To be able to go to the top of the hunt, not only on his own horses, but on other people's, is quite unique,' said a famous early Master of the Quorn, Major Algernon Burnaby, of Charles's grandfather, the future George VI.

Charles's own hunters have included Mexico, Reflection, Collingwood and Princess Anne's favourite, Candlewick (on which Charles sat for an equestrian portrait). Then there was Highlight, the big 18-hand thoroughbred mare owned by a Nottinghamshire farmer who hunts with the Quorn and let Prince Charles have her on loan. Charles loved Highlight so dearly that she received a Christmas card from his ski-ing holiday.

Now he is galloping on Reflection across the grassy pasture at Muxlow, as hard as he would go when out team-chasing – the cross-country version of the point-to-point to which he was introduced by his friends Lord and Lady Tollemache. In 1979, he was invited to join the Ratcatchers team by its captain David Tatlow.

'You wouldn't mind going over the wire with him,' said Tatlow of his royal team member. 'He really kicked on, and showed us what he is made of. That TV programme *Spitting Image* gives Prince Charles a lot of stick for being "wet". They just don't know what they are talking about . . . I tell you, Prince Charles is a man's man.'

As Charles rides to hounds, the steely concentration of mind, the physical force of the wind rushing past the ears, tearing at the thick cloth of his coat until it opens in a peacock fan at the back, offer an exhilarating escape from the tight boundaries of royal life.

This sense of freedom in speed, exercise and danger, is the real attraction of hunting for Prince Charles – as it was for his royal ancestor before him. 'Had I been of a studious nature, I might have sought refreshment in highbrow circles . . . But it so happens that I prefer physical to intellectual exercise,' said the Duke of Windsor. 'In the hunting field I could forget my round of duties. I was too busy riding my horse and scanning the next fence for a place to jump to worry over my next engagement or my next speech.'

17

There are other ways of breaking out of the royal straitjacket. 'That flying descent was exhilarating beyond description,' said the future Edward VIII of a switch-back bicycle ride from Sandringham to the railway station at Wolferton. 'The most exciting part of the ride was down a steep hill, with crossroads at the bottom. Arriving at the crest, I would crouch down over the handle bars as racing cyclists do; then . . . I would race downhill with Mary and Bertie tearing along behind.'

In the hunting field, the sense of wild escape was expressed in the words of Jorrocks, the wisecracking cockney character invented by the writer Robert Smith Surtees (1803–64):

> NOW, vere are all your sorrows and your cares,
> ye gloomy souls? . . .
> One Holloo has dispelled them all.

The dog fox is providing remarkable runs across the springy turf by Parson's Thorns; up to the brow where tufts of grey-green grass merge with the winter sky; and then a wild dash downhill on a screaming scent into the valley.

'Like a swallow on a summer evening' was the description of Prince Albert,

out to hounds in the Vale of Belvoir with the Duke of Rutland in 1843. His swooping ride won him the admiration of the local gentry who had previously dismissed him as an effete German princeling.

'Albert's riding so boldly and hard has made such a sensation that it has been written about all over the country,' wrote Queen Victoria to her Uncle Leopold in Belgium. 'And they make much more of it than if he had done some great act.'

He was not the only royal prince to make a name for bravado on the hunting field. 'Come back, young feller,' Major Burnaby would cry, when a foxhunter rode wildly in the 1920s. 'Who do you think you are, the Prince of Wales?'

'He went like a bomb,' says Ulrica Murray Smith of the future Edward VIII. 'As does his great-nephew now.'

Prince Charles is taking with ease a timber fence at Parson's Thorns.

'Bloody Hell!' said the Prince when faced in 1977 with a thorn hedge with ditch and deep drop in Portman Vale in Dorset. The notorious jump has been called by that name ever since.

For Charles, learning to take every obstacle in his stride has been a personal triumph, part of a character-building exercise in which his determination has

LEFT: *Charles at 'the sharp end' of the hunt when he is ahead of the mounted field, taking the fences in his own stride. His sister Anne, the Princess Royal, helped him to overcome his early fears of jumping.*

BELOW: *The future Duke of Windsor out with the Pytchley, by Cecil Aldin. 'Why doesn't my son ride like a gentleman?' complained his father, George V, of the Prince of Wales's untidy seat.*

'Jokes about the Prince of Wales falling off his horse became commonplace in American vaudeville,' said the future Duke of Windsor. Charles has taken a few tumbles, including jumping into a bog when out with the Quorn.

overcome lack of natural prowess. As a child, his sister Anne outclassed him in the saddle, just as Harry today rides more fearlessly than William.

'The whole idea of taking off scared me stiff in those days,' Charles admits of his childhood riding Bandit, a small grey pony belonging to Sir John Miller's sister, Cynthia Pitman. Bandit's habit of standing up on its hind legs made the Prince nervous.

'Not being nearly as brave as my sister – which very often happens – I rather got put off,' he says. A similar situation had occurred among George V's children. Princess Mary (like Anne, one girl in a family of boys) outrode her brothers. 'Loving horses, she rode better than either Bertie or I,' admitted the Duke of Windsor. 'Her yellow curls concealed a fearlessness that commanded our respect.'

Charles says the same about Anne. 'My sister was always far better, far keener and far more energetic than I was. Quite a lot of the time I was petrified. She used to hurtle past me, galloping flat out. My pony would go hurtling after her and I'd be yelling and screaming at her to stop.'

Anne, now Princess Royal, brushes off tales of her derring-do. 'My nerves,' she says, 'are a mixture of total fright and the fear of total incompetence.'

The hunting field is a good place to learn to overcome fear – which is why it has always been a popular training ground for army officers. 'There is little doubt that people will do things when they are hunting that they would never consider in cold blood,' said Beaufort. 'It is almost as if they had a shot of some sort of drug that dulls their normal fears.'

Michael Farrin is casting the hounds, and there is a sudden, unexpected moment of stillness, high up here on the backbone of hills, looking at a landscape fleshed by two thousand years of life: narrow brooks spreading like veins across the valley; a splatter of red-tiled village roofs; plump copses and wrinkled hills. 'There is this feeling, when you are out hunting in the middle of the countryside, of "England, my England",' says a Gloucestershire lady member of the field.

A deep feeling for the countryside is an integral part of foxhunting. It helps to explain Charles's addiction to a sport that might otherwise seem to conflict with his 'green' principles. He argues that hunting helps to conserve the traditional British landscape, with its patchwork of fields, fences, copses and hedgerows. It gives him an opportunity to escape from the city, exploring on horseback his far-flung kingdom. 'In a small way, it helps me to keep in touch with what actually happens in the British countryside,' says Charles.

The Duke of Beaufort agreed that the surroundings are part of the hunting experience. 'My love of the Chase comes from the thrill and challenge of a ride across country; from the skill and effort of a good pack of hounds; of the pleasure of riding an experienced or promising horse . . . and from the hours spent riding in a green countryside,' he said.

The Quorn's huntsman is waiting with animal patience for the hounds to find. 'Farrin is by no means a blue blood, but the Prince does love to talk to him about county matters,' says a hunting friend. 'They both share the same love of the countryside.'

'The Prince is a remarkable person,' says Farrin. 'He's got a wonderful outlook on the countryside in many ways. Not just hunting, but deerstalking, fishing and of course, farming.'

The exhilarating, fluting, doubling notes of 'gone away' are sounded as the entire pack sweeps out of the covert on the line of the fleeing fox, across the green turf in the rural heart of England.

Prince Charles puts his horse at a fly fence: up, over, and a vertiginous roll of sky, bare branches, fast-approaching grass and mud as the horse turns head-over-heels in a boggy patch.

'I went into the mud face first and got a bloody nose as well – quite a sight they all seemed to think. But it probably served me right,' says Prince Charles of a fall he had with the Quorn when he 'jumped straight into a bog and the poor horse turned about three somersaults'.

'Most of the bad falls I have had have been due to bog . . . the bigger and better a horse has jumped, the more likely he is to stand on his head or turn a somersault when his front feet are firmly stuck in the mud,' says Ulrica Murray Smith. She was rescued by Prince Charles in March 1988, after being trapped under her mount when it fell at a hedge near the village of South Croxton in Leicestershire.

Royal acts of chivalry become legendary in the hunting field: the man who

Princess Anne at the Burleigh Horse Trials. She is philosophical about falls from the saddle. 'The horse is the only one who doesn't know I am royal,' she says.

on High Peak in Derbyshire came round after a fall to find the future King pressing a flask to his lips; the Quorn lady who took a tumble and begged an anxious Prince Charles 'just kiss me'.

Royal tumbles have provoked the same response in different generations. 'Jokes about the Prince of Wales falling off his horse became almost as commonplace in American vaudeville acts as topical wisecracks on prohibition,' said the Duke of Windsor. 'People who ride to hounds or in steeplechases must expect their share of spills,' he said. 'The mere report from some obscure village that I had been seen with "mud on my back" or with my top hat stove in would momentarily assume world importance.'

'There was always so much fuss in the newspapers when he fell off,' his Duchess added.

Both Charles and his sister are philosophical about the public's reaction to falls. 'I disappeared over his head so frequently that people used to say, "Why is she riding that dangerous horse when she keeps falling off!"' says Anne, who aroused public anxiety when she fell while defending her European championship title on Goodwill in Kiev in 1973.

'It always amazes me to see the eventers and show jumpers taking on the massive fences that they do without the sound of hounds in front to stir their blood,' said Beaufort who, when he broke a leg, had a special stirrup made wide enough to take the plaster so he could continue to hunt.

Leicestershire, especially, seems 'to echo with the dull crack of breaking bones', as though courting danger at these 'hairy' fences were part of the thrill.

When Prince Charles fractured his upper arm in a polo accident in June 1990, an old debate as to whether a royal prince should risk life and limb for sport acquired a new lease of life.

'I hope, Sir, you will not risk your neck again,' Lord Stamfordham had said to the future Edward VIII when he rode (and won) a steeplechase at the Household Brigade meeting at Hawthorn Hill in 1921. Charles was subjected to similar pressure.

'Predictably there has been a call from some areas of the media for the Prince to give up "such dangerous sports",' said Michael Clayton, in an editorial in *Horse and Hound* that wished Charles 'the earliest return to the saddle'.

'Prince Charles has survived, without fractures, numerous falls in polo, the hunting field, and some in his brief forays into National Hunt riding,' Clayton continued. 'He has made no secret of the immense benefit he derives from his horsemanship in refreshment from official engagements.'

The future Edward VIII shrugged off the dangers, giving lucid instructions when he broke his collar bone, and learning tapestry from his mother while recovering from a riding accident in the 1920s. 'I became quite proficient with a crochet needle,' he said.

Sir Hugh Casson, ex-president of the Royal Academy and Charles's painting mentor, found that the Prince's broken arm did not impede his art. 'He taught himself to paint with his left hand,' said Casson. 'I think he really concentrates when he sets himself a task. I doubt if you could tell the difference.'

After a serious concussion steeplechasing in 1924, the subject of the earlier Prince of Wales's recklessness became a political issue. The Prime Minister, Ramsay MacDonald, begged the future King 'to refrain from taking chances that no doubt offer you an exhilarating temptation.' He added, 'Pray do not put me down as an interfering person who, having no zest in life himself, wishes to knock it out of others.'

But it was the Duchess of Windsor, not his father nor the Prime Minister, who finally persuaded her husband out of the saddle.

'The Duke loved horses,' said Laura, Duchess of Marlborough. 'When they

Prince and Princess Michael of Kent out with the Beaufort wearing the distinctive hunt uniform known as the 'blue and buff'. Princess Michael broke her nose when hunting with the Beaufort in December 1991.

were both staying in the country, I whispered to him one day, "Come out with me tomorrow if you want." But the Duchess was so angry when she found out she put a stop to it.'

Most royal wives have not found it easy to persuade their princes to dismount. Prince Albert spent Christmas on crutches after a hunting accident in 1842, and Queen Victoria was terrified by her husband's reckless riding. He finally gave up hunting in 1859.

The fracture in Charles's arm was fixed at the second attempt, by pinning it with a strip of titanium and making a bone graft from the Prince's hip in a Nottingham Hospital. 'Those of us who know about riding accidents wondered why on earth he didn't come up to hunting country earlier, where the doctors know what they are doing,' a Quorn follower said. The operation was in September and three months later Charles was back in the saddle, taking it easy on Reflection as he hacked about with William and Harry at Sandringham. By New Year 1991, he was out with the Quorn again and in the first flight, lifting his injured arm at each jump in order not to jar the bones.

'Like most men, he does what he wants to do,' Diana, Princess of Wales said of Charles's urge to get back to riding after his accident.

There is no doubt that Charles is dicing with danger every time he goes hunting. Among many serious accidents, the royal family has the sad example of Major Dick Hern – the Queen's racing trainer until 1989 – who broke his neck here with the Quorn in November 1984, when his horse jinxed in mid-air and threw the Major near Whites Barn. Hern remains partially paralysed and now runs a yard from his wheelchair rather than in the saddle. On the last weekend of 1991, Princess Michael of Kent, out with the Beaufort, broke her nose when she fell on her chin, her hat hitting her face in an ugly accident.

But the urge to succeed in sport beats fear – and sometimes even good sense

Prince Harry with his mother at a gymkhana near their Gloucestershire home. Harry, fearless in the saddle, went out with the Junior Beaufort in autumn 1990 during half-term.

Anna Wallace, daughter of landowner Hamish Wallace, watching Charles compete in a Cheshire cross-country team event during their romance, the year before the Prince married Diana.

– in a family which is showered with lavish praise at the most minor achievement.

'At least in matters where physical boldness and endurance counted, I could hold my own,' said the Duke of Windsor.

Princess Anne expressed the same spirit when she said: 'When I am approaching a water jump with dozens of photographers waiting for me to fall in, the horse is the only one who doesn't know I am royal.'

Or, as Shakespeare's contemporary Ben Jonson so succinctly put it: 'Princes learn no art truly but the art of horsemanship. The reason is, the brave beast is no flatterer. He will throw a prince as soon as his groom.'

Hounds are running so hard over the plough that, for the mounted field, a rut causes the teeth to rattle and a whistling intake of breath.

'You throw yourself over obstacles; you don't know what's coming; you have to shut your eyes and take a deep breath very often – I do,' says Charles.

Faster goes the field, scudding over a sea of grass, tacking with the pack, a ripple of riders engulfing each fence. A physical pleasure relieves taut muscles and hammering heart. The horses sweat and steam.

'There is no thrill,' said the Duke of Windsor, 'equal to that of riding a good keen horse on a line of one's own, as he takes in his stride the stake-and-bound fences standing out black in the wintry light.' No thrill, except perhaps for skiing, with its same tremulous sense of speed and risk; the intoxicating gulps of air; the awesome expanse of nature; the sheer physical effort to keep in control – just – on terrain that is familiar yet always fraught with incipient danger.

Charles will hurtle at hunting fences in Meynell country with Diana's sister Sarah, just as once, long ago, these two close friends would hurl themselves down the ski slopes. This hunt today is a spectacular ride – with a seven-mile point and a final run including ten hard miles across country. There have been other wild gallops through the Vale of Belvoir with Anna Wallace – daughter of the landowner Hamish Wallace and a former flame of Prince Charles. 'A marvellous-looking girl with a sparkling personality,' said Stephen Barry. 'She is as mad about hunting as he is.'

The romance ended with a jealous row at Windsor during a dance in honour of the Queen Mother's eightieth birthday. Anna left early claiming that Charles had not paid her sufficient attention in August 1980. Charles was engaged and married to Diana within a year. As his fiancée she played the more traditional woman's role of staying home. 'I drove her to Gloucestershire three times that autumn before they became engaged,' said Barry. 'The Prince was generally out hunting when we arrived, and Lady Diana would walk around the house and gardens waiting for him to return.'

Ah! the titillation, the thrust, the thrill of the chase, the excitement 'of a screaming scent when the hounds fairly flew', as the future Queen Alexandra put it. She shocked her mother-in-law by riding to hounds with a baby on the way.

The widowed Queen Victoria remembered Prince Albert, 'a beautiful figure, broad in the shoulder and fine waist', charging up the hill after hunting before she proposed to him on 15 October 1839. 'We embraced each other over and over again,' she wrote in her journal. Albert, 'rosy and wind-swept from hunting', seized her hand 'with the most graceful smiling bow'.

'Hello, been rat-
catching?' George V
joked to a friend dressed
in country tweed. The
name has stuck for the
hacking jacket Charles
wears for recreational
riding or for cub-
hunting, before the
season opens at the
beginning of
November.

Even the royal cook Mrs McKee, who published an authorized book, recognized the sexual charge of hunting. 'I can't help thinking,' she said, 'that the thunderous exercise that takes place during the hunting season, also has something to do with the wild abandon that goes on at some hunt balls.'

Generations of young girls – and not least royal princesses – have had a crush on horses in their pubescent years. 'I would like to grow up like mother, give lots of cosy parties – and hunt for six days a week,' claimed the young Princess Alexandra of Kent.

Royal males, hooked on hunting, have found it hard to give up the chase. 'I'm missing my riding terribly,' the future King Edward VIII wrote to George V from Balmoral, after his father had forced him, for safety's sake, to give up point-to-point racing. 'Stalking seems very tame after riding, as everything else does.'

His brother felt the same when forced to sell up his stables. 'It has come as a great shock to me that with the economy cuts I have had to make, my hunting should be one of those things I must do without,' said the future George VI. 'And I must sell my horses too. That is the worst part of it all, and the parting with them will be terrible.'

Nobody, except perhaps Diana or his fellow foxhunters, understood what it meant for Charles to be kept out of the saddle when the 1990 hunting season started. 'He just could not cope with the broken arm or with himself,' says a friend. 'That is why he went dashing off shooting at Sandringham all autumn. He missed the riding, missed the country, but above all he missed the hunting. It's like any addiction – he had terrible withdrawal symptoms.'

The fox has gone to earth, and the huntsman, after a brief discussion with the whipper-in and the terrier man, has given him best.

Given the vocal and increasingly active anti-hunting lobby, it is always a relief to Prince Charles's advisors if he can avoid being in at a kill.

'I do not enjoy the killing part, but I know it has to be done,' says Charles. 'I just wish *they* could realize how much more horrible and painful all other known methods of control would be.'

Known to his mostly urban subjects for his stand on ecology, Prince Charles is defensive about hunting – and those he hunts with close ranks so tightly on the subject that the extent of his riding to hounds is not widely known. By contrast, his sister Anne, because she is identified in the public mind with a hunting-and-shooting lifestyle, has been the butt of criticism. 'I caused a major row in the seventies by going out hunting,' admits the Princess Royal.

When a member of Highgrove staff quoted to Prince Charles Oscar Wilde's ironic jibe about hunting as 'the unspeakable in full pursuit of the uneatable', the Prince was icily angry. He has evolved a justification of the sport on conservationist lines. 'I try to look at things with a reasonably open mind,' he says. 'It is not always easy, I agree. Sometimes it is very hard to square one's attitude to things. I believe it is necessary to have some sort of fox control because otherwise everything becomes completely out of hand.

'I find with hunting it is much easier to justify it to myself because you are taking much more risk.'

In spite of his long-term work for wildlife conservation, Prince Philip also stands up for the chase: 'Everyone has views on hunting, which, if properly conducted, is a sustainable use of resources.'

This fine day out with the Quorn ends with an uncontroversial hack along Bridle Road and over the Clawson Lane, and with the customary 'goodnight' – although it is scarcely time for tea. When he is hunting in Gloucestershire,

Prince Charles riding back at the end of the hunt, his boots and breeches flecked with mud and his horse sweaty with effort.

the Prince will go back to Highgrove, take a quick drink from a tray in his study – and eat a substantial tea.

Here in Leicestershire, he waits while the horses are boxed, then sits down in mud-flecked breeches with Sir John Miller to eat a couple of sandwiches and take a nip from the flask. The orgasm of excitement over, it seems easy to discuss the pleasure of hunting in rational terms, as though it were not much more than a glorified ride out.

'On a good day, I think it is the thrill of trying to get across the country in one piece that I like best,' says Charles. 'Then I suppose that I "hunt to ride" rather than the other way round. But even when nothing much happens, I still just love being out.'

Mr Jorrocks made a more cogent judgement on this sport of dash and fire, of cut and thrust, of chase and escape, capture and kill. ''Unting is all that's worth living for,' he said, 'it's the sport of kings, the image of war without its guilt and only five-and-twenty per cent of its danger.'

SHOOTING

*From Sandringham's woods to wetlands
on the Wash, Edward VII's
shooting parties live on*

ABOVE: 'A Big Shoot at Sandringham',
painted by Thomas Jones Barker in 1867.
The future Edward VII in formal tweeds
among russet foliage, with his shooting
cronies from the Duke of Beaufort to Lord
Chesterfield.

RIGHT: Diana, Princess of Wales, with
William, surrounded by beaters and keepers,
at the Barbour-and-wellies Sandringham
shoot of modern times.

PRECEDING PAGES: Prince Charles
takes aim at a pheasant overhead, watched
by the Queen Mother and Lord and Lady
Romsey.

CHAPTER 2

Birds of a Feather

If a sportsman true you'd be
Listen carefully to me:
Never, never let your gun
Pointed be at anyone;
That it might unloaded be
Matters not the least to me.

You may hit or you may miss
But at all times think of this:
All the game birds ever bred
Won't repay for one man dead.

'A Father's Advice', verse given by King George V for his son to
memorize, quoted in *A King's Story* by HRH THE DUKE OF WINDSOR

FATHER TO SON

SANDRINGHAM HOUSE stands sturdy and florid against the Norfolk winds, as though its ruddy bricks still glowed with the *bonhomie* of an expansive Edwardian past. 'The quintessence of all that was amusing and gay,' said the Duke of Windsor of his grandfather's years at 'the Big House' where Edward VII was squire of Sandringham.

On this New Year morning, at precisely 9.30 A.M., a royal shooting party is walking towards the encircling woods – Prince Philip with his sons Charles and Edward – three specks of plain plumage against snow-stippled soil. Like the pheasants which will soon be scudding overhead, driven by the beaters from the coverts, the 'guns' are well camouflaged – Philip in a tweed Norfolk jacket the grey-green colour of lichen on a tree stump; Charles in a woodcock-brown shooting suit and grey-green wool socks. 'We'd be dressed in tweeds trying to blend in with the landscape,' said Stephen Barry, of partridge shooting on the Spanish estate of the Duke of Wellington when Charles was courting the Duke's daughter Lady Jane Wellesley. The only splutters of royal eccentricity on display in Norfolk today are Prince Edward's flat tweed cap worn with a military-camouflage combat jacket. His career with the Marines came to an explosive end here at snowbound Sandringham, as father and son argued out Edward's decision to resign.

The motley of gnarled tweed and waxed coats, speckled knickerbockers and worn cord breeches on show today are but a sepia shadow of the resplendent Edwardian shoots recorded in the royal family albums. 'Faded photographs of portly groups surrounding His Majesty King Edward, of beards and gaiters, of tweed capes, stiff-collared head keepers, and a strange assortment of headgear,' says Prince Philip's good friend Aubrey Buxton, who wrote a sportsman's memoir of George VI.

At the Edwardian shooting parties, Lord Knutsford described King Edward

Prince Philip is a keen shot even though arthritis stiffens his fingers and he is forced to carry a battery-operated hand-warmer.

After he broke his arm and was forced to shoot left-handed, Prince Charles put a patch over his right eye in November 1990 to force his left eye to focus on the bird.

VII in 1909 as wearing 'a thick brown suit, Tyrolese hat, and wonderful shooting stockings with stripes on them'. Colourful sock and garters – worn so low down on the body – are deemed not to be visible to birds in flight.

'The bright tweeded opulence of my grandfather and his friends, while out shooting at Sandringham, was always a wonder to me as a child,' said the Duke of Windsor, who inherited Edward VII's quixotic flamboyance. Lady Diana Cooper spotted the future Edward VIII in 'plus 20s with vivid azure socks', and the Duke of Windsor was still sporting these enormous plus fours ('my short stalking trousers in Balmoral tartan') in the 1950s, while his grandfather's voluminous Inverness cape moved a Paris gendarme to exclaim 'Sherlock Holmes!' when he saw the Duke wearing it.

Even his more conventional brother had a dapper elegance. Lord Buxton saw George VI step out of the maroon royal shooting brake, 'a trim figure in a Norfolk jacket made of his own cloth, his tweed cap at a jaunty angle . . . a merry monarch on this sunny morning'.

The royal party take up their pegs for the first drive – Prince Philip at four, with Charles to his left and his friend Nicholas Soames on his right. Edward is more awkwardly placed at number eight, his birds are likely to curl away right and left around the corner of the wood, or plane down and run, even though the 'stops' are already in position – two old men with wizened faces and battered tweeds, hitting the trees with a loud, rhythmic thwack.

'The Duke of Edinburgh and Prince Charles are excellent shots, though Charles doesn't do much shooting now,' Jack Clark said after he retired as a Sandringham keeper in 1988. He had worked 51 years on the royal estate.

Prince Charles shooting in a style that resembles his great-grandfather George V. Bright socks, deemed to be out of sight of the birds, are in the family tradition set by Edward VII and the future Duke of Windsor.

'Today I would say that the three best regular shots at Sandringham are Hugh Van Cutsem, Anthony Duckworth-Chad of Pinkney Hall, Norfolk, and Lord Tollemache of Helmingham Hall, Suffolk. Prince Edward is not a particularly good shot.'

Van Cutsem, heir to his family's Northmore bloodstock stud in Newmarket, shoots at Sandringham with Prince Philip and is a close friend of Charles, who gave special thanks to Hugh and his wife Emilie in his book of water-colours. Van Cutsem established a new breeding complex, the Hilsborough Stud, near Thetford in 1991.

A network of royal family connections is bound up in shooting. Diana, Princess of Wales, was brought up at Sandringham's Park House (built by Edward VII to take the overflow of guests from the Big House) and her father and grandfather (Viscount Althorp and Lord Fermoy) were shooting companions of George VI when the King shot his thousandth woodcock in 1951. Lord Spencer, who died in 1992, inherited the family estate of Althorp in Northamptonshire in 1975, and it was there, two years later, that a shooting party brought 16-year-old Diana, at home from boarding-school for the weekend face-to-face in a muddy field with Prince Charles.

'A very jolly and amusing and attractive sixteen-year-old – full of fun,' was Charles's opinion of Lady Diana Spencer. He cannot have been so impressed by her shooting ability.

'She was a pathetic shot, simply dreadful – and she was only using a single-barrelled gun,' said a sportsman who saw her shooting at Althorp.

Since Edward has been coming down regularly to Sandringham, staying at Wood Farm on the estate, the timing of his shots has improved. And Charles has done a deal of shooting, especially since he wrecked his arm at polo and needed an outdoor recreation while he was out of the hunting saddle. His normal action, like most guns, is to shoot right-handed on the trigger, with his left arm holding the gun, rather like George V's distinctive technique, which involved jumping into a change of feet when he turned to shoot behind him. But in November 1990, with his broken right arm mending, Charles shot left-handed, with a patch over his right eye to force his left eye to focus.

'He is an excellent and stylish shot with a fine sense of sportsmanship, showing great consideration for others,' said Sir Joseph Nickerson. 'A legend in his own lifetime,' claimed Mark Phillips of 'Sporting Joe' Nickerson who was the finest all-round game shot of modern times until his death in 1990.

In its glory days, when the future Edward VII was Prince of Wales, the weeks of formal sport at Sandringham were around the royal birthdays: Princess Alexandra's on 1 December and Edward's on 9 November, when the pheasants that had been reared during the spring and summer were driven from Dersingham Wood and produced a mighty birthday bag – 2,758 pheasants in one day's shoot in 1905.

Shooting at Sandringham now takes place mainly in two weeks in early January – although Anne, Edward and especially Charles all have autumn weekends booked when they invite their own friends to stay at Wood Farm. Even the Queen, when she does not want to open up the big house, increasingly takes over Wood Farm nowadays. It became a family refuge before Charles and Diana were engaged. On Charles's 32nd birthday, 14 November 1980, Diana joined the royal family there for a country weekend, but it was ruined by the Press on the scent of a royal love story.

'The reporters turned up in a pack, disrupting life for the Duke of Edinburgh's shooting party,' said Barry. 'He was so angry that it was amazing that none of them got shot along with the pheasants.'

The Queen, distraught that her rural retreat is invaded by the press, has been heard to say: 'You are despicable.'

'I think it is a sad reflection of our times that the Queen and members of her family . . . who spend so much time in the public eye are subjected to continuing scrutiny from the media and a curious public,' says Anne, who regrets that her mother has been obliged to move her riding horses away from the open paddock at Sandringham.

Philip's irascible temper will be vented today on the birds – just as in the early years of his married life, when he first learned to shoot. 'I also discovered that he could swear . . . He exercised it most often, to the four winds of a blasted heath, when shooting, a sport of which he was becoming increasingly fond,' said the Duke of Edinburgh's former valet John Dean.

'Philip, don't get so *annoyed*,' Princess Elizabeth would say to soothe him.

Her grandfather, George V, a legendary shot, had a more equable response on the rare occasions that he missed a hit. 'I can't hit a feather!' he claimed on a day he brought down a thousand birds. 'But I've been at sea for a good many years and one doesn't see many pheasants there!'

Edward VII made the shooting party a social fulcrum, mixing old aristocrats with new money; stirring in landowners and politicians; adding a sprinkle of adultery and a dash of diplomacy. Sandringham shooting parties today are for family, shooting friends and Norfolk neighbours.

Philip's regular shooting companions include Timothy Colman (of the mustard family) who is Lord Lieutenant of Norfolk and whose wife Lady Mary is a cousin of the Queen on the Bowes Lyon side. Philip shoots too with Lord Brabourne (married to his cousin the former Lady Patricia Mountbatten). Jack Clark described Brabourne as 'perhaps the best shot I've seen, though he can be a bit greedy'.

Charles's shooting chums are Nicholas Soames, Gerald Grosvenor, Duke of Westminster, the Duke's former brother-in-law Guy Roxburghe and Lord Brabourne's eldest son Norton Romsey, heir to the Mountbatten estate at Broadlands in Hampshire, where Elizabeth and Philip spent their honeymoon and Charles and Diana started theirs in 1981.

'To me it has become a second home in so many ways,' Charles told his 'honorary grandpapa', Earl Mountbatten of Burma, the royal family's 'Uncle Dickie' who was murdered by the Irish Republican Army in 1979.

Charles has had memorable shoots at Broadlands. In 1968, when he was 19, he bagged 500 pheasants there in one day – but earned the wrath of the veteran headkeeper Harry Grass – known as 'King of the Gamekeepers' – by shooting after the whistle had been blown on the final drive. 'I was so shocked, as my word was law and everyone knew it,' says Grass. 'So I marched over to the guns to find out who the guilty party was.'

'I'm sorry,' said Prince Charles. 'But I'd killed 499 when the whistle went and I don't suppose I'll ever do that again.'

William and Harry already brandish toy guns and help to pick up the fallen birds, and William joined the beaters in the 1991 season. Both boys will be taught to shoot by their father. Those who object to a new royal generation being introduced to field sports reckon without the power of tradition and example. In the country, children learn to handle a shotgun from their fathers and are brought up in an 'atmosphere of shooting'.

The Duke of Windsor remembered that he bagged his first rabbit at the age of 12. 'My father's favourite recreation was shooting, or what I used to call "banging", which occupied his leisure for six months of the year,' he said. 'Before I went to school I used to hire out as a beater and was paid two shillings a day,' he added. 'My father was almost a fanatic on the subject of the handling of firearms.'

Prince Charles worked the beaters' side during Sandringham's New Year shoots before graduating to the guns as a teenage badge of honour. He would be taken by his father to walk-up the hedgerows with a .410 shotgun, until he learned to use a lightweight but powerful 20-bore.

Peter Phillips has already been allowed to join the Sandringham Christmas shoot at the age of 12, after training with his double-barrelled gun on clay pigeons – at which his father is expert. Mark Phillips made up a royal clay pigeon team with Prince Andrew and ex-King Constantine of Greece in the mid-1980s.

'My two eldest sons enjoyed their first day's shooting,' the future George V told his Private Secretary. 'The eldest got twelve rabbits and the second got three.' He was talking about two future Kings of England: Edward VIII and George VI.

'December 27th. My first woodcock,' Bertie wrote at Christmas 1911 at the age of 16. In his game book, the future Duke of York and George VI noted with tidy accuracy the date, the place, the other guns, the bag and his personal score – as he did for the rest of his life. 'From the first woodcock he secured, he marked up his own total separately in red ink, immediately above the party's total, which was in ordinary ink,' says Buxton. The woodcock, a migratory bird, breaks cover with an erratic and unpredictable line of flight, and is therefore a difficult and dangerous shot to take.

George VI longed to teach the next generation and recorded in 1945 that 16-year-old Lillibet had shot a pheasant at Balmoral. As a wedding present, along with a sapphire and diamond cluster necklace and matching earrings, George VI gave his daughter 'a pair of Purdey guns'.

King George V by 'Spy', the nom de plume *of Sir Leslie Ward, pictured in 1910 in his impeccable shooting suit and spats, carrying his Purdey gun.*

Tap-tap-tap go the beaters' sticks. There is a crackle of parchment-dry leaves as a pheasant scuttles out towards the line and then back in a flurry of tail feathers into the undergrowth.

The smooth walnut stock of his Purdey gun – an heirloom from his grandfather – is grasped firmly by Charles as he waits at the peg. The panelled premises of James Purdey and Sons in South Audley Street in London's Mayfair have the fusty grandeur of a country house gunroom. The walls are peppered with photographs of the royal family at play, and in its brace and a half of royal warrants, the firm announces its credentials: gun and cartridge makers to HM the Queen and to HRH the Prince of Wales; gun makers to HRH the Duke of Edinburgh.

'Everything about him was always of the best – his clothes, his fine hammer guns by Purdey, his food, his stationery, his cigarette case by Fabergé,' said the Duke of Windsor of his father.

'I'll tell the office to make sure you go on a course at Purdey's so you know what you're doing. We don't want you killing anyone,' Charles told Stephen Barry when he first took him shooting at Balmoral as a loader.

Royal patronage is also given to Holland & Holland of London's Bruton Street, which make fine rifles for the Duke of Edinburgh and offer the inimitable English countrywear – tweeds, Barbours, checked caps and shooting sticks.

'These days I tend to use a 12-bore Holland & Holland Royal 26,' says the Duke of Westminster, whose shooting skills were taught, like Prince Charles's, 'by father and the gamekeeper'.

Just behind the line are the loaders, one for each gun – no longer a pair or even three for each sportsman as in the days when servants were as plentiful as game on the royal estates. 'He is the best shot I ever saw, though I think if I had three guns and men to load I could run him hard myself,' said Lord Ellesmere, English statesman and translator of *Faust*, about Prince Albert, who was accused of turning the gentlemanly art of shooting – a couple of guns, a loader, a beater and a pair of dogs walking-up coverts – into the ritual *battue* favoured in his native Germany.

Prince Charles inherited his grandfather's guns and is described as 'an excellent and stylish shot with a fine sense of sportsmanship'.

Today, anyone on the palace staff might be dragooned into beating up or acting as a loader – as Dean discovered. Prince Philip teased his valet for his misery in the shooting field. 'One cold and clammy day when I was looking more than usually miserable, he burst out laughing and said: "I must say it's a nice thing to come out for a day's shooting and have a face like an old boot looking at me,"' Dean recalled.

The birds are up!

'Years ago whenever a bird got up someone used to shout "Over!" as if the guns weren't on the look-out from the start of the drive,' says the Duchess of Devonshire, a keen gun in a sport where women are not often welcomed.

'Cock forrard!' was once the exultant cry. Today, the beaters still shout 'Over!'

Where? Here! High! A flush on the left, swarming across the line; heart-thumping; arm outstretched; both eyes quiveringly focused; a recoil on the shoulder; two birds plummeting straight, another drifting; the crack of guns broken and reloaded; two more bright bundles tumbling in the air; ears ringing with the echo of the fusillade; a mouth full of saliva; the sour smell of spent cartridges; a sudden silence.

'My left arm ached from lifting my gun, my shoulder from the recoil, and I was deaf and stunned from the banging,' said the Duke of Windsor after a famously large shoot with his father on the estate of Lord Burnham at Hall Barn, Buckinghamshire, in December 1913.

In the competitive Edwardian era, the end of a drive would be a time for exultation – or even recrimination, as when Lord Ripon was 'much astonished' to see a 'gun' bombarding his neighbour with dead birds, claiming that some of his had been 'stolen'. 'Take the damned lot! I don't care!' shouted the so-called sportsman. 'Take the lot, damn you!'

No passionate cries of rage or joy echo through Dersingham Wood this morning. Instead Nicholas Soames bends his portly form towards a bird that has thudded between the pegs. 'Yours, your Royal Highness,' says Soames, with a courtly bow.

'No, yours, your Royal Hugeness,' replies Charles.

WORKING THE DOGS

THE QUEEN has arrived at the shoot after her morning ride and steps forward at the end of the drive: – mud-spattered boot; stout tweed skirt with rust checks overlaid on green; quilted body-warmer; and, as she bends down to whisper quiet instructions to the golden labrador waiting at heel, there is a pink, powdered face and wiry curls escaping from a silk scarf patterned with feathers.

'The Queen never shoots, but what a keen gun-dog lady she is,' said Jack Clark. 'All the dogs love her and make a great fuss of her. She had handled my old bitch Pendle and now whenever the dog sees Her Majesty she will make straight for her – even if she is a hundred yards away.'

Now they are off to pick up – a skittish, snuffling dash to where birds have dropped or run off, disappeared deep back into the coverts.

'The dogs are part of the pleasure,' says the Duchess of Devonshire. 'The little triumphs which only the owner notices are intensely satisfying and make up for all the bad behaviour which everyone else notices.'

'I reckon that about one-third of my pleasure in shooting derives from working my gun dogs,' said Joe Nickerson.

The royal gun dogs are professionals, even champions. The Queen is patron of the Labrador Retriever Club and she gains much satisfaction from the dogs she has trained and bred in the kennels here at Sandringham, carrying on a family tradition started by Edward and Alexandra, and passed down by her father and grandfather.

On the eve of her 65th birthday in April 1991, the Queen spent the day at Sandringham watching the gun dogs in action at private retriever trials, just as in the past, with her labrador Wren, she took part in the retriever trials on Deeside staged by the North of Scotland Gun Dog Association. She spent five hours trudging through the Norfolk sugar beet with Sandringham Ranger back in 1962 when the National Gun Dog trials were first held on one of the estate farms.

'She really has marvellous control over the gun dogs, which is more than could be said for those corgis!' says a Sandringham house guest who claims to give the little dogs a surreptitious kick when he is wearing his shooting boots, in revenge for nipped ankles.

In November 1991, when she was watching the Yellow Labrador Club gun dog trials in Windsor Great Park, the Queen was surprised – but then amused – to find that the emblem on the club flag, usually a yellow labrador, had been mysteriously replaced by a corgi.

But in truth labradors – especially golden retrievers – are as much part of royal family life as corgis. The Queen has memories of Mimsey, the yellow labrador her father singled out as his personal gun dog, and of Mimsey's puppies Stiffy and Scrummer that she and Margaret played with as children. Charles has a golden labrador called Harvey – bred by the Queen and named after the rabbit he had as a childhood pet.

'I don't like corgis; I like labradors,' Charles has claimed. Harvey has disgraced himself by soiling 'some of the best carpets in Britain'. Barry said that 'when we went away for weekends, I'd have to follow him around with soda water and blotting paper.'

The Queen takes a continuing interest in the dogs that she has bred. When Barry was exercising Harvey in the Buckingham Palace grounds, he tried not to disturb the Queen's privacy, dodging her and the pack of corgis over the 40 acres. Finally they came face to face.

'I've been trying to catch up with you for the last half hour,' she said. 'I want

The Queen using a whistle to work her gun dogs at Sandringham in November 1991, wearing waxed jacket and overtrousers on the five-hour shoot. She personally selects the stock for breeding in the labrador kennels and helps to train young dogs in the field.

to see how Harvey's getting on. I hadn't realized he was in London.'

On small shoots with friends, Prince Charles will take out his Jack Russell Tigger. On formal shoots, guests are encouraged to leave their dogs at the Sandringham kennels – 14 self-contained units in Queen Alexandra's original building, where wooden kennels and chain-link fencing were installed in 1968. There, 20 full-grown dogs and up to 20 puppies in season are under the supervision of Sandringham's gamekeeper Bill Meldrum. The dogs are fed with military precision at 6.30 in the morning and at 4.30 P.M. when the guns come back. Occasionally Meldrum will show parties of local school children round the kennels and display the dogs' obedience.

There is money in breeding, and Harvey, like most of the Queen's dogs, has helped to pay for the upkeep of the kennels. 'People keep writing to the kennels in Sandringham for him to service their bitches,' Barry said. 'Harvey always obliges. He has progeny all over the place.'

All the Queen's champion gun dogs have had the same prefix: Sandringham Flora, Sandringham Sydney, Sandringham Slipper. The tradition was started by Queen Alexandra for her puppies – the borzois and basset hounds, Great Danes, bulldogs, pugs, dachshund, terriers and wiry clumber and springer spaniels that her husband claimed could 'do the work of three beaters' as they flushed pheasants out of clumps of rhododendrons.

For his dogs Edward VII used the prefix 'Wolferton', after the local village, and that was taken up by George V, who had two prize-winning labradors named Wolferton Jet and Wolferton Ben. The Queen's own Field Trial champions have been Sandringham Ranger, Sherry of Biteabout and her son Sandringham Slipper.

The Queen is getting her dogs to work from heel to bird, using a whistle to instil total discipline, giving a pat and a smile of encouragement for each retrieve. She marked the birds as each fell, but prefers to trust a well-trained dog.

Prince William joined the beaters in the 1991 shooting season. Like his father before him, he will graduate to the guns as a teenager, first walking-up the hedgerows before he takes part in a big shoot.

'He knows the likely places to search and stays as long as he, not you, may think necessary,' explains the Duchess of Devonshire. 'He hunts the familiar ground and usually comes back carrying something.'

If Sandringham Scrum failed to pick up game, no other dog would find it, boasted George VI of his 'most accomplished retriever, distinguished by the excellence of his nose'. On the last evening of George VI's life, in February 1952, he went down twice to the Sandringham kennels to see a favourite labrador which had injured a paw on the Keeper's Day shoot. The King filled in his game book, went up to bed and died in his sleep, leaving his fine legacy of sporting dogs to his daughter.

Now Princess Anne, in waxed jacket and wellies, cap pulled down in workmanlike fashion, walks towards her father holding a brace of pheasants. 'The Princess Royal does not shoot but enjoys picking up with labradors, which work well for her,' said Joe Nickerson. She learned from her mother how to work her dogs – Baskerville, the Gascony Hound, the gun dog Fox, the black labrador Moriarty and Mark Phillips' lurcher Laura, whose death devastated Prince William and Harry when the dog was put down at Balmoral after an accident.

'She gets everybody organized in typical Brownie pack fashion,' say friends of Anne's who used to be invited for a day's shooting when Mark Phillips was still with his wife at Gatcombe Park. Mark was brought up to shoot in the country tradition. 'He really enjoys his shooting and does it well, improving every year,' Nickerson said of him.

Anne was out with the gun dogs after dancing the night away at the surprise party she gave for Mark's fortieth birthday celebration in December 1988. 'My feet haven't recovered from last night,' she announced.

While her mother has focused, like her father before her, on breeding labradors, Anne, the Princess Royal, has followed another Sandringham tradition. In 1990, she bought her daughter Zara a clumber puppy bitch, Venaticus Edwina – known as 'Splodges' – which was then trained by the Gatcombe gamekeeper Graham Cummins. The following year, Anne became President of the 100-strong Working Clumber Society. Controversy now surrounds this sturdy spaniel breed. In 1934 George V's Sandringham Spark was a winner at Cruft's, but working clumbers – white with lemon or orange markings round nose, ears and tail roots – are not now recognized by the autocratic Kennel Club, which in 1986 changed the standards, encouraging a heavier breed weighing up to seven stone.

The whistle goes for the second drive; the dogs are called to heel; the royal males check their guns and are silent as they concentrate. Although Anne will stay with the guns for all four drives before lunch, shooting at Sandringham remains a male preserve. Sarah, Duchess of York, enjoyed watching a shoot during her brief royal marriage. The Princess of Wales will bring William and Harry out to watch their father and grandfather. Her supposed distaste for shooting has been exaggerated, but – like Queen Mary and Wallis Simpson before her – Diana does not rate shooting highly as a spectator sport. 'Bor-ring,' she will intone to friends, although she quite enjoys larking around with her boys and the beaters.

'This is the shooting season,' the Duchess of Windsor wrote to Major Gray Phillips in 1958. 'Fortunately women are not often included. Yesterday the Duke left here at 8 A.M. and returned at 9 P.M.! He had good sport.'

'My mother, tired of shooting parties and anxious to escape those to which my father was invited, would bring us kids here to Frogmore each year,' said the Duke of Windsor, 'while my father "banged" relentlessly away in the north.'

Prince Charles with his golden labrador Harvey, named after his childhood pet rabbit and bred by the Queen. Her father had a yellow labrador, Mimsey, as his personal gundog.

FACING PAGE: *The Queen at the Yellow Labrador Gun Dog Trials in Windsor Great Park in autumn 1991, with head keeper John Stubbs.*

Andrew, Duke of York helping to pick up. The bag at an average Sandringham shoot is 350 birds, but all the pheasants are wild, not reared.

A BIG BAG

A COCK PHEASANT is coming straight over, very high. Prince Philip raises his gun and misses with both barrels, cursing into the wind as he rubs painful fingers together. 'Philip gets bad arthritis in his hands; you always know when it's playing him up on a cold day because he misses more than usual and then swears a lot,' says Clark. The Duke uses a battery operated hand-warmer against the searing Norfolk wind.

Does missing matter? Today's guns are quick to say – at least in public – that it is the sport that counts, not the bag. Yet Prince Philip still likes his picker-up to use a 'clicker', an automatic counter, just as George V's detective would record each royal bird.

'A "Norfolk Liar", that's what they are known as,' says a fellow gun. 'Most people of my generation don't think counting the birds should be part of the sport.'

'Anyone who has the interests of the pickers-up at heart still carries a counter,' claims Philip.

Shooting prowess, reflected in the size of the bag, used to be the measure of success on the royal estates. 'I watched the King and kept count,' Lord Burnham's agent reported of George V. 'He brought down thirty-nine birds with thirty-nine consecutive cartridges and only with the fortieth did he miss.'

A carpet of cartridges would surround the King; 30,000 a year; 1,700 in one day to kill 1,000 pheasants. George V would even send his son his game cards – the official tally in the numbers game.

'Can this terrific slaughter possibly go on?' asked Lord Stamfordham, the new King's Private Secretary in 1912. But the big bags went on right through the 1930s and beyond. As late as 1970 Prince Charles was one of ten guns at Broadlands who brought down 2,000 birds, an achievement for Lord Mountbatten and for his keeper Harry Grass – but also the end of an era.

Today, a debate between landowners about shooting and conservancy is carried on in the shooting press and in *The Field*.

Lord Romsey has made conservation and habitat improvement hallmarks of the Broadlands estate, where the Queen and Prince Philip shoot, as well as Prince Charles. 'When I took over I changed the whole philosophy of the shoot, especially when Grass retired,' Lord Romsey says. 'I wanted to do away with Broadlands' reputation as a blunderbuss shoot, grandfather's huge monolith.'

Norton Romsey is a sportsman of Prince Charles's generation, one of the new breed who have no truck with 'aerial slaughter' and make conservation a priority. His contemporary, the Duke of Roxburghe takes the same position. 'On a shooting day, it's as important as anything else to have very pleasant surroundings and good company,' he says. Guy Roxburghe is chairman of the Scottish Wildlife Trust, and it was at his Scottish estate at Floors Castle that Prince Andrew proposed to Sarah Ferguson in February 1986.

'I don't think you can think of a day in terms of bag size,' says Gerald Grosvenor, Duke of Westminster, whose sister Jane married Roxburghe in 1977 but divorced in 1990. 'Provided that you have good fun in very good company and have challenging sport, it matters not what you shoot in numbers, either of pheasant or any other game.' The Duke is President of the Game Conservancy Trust.

Privately, shooting enthusiasts admit that many guns do still keep a score, and never more so than when an estate is playing host to a royal shot. 'There is still a tendency to go for the big bag when royal visitors come,' says a shooting colleague of Prince Charles. 'I suppose it goes back to the Edwardian era. And although everyone is supposed to draw lots as usual, in practice, the Prince of Wales gets pretty fed up if he doesn't get good birds. And his hosts make pretty sure he does. Why do you think the best peg is called "the King's stand"?'

Sandringham is a well-managed estate: 14 full-time keepers; anti-poaching trip wires which fire 12-bore blanks; ferrets fitted with bleepers to assist retrieval when they are rooting out vermin. The result is that the royal estate is flush with pheasants, and bags have climbed through the 1980s from a total of 5,000 game birds to nearly double. A day's bag may be limited to around 350 but it will go up to 1,000 birds on big days – especially the cock shoot which closes the season, when 10 separate parties of five guns cover the estate.

To most ordinary people, there is contradiction in the idea that royal father and son, both of whom preach conservation and ecology, should stand on the Sandringham Estate, guns at the ready as the birds are driven towards them. But Prince Philip is impatient with critics who believe that conservation and care for wildlife are incompatible with field sports.

'What they appear to find so difficult to comprehend is that an interest and appreciation of nature is not the same thing as an attachment to pet animals,' he says. 'I came into contact with the natural world through these sports, and while learning about the conservation of game species I began to take an interest in wild animals and their habitats.'

As Patron and a former President of the Game Conservancy, Philip thinks of the keeper as a steward of the land, a protector of the birds in their natural habitat. 'Conservation and shooting are the same thing,' he says. 'You won't get wild pheasants unless you get a good habitat and that is good for conserving all forms of wildlife.'

Princess Anne learned how to work dogs from her mother, and on her own Gatcombe Park shoots she 'gets everybody organized in typical Brownie pack fashion'.

Prince Charles has also served as President of the Game Conservancy. 'The Conservancy was the first organization to regard game quite rationally as a "crop", a valuable by-product of the land which deserved good husbandry as much as corn or cattle,' he says.

At Sandringham today, there is an attempt to re-establish the balance of nature. In the past, all the gamekeepers' energies went into rearing birds to be slaughtered – the eggs hatched, the chicks crated and coops set out in long lines in the rearing fields to get fine healthy poults. That intensive effort stopped at Sandringham in 1939 with the Second World War; all the birds downed today are wild.

'There was no going back to the old days of heavy rearing, when they thought nothing of shooting 2,000 pheasant or 300–400 brace of partridge on a single outing,' said Jack Clark. 'The total number shot must have been enormous and we always wondered how accurate the gamebooks were. Large quantities were sent off to market and we always reckoned that someone must have made fortune.'

In those days, when a million head of game was reared annually at Sandringham, the whole estate was treated as a vast game reserve. Louise Cresswell, a tenant of Appleton farm, described the birds being 'brought up in hen-coops and turned out tame into the woods to be shot down in thousands'.

'The place is literally crawling with them,' claimed Queen Alexandra's courtier and comptroller Sir Dighton Probyn.

Prince William and Peter Phillips still find pheasants everywhere at Sandringham, chasing them through the woods, imitating their pernickety running walk or shooing them up into the air with whoops of encouragement that would never be allowed on this morning's silent, professional beat.

Clark claims that today's plentiful supply of pheasants is still nothing compared to the past under the regime of head keeper F. W. Bland ('You wouldn't have dared address him by his Christian name,' Clark said of Bland,) a stocky Yorkshireman who 'looked just like George V' and ran the Sandringham estate with sergeant-major efficiency for half a century.

'There were so many birds here then,' says Clark. 'Why, on my mile and a half walk to school I could spot about thirty partridge nests in the hedgerow, but today you would be lucky to see half a dozen.'

In the 1960–61 season, Lady Fellowes (wife of the former Sandringham agent and mother-in-law of Diana's sister Jane) decorated a commemorative game card with delicate water-colours of all the birds bagged. Under the Queen's EIIR crest are listed: pheasants 16,188, partridges 6,023, hares 809, rabbits 127, woodcock 106, snipe 3, wild duck 63, teal 12, wood pigeon 553. The total bag for the year was 23,900.

Thirty years on, Anne, the Princess Royal, still sees while out riding 'golden pheasants in the rhododendron bushes', hares, geese 'back in vast numbers' and wildfowl.

'The tiny snipe and visiting woodcock still create their own special excitement when you catch a glimpse of them,' she says.

Charles believes that today's estate owners must respond to the situation each season, and cannot set shooting targets. 'Some people treat game as a marketable commodity, and once you have placed an advance order it must be delivered, whatever Nature decides, because it has been paid for,' he says.

But even in the days of the big shoots, conservation was part of managing the estate. 'Judging from your letters and from the number of days you have been out shooting, there can't be much game left at Sandringham,' George V grumbled to his son. 'It also seems a mistake to shoot the coverts three times over. I never do that unless a few more cocks have to be killed. I can't understand Bland wishing you to do so.'

FACING PAGE: *Gerald Grosvenor, Duke of Westminster, who learned to shoot at the age of eight, was voted one of the country's best shots by* The Shooting Times. *He uses a 12-bore Holland & Holland Royal 26. 'I don't think you can think of a day in terms of bag size,' says the Duke who, like his close friend Prince Charles, is a convinced conservationist.*

Prince Harry with his father at
Sandringham, where Prince Charles
believes that a well-maintained shooting
estate enhances the landscape.

George VI set out what has become the modern sportsman's creed: 'The wildlife of today is not ours to dispose of as we please,' he said. 'We have it in trust. We must account for it to those who come after.'

'Rather wild-looking, flat, bleak country,' said Queen Victoria on one of her rare visits to Sandringham. 'How anybody can say that Norfolk is flat round here I don't know!' said the present Queen as she drove a Land-Rover down a bumpy road. Today the seven guns waiting for the birds to be beaten towards them can survey a traditional English landscape – woodlands, copses and spinnies threaded across bare fields. Most of the clusters of trees have been planted to improve the shooting.

The fact that the keepered estate enhances the landscape is one of the arguments put forward by the shooting lobby. 'The Sporting' has determined the look of the land, says the Duchess of Devonshire, of the Chatsworth estate. 'Professional foresters frown on such uncommercial woods, but the country would be poorer without them,' she says.

'I think this is absolutely true,' says Charles. 'Again, it is easy for people to say that this is just an argument, an excuse to maintain field sports. But I honestly do believe that otherwise there would be no reason to prevent the countryside becoming a prairie.'

Charles has captured in a wash of water-colours Sandringham's brown foliage and rounded thickets. He admits that he loves this part of Norfolk 'with a passion'. In 'Winter Scene', a pink-tinged hedge spans his painting, dividing a snow-covered foreground from the bands of copse and woodland behind.

'Why would you add coverts, little woodlands, hedges and similar features, if you did not want to see wildlife?' says Charles. 'Unless there is a bit of shooting, hunting and fishing taking place why should such forms of conservation occur?'

A century earlier, this royal argument might well have provoked derisive laughter – or even bitter tears, for the destruction caused by game in Edward VII's era was a disaster for Norfolk's farmers. After her husband's death in 1865 Louise Cresswell went to the county court to claim compensation for her ruined crops from Sandringham's royal squire. By the time her case was taken up in parliament, her struggle had become a *cause célèbre*. The satirical magazine *Punch* summed up aristocratic attitudes:

> Hurrah! Hurrah! For our game preserves,
> Hurrah for the fat *battue*, –
> A flush of pheasants at every hedge,
> And for each man loaders two! . . .
> What property so stands in need
> Of law's protecting arm,
> As pheasants, hares and partridges
> That do nobody harm, –
> Save grumbling tenants who complain
> That they won't let them farm?

Mrs Cresswell finally sold up her bankrupt stock at Appleton Farm (now managed directly from Sandringham), left for America, and published her story in a book, *Eighteen Years on Sandringham Estate*, in 1887. Almost every copy was bought up and destroyed by Sandringham's land agent. It told how wheat, rye, mangolds, turnips and clover were all flattened, eaten or damaged; how hares – already 'a swarm of little brown ears in the corn' – were being brought in as fodder for the guns.

'They would start up at my pony's feet, gathering like a snowball, and run along before me like a little pack of hounds . . . as if they knew they were royal property and dared me to touch them,' said Mrs Cresswell. Princess Anne says that she and her children are often startled by hares which 'wait until your mount is almost on top of them before moving – fast!'

The Duke of Windsor was suspicious about Sandringham's teeming game. 'I always suspected that in addition to the birds raised on the place, a good many hundred pheasants were brought in and released for the King's benefit,' he admitted.

The third drive starts with one single bird flushed out of the thorn thicket and climbing, climbing, climbing – a cloud of pheasants rising behind. The guns wait until they are high in the sky, and then the barrage rattles for ten full minutes, barrels burning through gloves, the loader struggling to keep up, birds cartwheeling down, the dogs panting at heel. At the end of the drive, there is a sudden stillness and the ringing reverberation of gunfire. An eddy of wind makes the leaves pulsate – bright dabs of molten yellow on skinny branches.

The mixture of callousness and sentimentality that characterized Victorian attitudes to animals has been reflected in the royal estates. While Edward VII joined the big *battue*, his wife Alexandra would tame wildfowl to eat from her hand. George V, so proud of bringing down 1,000 pheasants in a day, would come down to breakfast each morning with his pet parrot Charlotte on his finger, and the Duchess of Beaufort, walking with him at Windsor, saw his eyes fill with tears at the sight of a dead bird in the garden.

Outside Prince Philip's private rooms in Buckingham Palace, he has bird trays so that he can watch London's bird life from his study. Today his loader

Prince Edward during the Christmas 1990 holiday at Sandringham. Like Charles and Anne, he has shooting weekends with friends, when he stays at Wood Farm on the Sandringham estate.

has struggled to keep up with him as he has relentlessly downed the pheasants on this drive.

'HRH Prince Philip, the Duke of Edinburgh, is high on my list as a good sport,' said Joe Nickerson, whose memoirs are labelled *A Shooting Man's Creed*.

Charles watches a retriever bound back with another bird. 'It must be very difficult for people not brought up in the countryside to understand the strange, paradoxical relationship between shooting gamebirds and the conservation, or stewardship of a diverse and beautiful natural habitat,' he admits. 'It must be equally difficult to comprehend the possibility of someone enjoying shooting while at the same time having a great love and intimate knowledge of nature and of wildlife in general.'

A Sandringham shoot used once to be a private battlefield, where games of power and glory were played against neighbouring country estates, each army identified by a different uniform, like the fiefdoms of medieval barons.

Louise Cresswell watched a shooting party get under way: 'A band of gamekeepers in green and gold, with the head man on horseback, an army of beaters in smocks and hats bound with royal red.'

The Duke of Windsor remembered the keepers' hats: 'They wore bowler hats with gold cords round the base of the crown, and gold lace acorns on the front,' he said. 'But the headkeeper wore one of those half top hats, a "cheerer", and carried a silver horn – on a cord of red braid with tassels slung over his green brass-buttoned coat of melton cloth.'

The uniforms – green-velvet coats worn with tight cord breeches and gaiters – had been introduced by Prince Albert, who trained an army of under-keepers at Windsor and brought them to Sandringham to police his son's estate. They were dubbed 'Velveteens' by the Norfolk locals. A farmer complained to Louise Cresswell that the keepers were 'always a-spyin' here and a-pryin' there and a-watchin' everything I du'.

Albert's ideas were inspired by the shooting costume of Germany, and the Norfolk locals were in for an even greater shock when Kaiser Wilhelm – Albert and Victoria's grandson – visited Edward VII at Sandringham in an unequivocally military shooting costume. 'A dark green loden suit of jacket and knickerbockers, worn with high black boots,' said the Duke of Windsor. 'It had an ornate leather belt, from which hung an elaborate short sword, and a stiff green homburg hat surmounted by long feathers.'

Today's keepers wear green tweed suits with waistcoats and plus fours, tweed caps or hats, thick socks and stout shoes. Country ties are knotted against Tattersall check shirts. The military precision of sporting dress has quite gone, although the beaters travel in an army-style green canvas waggon, pulled by a tractor. Diana often travels with the beaters when she comes out on a shoot, her merry face peeping out from the hood of a parka.

Inside the Big House, both ladies and gentlemen once made endless changes of outfit – morning costumes, walking dress, tea gowns and dinner suits. So it was for the gamekeepers up to the war. 'Father had a lighter suit for partridge shooting,' says Jack Clark. 'But for pheasant days, he wore a big, dark green beatkeeper's coat. It was ever such a heavy coat. What it would cost today goodness only knows.'

Charles is chaffing a keeper, echoing the relationship his grandfather had with Bland.

'Well, Bland, all the partridges downed, I suppose,' George VI would say to the lugubrious royal gamekeeper.

So much has changed here at Sandringham. Firstly there are the pheasants themselves, wild and supposedly able to fly fast and high, compared to their Edwardian counterparts 'ridiculous in their slow flight'.

'The King is having good sport,' said Sir Dighton Probyn. 'They call it sport!!!! Shooting tame pheasants. It does puzzle me.'

In that earlier era, guns whom a Sandringham guest described as 'perhaps only just more mobile than the pheasants from which they were hidden', sat complacently behind a dense screen of seven-foot-high evergreens, moving on like a battle convoy from drive to drive. 'The coverts which he planted were designed with no intention of producing pheasants which could possibly fly either high or fast,' said a Sandringham gun of Edward VII's thicket of broom, snowberry and privet.

Now the coverts have been replanned and Dersingham Wood replanted, but still a current gun claims that the topography of the estate offers too much

The Queen Mother does not actively participate in the shoot, but she enjoys watching the guns as a spectator.

Sarah, Duchess of York at Sandringham with her dog Tarn in December 1989, when she was expecting Eugenie. She enjoyed shooting days during her ill-fated royal marriage.

cover set close together. 'Sandringham is not really a good shoot – that is, you don't get good birds flying high, which is what the sport is all about,' he says. 'Of course, there is no question of refusing a royal invitation. One is pretty pleased to be asked. But it is the idea of rubbing along with royalty, not the quality of the shoot.'

A Norfolk landowner criticizes the royal guns as much as the shoot. 'Prince Charles is known round here as a bit greedy,' he says 'And his father always goes for the big bag.'

'Sandringham and all it stands for is dead,' claims another Norfolk shot. 'The Duke of Edinburgh is very Germanic in his attitudes. They don't rear birds, but there is a whole vast gamekeeping staff dedicated to beating up those pheasants for a few weeks in the year. In a sense they owe it to the keepers to shoot in that way. The whole estate is in a time warp. It belongs to another era.'

Although Sandringham would never be made into a commercial shoot, it was rented out to a party of Americans in aid of the Game Conservancy in the 1991/2 season.

Royal guns have not always enjoyed the set-piece driven shoots. George VI, when Duke of York, discovered the pleasures of rough shooting when he went to stay at Glamis Castle with Lord Strathmore, his future father-in-law. 'It was in the Glamis pattern of sport that the King found a new and lasting appeal – mixed and varied days, snipe drives, and so on,' Lord Buxton recalls.

Prince Charles too rejoices in a small day at a rough shoot on Duchy of Cornwall land, sharing the beating up, talking to the locals and the ladies from the local gun dog society.

'He's a much better shot than us!' says a farmer in Devon where Charles has been out with the guns. 'When he first came, we gave him the best stand. But now he draws lots for his peg. He seems to like just being one of us.'

THE SHOOTING LUNCH

Lunch at last! The shooting lunch – once held in a giant marquee – now takes place in the timber shooting lodge built in the mid-1980s by the Queen in a belt of trees on Flitcham hill.

'It's part of keeping the controversial shooting business out of the public eye,' says a local who remembers when the royal family would lunch among the notices for Church Bazaar and Women's Institute in the village hall at Anmer – one of the seven villages on the estate.

'When I first went to Sandringham, I couldn't believe it,' said Barry. 'There we were in a bare-boarded hall with an enormous table covered with linen cloths, napkins and silver. It looked like the dining room of a West End Hotel.' But in recent years, he explained, 'The royals now help themselves to food; the footmen are no longer required.'

Today thick white plates are sent to the lodge by jeep from Sandringham in blankets to keep them warm. There are hot jacket potatoes in crumpled silver foil, Thermoses of soup or stew, and a slug of sloe gin to stave off the chill. Depending on numbers, the shooting party either sits formally round the long table on the high-backed rush chairs, or there is a serve-yourself buffet lunch.

But some traditions never change, and this is the moment when the guns are joined by the ladies. 'The guns would go out in the morning and the Duchess of Wellington and Lady Jane would come out to join us for lunch,' said Barry of shooting in Spain with Prince Charles and his former girlfriend. However, if Charles is shooting at Sandringham with a few friends, they might not stop for lunch, but follow instead his hunting regime: a hearty breakfast, drives right through the daylight hours, a sandwich on the hoof and home for a substantial tea.

At this royal family shoot, Sarah Duchess of York in her green husky, cord

The timber shooting lodge built by the Queen. Inside there is a wood-burning stove, leather fender seats round the fireplace, framed pictures of birds, and a pine table with rush-seated chairs.

trousers and Davy Crockett fur-tailed hat, is the modern equivalent of the elegant Edwardian lady in ankle-length tweed shooting costume and be-feathered hat that the Queen Mother alone still wears. She has on a delphinium blue felt hat with a jaunty feather clasped by a silver buckle on the band, a blue tweed suit and a triple string of pearls. They will all be enveloped by a hooded raincoat when, after lunch, she watches a couple of drives.

Diana is rounding up her own boys and Anne's Peter and Zara to serve them from the buffet. She might have preferred to stay back at Wood Farm, but a shooting lunch is still a royal summons.

'Luncheon out shooting was in a large tent and everybody staying at the house had to come no matter what they might have been doing during the morning,' said the courtier Sir Frederick (Fritz) Ponsonby of Edwardian Sandringham. 'Carriages were ordered and we all had to have luncheon in a damp tent.'

The idea of a full, formal, hot shooting lunch was an invention of Prince Albert's in Victorian times. 'Heaven defend my stomach,' he said to his wife at the prospect of the cold food at English shooting parties.

'He stops shooting to devour his German *Mittagessen*,' complained Lord Lonsdale, who saw the fancy meal, like the set-piece shooting *battue* as an unwelcome introduction from Albert's native Germany.

The shooting lunches became increasingly elaborate, and by George V's reign, a visiting parson noted ten liveried serving men – half in dark blue with gold buttons, the others in red – waiting at lunch on a shooting party of eight. Such palatial grandeur destroyed the idea of a day's sport in the country.

'Sometimes when I am sitting in a tent taking part in a lengthy luncheon of many courses, served by a host of retainers, my memory takes me back to a time . . . when seated under a hedge, our midday meal consisted of a sandwich, cut by ourselves at the breakfast table in the morning, which we washed down by a pull from a flask; and I am inclined to think those were better and healthier days,' said Lord Ripon.

The shooting servants made do with the sandwiches in the hedgerows. 'A great chunk of bread – about half a cottage loaf, cheese, meat, beer and mince pies – all wrapped up in a little parcel,' says Jack Clark of the keepers' lunch back in the 1930s.

Twenty years later, the Duke of Edinburgh's valet John Dean complained about the pecking order. 'We were out from about nine until four-thirty in the afternoon,' he said. 'The loaders lunched on sandwiches, beer and coffee behind a hayrick or anywhere else that offered shelter from the knife-like winds that blew across the fens. How envious we were of the steaming hot foods which footmen carried from the house to some village hall for the shooting party.'

In shooting's heyday, there was a rigid hierarchy: the King in the large lunch tent; keeper Bland in 'his own little tent adjoining it', while 'Mother did our big front room for the loaders of the guests,' says Clark. 'We used to be all right for grub for about a fortnight afterwards, what with sauces, cold meats, pickles, chutney and suchlike.'

The talk today is inevitably of birds, dogs and retrievals. Although it is considered bad form to boast about the bag, there are still heroes and duffers, as in the days when Bland would emerge from his tent to give the King the scores, his face 'as solemn and grave as that of an ambassador presenting his letters of credence'. Edward VII would read out the scores himself, inviting the ladies to applaud heroic bags. 'This may have been very amusing for the good shots, but it seemed to hold the bad shots up to ridicule when the totals were read out at luncheon,' said Ponsonby.

Now Diana is serving coffee from the line-up of Thermos flasks on the trestle table. The Queen has done away with the silver coffee pot kept warm over a small burner, which, according to family legend, nearly sent Princess Margaret up in smoke when a young footman went to refill her cup.

Not so long ago, the royal cook Mrs McKee would plan a shooting luncheon of lobster salad, curried eggs, veal and lamb cutlets in aspic followed by apple turnovers and cheese.

'The great function for me was the hot luncheon in a barn. Sat next to the Princess [Alexandra] at dinner, most charming of all Princesses,' was Sir Henry Keppel's judgement on a Sandringham shoot on 10 January 1865. Ten years before he had commanded the British fleet at the siege of Sebastopol in the Crimean War.

'Well, Sir, the shooting was not much, but the lunch was excellent,' said Lord Curzon, one-time Viceroy of India, to Edward VII. He was not asked to Sandringham again.

Diana, brought up at Sandringham's Park House, is familiar with shooting and enjoys taking the boys in the beaters' wagon. Her father (then Lord Althorp) and her grandfather, Lord Fermoy, were shooting companions of Charles's grandfather George VI.

Princess Anne's son Peter Phillips was allowed to join the Sandringham shoot at the age of 12. He was taken wildfowling on Wolferton Marshes by his grandfather, Prince Philip in November 1990, bagging teal and mallard.

ON THE MARSHES

THE PARTIES have split up, Prince Philip keeping a promise to take duck shooting Anne's son Peter ('absolutely his favourite grandson', says a friend). The Princess Royal takes Zara and William along the Norfolk shore for a windy walk, while the Queen and her house guests have returned in a posse of Land-Rovers to Sandringham. Charles and the other six guns go on with the shoot, the Queen Mother, Sarah, Diana and Prince Harry joining them as spectators, although if Harry is out in the morning he will usually 'pack it in' at lunch time.

Above the marshes a string of flighting fowl are battling across the Wash to make headway against the wind. In the failing light, they are just faint stains on the sky, then a clearly defined wingspan, a duck bill in silhouette, a familiar

Anne, her daughter Zara, Prince William and royal dogs on a windy walk at the sea shore at Wells in Norfolk, 18 miles from Sandringham just before New Year 1991. They stopped at the Queen's beach bungalow for tea.

BELOW: *Prince William at the water's edge. A few moments later, a gust of wind bowled him over.*

quacking call, the hissing of the wings. There is a crack of gunshot and a mallard drops to where Prince Philip and Peter are waiting in the eerie half-light for the evening flight.

The marsh has been preserved as a wildfowl reserve, not just for ducks, but for the teal – that small, agile bird which Peter will bag today – and the elusive widgeon. In 1985, Philip the conservationist helped to launch a campaign called 'Life at the Water's Edge'. Here in Norfolk it is strange, wild, uncompromising territory.

'It is quite wrong to think of them as a wasteland that must be drained to be productive,' says Philip of the wetlands that stretch to the Wash from the outer edge of the Sandringham estate. This salty wilderness of reeds and creeks, of mud flats rhythmically engulfed by the tidal flow, has a strong appeal for the ex-naval Prince.

'Today it was a harsh spectacle, the dykes lifeless and solid with ice, reeds and long grasses frosted and fast. No birds spoke in the bleak afternoon on the marshland,' said Aubrey Buxton of a day wildfowling with George VI.

'There are plenty of duck in now,' said George VI. He had been reading a report from Sandringham as he looked out towards St James's Park in London, where his royal ancestor, King Charles II, had created a lagoon stocked with waterfowl. 'His mind would have pictured other duck in Norfolk, against a wilder sky on the marshes, and his men watching the duck on the ponds and pools,' said Buxton.

George VI would escape from royal protocol to keep a lonely vigil at the flighting ponds on the estate – Frankfort Pool, where the dawn flight in 1937 brought the new King a flock of 150 teal; or Wolferton Splash, the pool carved out by a Zeppelin bomb in 1915, where he and a colleague together shot 69 mallard. In 1937, when he took over at Sandringham as King, he started a new game book especially for duck shooting, recording the date, place and weather, his bag ('48 mallard, 2 teal, 1 widgeon, 1 various'), and his comments: 'Duck came in steadily in small lots' or 'The guns were too close' or 'Mallard very chary, but a lot of teal came in.' The King became an expert on wildfowl and hung illustrations of different species of duck in the estate

office, so that his head keeper Alfred Amos and the staff could recognize them.

'I really think he was more fond of duck shooting than anything else,' said a shooting friend.

'George VI really liked duck shooting and rabbit shooting best, but he had to slacken up in the last few years when he became ill,' says Jack Clark, who on a bleak February day in 1952 marched in the gamekeepers' procession to Wolferton station behind the King's coffin.

Princess Elizabeth had joined her father on his last wildfowling expedition. On 18 October 1949, they had set off at dawn, crossed the bridge to the reed-tipped island of Frankfort Pool and waited for mallard and teal, widgeon, gadwell, shoveller and pintail to come in. 'There is poignancy in the thought that here, in the depths of England, George the Sixth was out after the fowl before sunrise, while Elizabeth the Second crouched by him to see how these things should be done,' said Buxton.

In Edwardian times, even the desolate marshes could be taken over by a shooting party, with hides and shooting platforms built among the reeds. Kaiser Wilhelm, invited by Edward VII to Sandringham at the start of the Edwardian era, was entertained with duck shooting on the marshes. Although the King told his German uncle that 'it is not customary to wear uniforms in the country in England,' the Kaiser still wore his duck-hunting suit the pale blue of a rainwashed sky and a feathered Tyrolean hat.

George VI enjoyed the solitary motionless wait for wildfowl, calling Wolferton Splash 'a one-gun place'. So it is for Philip, who likes to come alone to the Wash, using the viewing window of a shepherd's hut perched on the old sea-wall as a look-out. Even before the birds are flighting, there is the sting of salt on the spray, the swell of the sea and a far horizon of memories.

'He came into the Palace like a refreshing sea breeze,' said the royal governess Marion Crawford. As a young naval cadet at Dartmouth, Philip had showed off to the two Princesses by rowing after the royal yacht as it turned out of the harbour and into the Channel. In the last carefree summer of 1951, the sailor prince had taken command of HMS *Magpie*, and stood on the bridge while Princess Elizabeth on the quay in Malta waved him goodbye, like any naval wife.

The Queen taking her corgis for a walk along the sandy beach. She likes to give them a good run to stop the vicious scraps that break out among the dogs.

ABOVE: *The royal beach chalet among the sand dunes at Wells in Norfolk – a favourite for family picnics.*

ABOVE RIGHT: *The Queen Mother surprised a party of nudists on the North Norfolk beach after a picnic with friends she had invited for the King's Lynn Festival.*

Anne, as well as Andrew, has inherited Prince Philip's love of the sea. 'Sailing on a sunny day, with a fresh breeze blowing, with maybe someone you really care for, is the nearest thing to heaven I will ever get on this earth,' she says.

Anne also understands the problems her father faced by marrying into the royal family. 'I think there is a special difficulty,' she says. 'After all, we normally still think of the husband as number one and his wife as number two, whereas in the case of a royal female who has public duties to perform it's rather the other way about. There has got to be a problem, hasn't there? My father had a naval career and eventually had to give it up.'

The panoramic view is over sea and salt marsh, where there have been bawdy outings in a punt for Philip, duck-shooting with his good mates the writer and country commentator Maxwell Hastings and James Robertson Justice, the former actor and a lover of field sports.

Now Philip concentrates on protecting the area from the public. 'Simple access in wetland areas is very disturbing to wildlife,' he says. 'You've got ground-nesting birds on the shore at Blakeney Point. If people just swarmed down there and treated it as a beach, that would be an end of the terns.'

Farther along the coast, Anne, with seven dogs – her Staffordshire bull terrier and a bunch of labradors – is taking the children on a gusty walk to the Queen's beach bungalow near Wells, where sometimes they have tea. It is 'a little beach chalet perched on top of a sand dune and overlooking an enormous beach', said the late Prince Jean-Louis de Faucingy-Lucinge, one of the Queen Mother's friends who used to come over from France for a summer stay at Sandringham during the annual King's Lynn festival of the arts.

The Prince remembered one picnic at the Norfolk beach hut when, after a grand picnic, he walked with the Queen Mother and the corgis along the sand dunes. The royal party (mostly aged over 80) discovered that the beach was occupied by nudists.

'They got up from their nest in the sand and, when they saw us coming, fled as fast as their legs could carry them,' said the French Prince. 'But others, just to prove that a Queen walking by wasn't going to change their habits, stayed there, being just a little bit provocative. It was amusing for us. Alas, nudists were banned after that.'

Far from being embarrassed, the Queen Mother had enjoyed the diversion. 'The royals love anything that upsets the even tenor of their lives,' says Barry.

Today Prince William, in his red anorak, walks along the deserted beach watching the waves boiling and foaming along the shoreline. The wind is so powerful it bowls him clean over, sand creeping under his check shirt and sweater and down his boots.

His grandfather is walking back from the marshes, to the roar of the wind and the weird whistling cry of a widgeon.

Prince Philip is passionate about protecting this fowler's paradise. 'But what's controversial about this?' he asked angrily in an interview in *The Times*. 'Is what you are saying that because of critics we should go on squirting all this shit into the North Sea: or take all the fish out of it? Or reclaim all the wetlands so that there is nowhere left for the wildfowl to go? Is that what you want? Saying we want to keep the North Sea healthy is like saying we want to keep children healthy. Why is that wrong?'

Prince Charles tries to sum up the eerie splendour of the isolated Norfolk marshes. 'We must protect the land,' he says. 'We need, for all sorts of complex historical and psychological reasons, a sense of wilderness.'

EVERYTHING STOPS FOR TEA

A CACOPHONY of chimes announces 4 P.M.: one gilded clock tinkles above the massive carved fireplace in the saloon; another strikes from the pink-veined marbled mantelpiece in the small drawing room; yet another in the drawing room, where the Queen is walking purposefully, followed, like the Pied Piper, by her corgis and dorgis.

'Very long and handsome drawing room, with painted ceiling and panels with two fireplaces,' said Queen Victoria, when she made a rare visit to Sandringham in 1871 to see her son who was ill with typhoid.

Sandringham was bought by the newly-widowed Queen Victoria in 1862 for the Prince of Wales – the future Edward VII. The long three-storey Georgian mansion was extensively re-built by architect Albert Jenkins Humbert, emerging in 1870 as the red brick house with pepperpot turrets – its conservatory converted to a billiard room and a game larder with space for 1,300 birds.

Its heart is the grand entrance saloon, but the main rooms, which Queen Victoria admired, are the three interconnecting drawing and dining rooms. They have fancy mouldings and marbled fireplaces, and although Queen Mary had a clear-out of her mother-in-law Queen Alexandra's clutter, the rooms are still filled with family photographs and mementoes.

The Prince de Faucingy-Lucinge called Sandringham 'Edwardian and cosy'. 'There are marvellous salons, all in creamy stucco, with portraits of Queen Alexandra and her sisters,' he said. 'You see elaborate glass-fronted cabinets containing Fabergé and other wonders, and screens with photos of royalty, friends and famous people of that epoch.'

Queen Alexandra, looking down from the Edward Hughes portrait of herself in a shimmer of silk and lace, would have understood the important task her descendant, in checked tweed skirt and twinset, is carrying out on the hour this afternoon: she is going to feed the dogs.

When Alexandra was Queen, Edward VII insisted on having the clocks half

The Queen and Prince Philip outside Sandringham House, bought for the future Edward VII by Queen Victoria in 1862. The red-brick façade and pepperpot turrets were completed in 1870 and stand in 20,456 acres (8,280 hectares) of grounds. Except for the traditional royal New Year holiday, the family often stays at the smaller Wood Farm.

an hour fast. This was a trick learned from nearby Holkham Hall on the North Norfolk coast, where the Earl of Leicester, of the Coke family, had made a little more daylight time for shooting. Although Queen Victoria exclaimed 'It's a wicked lie!', in Norfolk the royal family kept 'Sandringham Time' for half a century.

'A little boy was born weighing nearly 8lb at 3.40 (S.T.),' George V wrote in his diary when his second son, the future George VI was born.

As George V's life 'was drawing peacefully to its close,' the future Edward VIII, in a symbolic gesture, ordered the local clockmaker to take a taxi to Sandringham where Greenwich Mean Time was to be restored. 'I'll fix those bloody clocks,' he said.

The corgis' meal is always at precisely 4 P.M. There are only nine bowls now on the tray, since dear old Chipper was fatally wounded by the Queen Mother's corgi Ranger in 1989 and the trouble-making Apollo was dispatched to Anne at Gatcombe. The plastic sheet is laid down as the Queen adjusts the volume in each bowl. The mixture of wheat and barley, with vitamins, protein, soya and dried meat, called Carta Carna, is delivered in sacks of 20 kilos from Clark & Butcher, royal warrant holders in Ely. The gravy is added as the dogs sit, salivating in a semi-circle, waiting to be called forward:

'Spark! Myth! Fable! Diamond! Kelpie!' Each one is fed in turn, the eldest first and youngest last. All the corgis are pure-bred Pembrokeshires directly descended from Susan, who was given to Princess Elizabeth as an eighteenth-birthday present in 1944, and was with her in the state landau as the newly married Duke and Duchess of Edinburgh drove down the Mall and off on honeymoon. Her grave is outside in Sandringham's grounds: 'For almost 15 years the faithful companion of the Queen' it says on the headstone of Susan, who died in January 1959.

'Phoenix! Pharos!' and then 'Harris! Piper!' the two dorgis – also descended from Susan, via Honey, Bee,

Caesar, Edward VII's terrier painted by Wright Barker. After the King's death in 1910, a book, Where's Master?, *written as though by Caesar, became a bestseller, running to nine editions.*

Heather, Foxy, Brush and Sweep – derive from a cross between the blush-red Pembrokeshire bitches and Princess Margaret's dachshund Pipkin.

The dogs are perfectly behaved, never a snap or a growl, but then they have been give a good run here at Sandringham, instead of being cooped up in the cars shuttling between Buckingham Palace and Windsor. Vicious scraps do break out, in spite of the Dog Stop alarm – an ultra-high-pitched 120 decibel whistle (designed as an anti-rape alarm). It was introduced to the Palace by the dog psychiatrist Roger Mugford, who was recommended to the Queen by Princess Anne. Yet the Queen was still bitten on the knuckles of her left hand – needing three stitches – after separating scrapping dogs at Windsor in the spring of 1991.

The Queen's theory is that corgis need children to stimulate and entertain them, just as she and Margaret, as children, would play with Dookie, the first of the royal corgis.

'He really is the greatest personality of a dog that I have ever known,' claimed George VI. 'So intelligent – and so marvellously patient with the children.' Later he admitted that Dookie – much given, like Ranger, to snapping at the ankles – was 'the black sheep of our family . . . and like most black sheep, he is probably the favourite'.

Kelpie, well fed, rolls over to have her tummy rubbed. The Queen's fondness for her dogs is in a fine tradition here at Sandringham, where Queen Alexandra would keep 20 dogs of all kinds from graceful borzois to chows, spaniels and pekinese. Her husband's faithful wire-haired fox terrier, whose collar carried the legend 'I am Caesar. I belong to the King', became a celebrity after Edward VII's death in 1910, when a sentimental book was published in his name entitled *Where's Master?*.

The royal dogs today know who is master. As the Queen goes off to preside over Sandringham tea, they follow her obediently, a pool of red brown lapping round her sturdy shoes.

'Horrible, yapping, snapping creatures,' says a house guest. 'I can't think of a good word to say about them – except they warn you that HM is on the way.'

The children are coming in for tea – Peter Phillips boasting of his prowess on the marshes, sparring with William, just as Anne and Charles, years ago, would play games of sardines and start scraps between the corgis.

'All of us who have been blessed with young families know from long experience that when one's house is at its noisiest, there is often less cause for anxiety,' the Queen claims. She is ignoring the jumble of children as she goes to greet new arrivals.

For Sandringham house guests, there is always a panic to arrive precisely in time for tea – but not too far ahead of the returning shooting party or at the moment when the Queen is walking the corgis in the grounds. From London it is an awkward journey, full speed down the M11 to Cambridge, then a crawl across the fens.

'A deuce of a way from London,' Lord Esher complained when Sandringham first became a royal residence. Then it was far more practical to go by train, especially on the Prince's Special that would pull into Wolferton station, which Queen Victoria found 'very prettily decorated' when she made a royal progress in Easter Week of 1889, then on through Sandringham's gates, hung with Venetian masks to celebrate the engagement of her granddaughter Princess Louise to the Earl of Fife.

'Our journeys to Wolferton, for Sandringham, were an enjoyable picnic,' said the Duke of Windsor. There were no dining-cars on this route in those days, so we took a well-stocked luncheon basket.' Labelled 'His Majesty the King', the baskets would be collected at Liverpool Street station. They are still used for royal picnics today.

The saloon has hardly changed since the Edwardians assembled for tea. There is still the same dark frowning panelling, the fretted minstrels' gallery, the shield and Brussels tapestries, a fireplace at each end. 'It's an inherited place – one's known it ever since one was a child,' the Queen explains. 'I knew how much my father had enjoyed it. Well, in fact, all my family ever since King Edward bought it.' Memoirs of the Edwardian age are filled with stories of travellers welcomed into the warm womb of Sandringham. 'The five o'clock family tea-table round which we all sat, the Prince of Wales pouring out tea,' said Lady Constance Battersea, daughter of Sir Anthony de Rothschild, a friend of the Prince of Wales.

'I arrived just as they were all at tea in the entrance hall, and had to walk in all seedy and dishevelled from my day's journey and sit down beside the Princess of Wales,' said Dr Magee, Bishop of Peterborough, in 1873.

'Everybody had assembled at tea in the hall, into which one bursts from the outside air,' said Wallburga, Lady Paget. 'The Prince was the first to greet me, the Princess was handing round the cups.'

Today the Queen is presiding over the tea pot, or, to be more precise, the silver tea kettle with ivory handle and silver blower to snuff out the paraffin burner underneath. The kettle tips forwards on a spindle to fill the pot as the Queen takes three spoonfuls of Twining's tea from the caddy and cooks crumpets in the automatic toaster.

'We are not very interested in alcohol,' says Prince Charles, 'but in our family everything stops for tea. I have never known a family so addicted to it.'

After 25 years of exile in France, the Duke of Windsor would still carry a Thermos of tea in a tartan zip bag. 'I too depend on my cup of tea, as most self-respecting Britons do,' he said.

Royal tea is above all a family get-together. 'Family tea with everyone sharing in the banana sandwiches and sponge cake,' says Mrs McKee of Princess Elizabeth's days as a young mother having nursery tea with the children.

The Queen Mother is famous for the teas she gives at Clarence House, Royal Lodge and, particularly, Birkhall, where a guest says that there is 'an enormous table, always much too much'. In earlier days, Lady Cynthia Asquith would talk of 'her Scotch skill in the making of scones and cakes' –

Prince Charles on the terrace of Royal Lodge, Windsor in 1954 with Honey, one of the ancestors of the present corgi pack.

FACING PAGE: *The Queen and Prince Philip with the corgis in the saloon at Sandringham. Behind them, the seventeenth-century Belgian tapestry depicting the history of Constantine.*

learned as a child in the still room at Glamis Castle. When they stayed at Glamis, Crawfie said that the two Princesses 'loved to go to taste the newly baked cakes and beg for coffee sugar'.

The royal tea menu is immutable: cucumber sandwiches spiced with a drop of tarragon vinegar; potted shrimps for Philip; crunchy ginger biscuits; McVitie & Price digestive biscuits; chocolate biscuits in silver wrappers; a sponge sandwich or the Queen Mother's perennial birthday treat: chocolate and coffee cake, rich dark slabs with a secret ingredient of a tablespoon of orange marmalade and a buttery filling flavoured with coffee.

Outside in the half-light, the returning shooting part forms black silhouettes, their guns like broken sticks, the dogs dancing shadows, the Land-Rovers hulks in the gloom.

Guests are thanking the head keeper Bill Meldrum for a fine day's sport, while he keeps to himself his feelings about the one gun who consistently failed to mark his birds. Notes are pressed discreetly into his hand. 'The average in my last few years at Broadlands was £10,' says Harry Grass. 'And royals tipped much in line with other guests.' Visitors today are giving Meldrum £20.

What happens to these bundles of feathers catching the dying light as they are hauled away? Some of today's birds will finish up on the royal dinner table. Van-loads of game from Balmoral and Sandringham arrive at all the royal residences.

'It was my job at Clarence House to think of ways of dealing with this rich stream of pheasant, grouse, partridge, etc,' says Mrs McKee. 'I was quite pleased when the shooting season was over.' Her recipes included pheasant pie, partridge stuffed with button mushrooms and bacon, roast wild duck and a galantine of game that used up a pheasant and a grouse.

Although the Queen is conservative in her tastes, hosts often present imaginative dishes. 'The Queen so liked the pigeon cooked in honey, when we served it for dinner, that "Young Porchie" (Lord Carnarvon), whom she was travelling with, called us to ask for the recipe,' says one of the Queen's hosts in France.

Joe Nickerson also entertained Prince Philip royally. 'We gave him a golden plover pie, a tremendous delicacy which he had never had before,' said Nickerson. 'It was quite a coup, I felt, to have been able to provide something novel for a man who attends so many dinners in so many lands.'

Sandringham meals today are not the bountiful feasts of the Edwardian era, when the actress Ellaline Terriss, appearing in a performance of *Scrooge* at Sandringham in 1902, exclaimed over the kitchens. 'In one corner ducks, woodcocks, snipe and other wildfowl were being roasted on an enormous spit, whilst a contingent of chefs basted them,' she remembered. 'We seemed to have stepped right back into the Middle Ages.'

Muddy boots are pulled off or scraped at the door using the porcupine brush rotating on a chain. This moment of stripping off wet-weather clothing outside can be hazardous – as Prince Philip found when he was removing his over-trousers and nearly got run down by a Land-Rover. 'I realized that he could not see the Duke bending down in front of the radiator and shouted to him to stop – just in time,' said Joe Nickerson.

'Thanks, that was a near one!' Philip said.

Inside, damp tweeds are exchanged for sweaters with cord trousers or jeans, still with a country shirt and tie, but nowhere near the sartorial standards of the past.

'Once, after shooting at Sandringham, I had gone to the kennels to look after one of my dogs, who was sick, and appeared for tea still dressed in my shooting clothes,' says the Duke of Windsor. 'This brought me an immediate reprimand from my father.'

'Is it *raining* in here?' the King asked his eldest son, on another occasion, glaring at the new-fangled turn-ups on his trousers.

George V would change after shooting, just for tea, into a velvet or tartan suit, like the striking Rothesay hunting tartan suit which the Duke of Windsor inherited. 'I had this altered to fit me, substituting zip flies – which I fear would have horrified my father – for buttons,' said the Duke.

The velvet suit was first introduced to royal households by Prince Albert. 'He wore a black velvet jacket without a cravat, and anything more beautiful – and more youthfully manly and perfect – never was seen,' recalled Queen Victoria. Its descendants are the buttermilk furrowed cords that Prince Charles favours, or Sarah's cord skirt and plush velveteen waistcoat.

Edward is adding a piece to the jigsaw – a Christmas present to the Queen – which has its straight outside edges of landscape already completed, but a blank patch in the middle where puffy white clouds should fill the sky and trees spread leafy branches. The puzzle is part of a long tradition.

'In the entrance hall there now stood a baize-covered table on which jigsaw puzzles were set out,' said Lady Airlie, Queen Mary's old lady-in-waiting, of the first Christmas at Sandringham after the war. 'The younger members of the party . . . congregated round them from morning till night.'

Sandringham at Christmas was once the quintessential country house party, famous for its hoaxes and horseplay, as when Edward VII arranged apple-pie beds and his teenage daughters Princesses Louise, Victoria and Maud, stuffed sticky sweets into pockets, set up buckets of water or served up soap as cheese. Princess Margaret, as a child, got up to similar pranks. 'I have seen an equerry put his hand into his pocket, and find it, to his amazement, full of sticky lime balls,' Crawfie claimed.

Modern-day Christmas frolics have included adult charades and a wild cabaret in which Diana, in a pair of falsies, and Fergie in a mask, set out to 'debag' Prince Charles. Tonight, the only entertainment will be a film screened in the ballroom (all staff welcome) and an early night before the morning start for the guns.

George V out shooting in 1905. His shooting pony Jock was at the head of Sandringham's mourning procession when the King died in 1936.

Outside, although it is only 6 P.M., a dank, dark chill already cloaks the estate. Winter at Sandringham has laid cold fingers on two Kings. George V wheezed out the last of his shooting days in January 1936. In 1952, a draughty New Year saw the death of George VI.

When George V returned to lie in state in London, the new King Edward VIII marched with his two brothers at the head of the Sandringham procession, along with his father's shooting pony Jock and the mourning beaters and keepers.

'Just as we topped the last hill above the station, the stillness of the morning was broken by a wild familiar sound – the crow of a cock pheasant,' said the Duke of Windsor. 'Had my father been vouchsafed the choice of one last sight at Sandringham he would have chosen something like that: a pheasant travelling high and fast on the wind, the kind of shot he loved.'

FARMING

**Royal agriculture includes
Windsor Dairy milk, Highgrove's organic
corn and Highland cattle**

Down on the Farm

The King asked
The Queen, and
The Queen asked
The dairymaid:
'Could we have some butter for
The royal slice of bread?'

From *When We Were Very Young* by
A. A. MILNE (1882–1956)

THE ROYAL DAIRY

THE MILK flows in a silent stream from the fluted jug into the white porcelain bowl. Outside in Windsor's Home Park, leaves are listless in the July heat; grass lush and still; the Queen's Jerseys immobile brown boulders. There is a desultory swish of tail from Sparkling Natalie (a big winner at the Royal Show) and a slow, rolling advance by two cows, both descendants of Pretty Polly, who was brought by Queen Victoria from the farm at Osborne on the Isle of Wight.

The Queen today – her impressive knowledge of breeding extending from racehorses to her Jersey herd – will reel off sire and dam of cattle she inherited from her great-great grandmother. 'Her Majesty is very interested in the stock – particularly the Jerseys,' says Bill Gibson, who manages the cluster of farms at Windsor. 'She has lived with the pedigrees and knows them well.'

'I like farming,' the Queen admits. 'It's not very easy nowadays. I like animals. I wouldn't be happy if I just had arable farming. I think that's very boring.'

In Victoria's time, it was her husband alone who took farming seriously, while the Queen and her eldest daughter Vicky played milkmaids at Osborne, giving a demonstration of butter-making to the Emperor Napoleon III and Eugénie, on a visit from France.

'We Agriculturalists of England,' proclaimed Prince Albert when he addressed the annual meeting of the Royal Agricultural Society in 1848. 'That damned farmer!' the head keeper at Windsor called Albert.

The monarch is still an important landowner – both on the private estates and in the vast tracts of tenanted farm land of the Duchy of Lancaster. But the Queen's mud-on-the-boots farming is – to her regret – curtailed by her royal duties.

'It therefore fell to me to assume the general responsibility for the Sandringham and Balmoral estates,' explains Prince Philip, who, like Albert, takes an interest in modern farming methods and the science of agriculture – with a particular emphasis on conservation.

'Who identifies with agriculture?' asked Prince Philip in a lecture on

The Prince Consort's Dairy built in 1858 in Windsor Home Park.

FACING PAGE: *Royal dairymaid June Williams in the vaulted splendour of Prince Albert's Dairy, with its painted ceiling.*

PRECEDING PAGES: *The Queen and Prince Philip with Highland cattle at Balmoral.*

A private supply of milk and cream made in the Windsor dairy from the Jersey herd is sent in monogrammed bottles and waxed cartons to the Queen, the Queen Mother, Princess Margaret and the Prince of Wales.

The majolica-ware water-nymph fountain, one of a pair designed by John Thomas, is part of a complex water-feeding system that can still work at the turn of a tap.

intensive farming. 'It is an abstract concept, useful maybe for economists and for the civil servants and scientists who work in government departments of agriculture, but I doubt whether farmers and landowners feel that it applies to them personally.'

The Victorian edifice shimmering today in a heat haze, is part of the model farmstead at Windsor created from a hodge-podge of old buildings by Prince Albert in the 1850s, designed by architect and sculptor John Thomas.

Inside the Prince Consort's Dairy, the vaulted room is deliciously cool, even though – since a rotary milking parlour was installed in 1973 – water no longer flows through channels in the exotic tiled floor or spouts from the fantastic fountain, a majolica water-nymph rising from a shell supported by a pink-tinged heron amongst asparagus-green bullrushes.

'The appearance of a Turkey carpet' said a contemporary describing the blue-green translucent tiles with their borders of dense, precise flowers and flowing arabesques.

Mrs June Williams, custodian of the dairy parlour, is in a plain white overall amongst the tiled splendour. She pours the milk, skims the butterfat, while behind her a milk-white statue is sculpted in a similar pose. The milk, the velvet-smooth cream and the cream cheese she makes in muslin bags, straining them on a stand decorated with Victorian curlicues, will all go off to the royal residences.

'Untreated Milk produced on Royal farms, Windsor' it says on the foil top to the royal milk bottle, stamped in royal blue with the 'EIIR' monogram and crown, and delivered to Buckingham Palace three times a week. The cream – thick, rich and too much of it for a cholesterol-conscious modern royal family – goes into a waxed carton.

'The Jersey herd produces so much fat that we could exceed quota,' said Mr Gibson in 1987. 'We may well have to make more productive use of it on the premises – possibly through ice-cream.' Royal farming is constantly under review – both for internal efficiency and economy and to fit in with general trends and the European Community's Common Agricultural Policy.

'There is a lot more to agriculture than the production of food,' explained Philip in his 1989 BBC Dimbleby Lecture 'Living off the Land'. 'The individual farmer naturally tries to make the most of his assets and to satisfy

A decorative frieze contains an ornamental medallion of the Prince Consort. 'A man of remarkable energy and vision,' says Prince Charles of his great-great-great grandfather Prince Albert, who was a member of the Royal Agricultural Society and laid the basis of scientific farming at Windsor.

his customers, but he also has to respond to the economic realities of pricing policies, international trade agreements, common agricultural policies, tariffs, quotas, quality controls, subsidies, penalties for over-production, demands for conservation of nature and a host of other factors that govern the economics of his enterprise.'

Both the Queen and her husband have come down in the Land-Rover from the Castle to discuss a problem raised in Mr Gibson's monthly report. The Queen, oblivious to the heat, is in deep discussion with her farm manager and pigman Tony Burton, who is mucking out the Large White/Landrace sows in the yard.

'She has never lost her interest in the farming and other activities on the estates,' says Philip.

Technically the Queen is tenant of the 2,000 acres (810 hectares) of farmable land on three different farms at Windsor, while the Crown Estates Commissioners are her landlords. The Duke of Edinburgh has an official title as Ranger of Windsor Great Park, which makes him overseer of the stock at Shaw Farm and Prince Consort Farm down here in the Home Park, as well as of the cropped acres at Clayhall Farm. In the Great Park are Norfolk Farm and Flemish Farm, west of the Windsor-to-Ascot road.

The Duchy of Lancaster is a quite different and more distant proposition, for the Queen is not involved personally with either the 51,560 acres (20,866 hectares) of land or with the tenant farmers who provided her with a total income of £3.1 million in 1990. The inheritance dates back to 1265 and the holdings were once far greater than today, although investments in agricultural land have been made over the last fifty years. Dairy farming is important to the estates, which are divided into four main units or 'Surveys': the Crewe Survey in Staffordshire, Cheshire and Shropshire; the Lancashire and Yorkshire Surveys, with high ground for sheep farming; and the South Survey in Lincolnshire and Northamptonshire, which has the largest arable acreage.

'Responsibility for Sandringham and Balmoral has been rather more direct,' Philip said of the Queen's two private estates in his introduction to a 1980 book about royal farms, 'And the challenge, particularly after six years of war, to modernize, and more recently in the face of inflation, to contain costs and increase revenue has been daunting.'

The Duke of Edinburgh's interest in both the scientific theory of farming and its practice make him a part of a royal tradition that goes back to George III. 'Farmer George', as the Hanoverian monarch was known, stocked the wastelands of Windsor with cattle and sheep, drained marshland and laid out the two model Norfolk and Flemish Farms – as well as contributing farming advice to the *Annals of Agriculture* in 1787 under a pseudonym. He even involved his children. 'I am never out of the field all day,' said George III's third son, who became King William IV.

But it was Queen Victoria's Albert who laid the foundations for modern methods of royal farming. He conceived the Great Exhibition of 1851 as a display of Victorian enterprise 'from paintings to machines for making buttermilk', the first germ of an idea for the exhibition coming from the Prince Consort's plan to advertise modern agricultural methods and stimulate British farmers.

His noble carved profile looks down from the lofty ornamental ceiling of the deserted milking parlour where 70 cows once stood head to head over the network of drainage channels.

'Prince Albert was clearly a man of remarkable energy and vision,' says Prince Charles of the farmstead at Windsor. 'It is extraordinary to think that he died at the age of forty-two – the same age as I am now – having accomplished so much.' Yet Prince Albert's thoroughly modern buildings have long since been overtaken by scientific progress.

'Fashions change fast now,' says the Duchess of Devonshire, another landowner who has had to move with the times. At Chatsworth, as at Windsor, a rotary tandem milking parlour was installed.

'People came to wonder at it and to see the cows on a moving carousel while the man who was milking them remained in one place in the middle,' the Duchess recalled. But it has now been replaced by a 16-cow herringbone parlour.

And so it is at Windsor, where the royal Ayrshire herd over at Shaw Farm had three different milking systems before the installation of a herringbone parlour in the Queen's Jubilee year of 1977. There the 160 cows could be milked in two hours, morning and evening. Both the Ayrshires and the 129 Jerseys are now milked through 14:14 herringbone parlours. It is all a long way from the pastoral and picturesque scene in which a nursery-rhyme dairymaid splashed milk into a shiny bucket.

'Poor cow!' exclaimed Prince Charles when faced with the data of high-yielding scientifically-bred cattle at a model farm in France. He tried traditional milking when working on one of his Duchy of Cornwall farms, but at Highgrove he is obliged to milk to the rhythm of modern times. On the Duchy's Home Farm, Charles keeps a 110-cow Ayrshire dairy herd 'because it is a traditional British breed which is well-established by Her Majesty at Windsor', and has a modern milking parlour. However, it did not impress a fellow farmer visiting Highgrove.

'The milking parlour is nowhere near what I would have expected for Prince Charles,' he said. 'The cheese was gathering up at the necks of the jars. I was quite surprised, although I know they are talking about a change of herdsman at Highgrove. The cows look very good though.'

Inside the parlour at Windsor, the tiles are as clean as a whistle. The modern commerical dairy operation there yields a combined annual quota of milk from the two herds of approximately 1,118,000 litres. Prince Albert's dairy dealt with about 240 gallons of milk a day, according to the contemporary records which he kept with meticulous efficiency.

The Queen is emotionally attached to the Jerseys and to the Ayrshire herd, which was founded by her father in the last year of his life, and has resisted all

Prince Philip sets policy as Ranger of Windsor Great Park and assumes general responsibility for the private royal farms at Sandringham and Balmoral. 'The urge to improve and to develop the estates is as strong in me as in any of my predecessors,' he says.

The Queen takes a close interest in Windsor's Jersey herd, founded by Queen Victoria in 1871 with stock from Osborne Estate, Isle of Wight. Windsor Loreen (above) was selected personally by the Queen in New Zealand from the Ferdon herd as an in-calf heifer.

suggestions to turn over to Friesians, which would give a higher yield. Her 120 Jerseys yielded at the end of the 1980s an annual average of 4,000 litres per cow, which a farming expert describes as 'on the low side'.

'The decision to retain the Jersey and Ayrshire milking herds was one we could take without having to get the "landlord's" approval,' says Philip.

Victoria and Albert complained about the bureaucracy that hedged the royal estates. 'The Plague of one's life,' said Queen Victoria of the Department of Woods and Forests, that had to approve all the farming at Windsor in her day.

Albert found farming at Osborne a relief from officialdom. 'A place of one's own, quiet and retired and free from Departments, Crown, Woods & Forests, etc,' he said.

Prince Philip is resigned to the delicate balancing act he has to perform at Windsor: 'That ambivalent relationship which always exists between someone in a titular position and an autonomous semi-Government department,' he has said.

The royal owners have to make tough, unsentimental decisions of their own. At Sandringham the pedigree herd of Red Poll cattle, founded by George V, could not earn its keep and went in 1959, but not before two cows – Royal Frolic and Royal Gladiolus – had romped home with prizes at the Royal Show of 1951. The herd of 200 single-sucker beef cattle was sold in 1986, and now all that is left of the proud stock at Sandringham are some Friesian cows whose job is to keep the estate's grass tidy.

'I call them the "Hoover" herd, said Julian Lloyd, land agent for the Sandringham estate until his role was taken over by John Major in 1991. Two hundred of the distinctive black and white cattle are bought annually in March and April when they weigh between 400 and 450 kg, run on the grasslands of Sandringham's 20,000-acre (8,000-hectare) estate during the summer and then put into the Appleton Farm fattening yards before Christmas.

The Duke of Gloucester, farming at Barnwell Manor, near Peterborough in Northamptonshire, has also been forced out of cattle: the herd of pedigree Guernsey cattle has gone because of uneconomic milk yields. 'We can't grow enough good grass here,' says Victor Vinson, farm manager at Barnwell since 1968. In 1977, a herd of Friesians replaced the Guernseys, but now the model dairy has been taken over by a mixed community of small rural businesses.

'I swapped architecture for agriculture,' says the Duke of Gloucester, who took over Barnwell when his elder brother Prince William was killed in a flying accident in 1972. 'Things happen more quickly in farming – the natural cycle of exactly twelve months compared to much longer periods for building projects. In architecture you have to live with your mistakes for years to come. In farming it is just for that season.'

Under the shade of the trees, the mechanized milking parlours and computerized data of butterfat yields give way to the age-old English rural idyll: a variegated green landscape with spreading trees, dotted with grazing cattle and crowned by the turreted castle, its flag flying to denote that the Queen is in residence.

Prince Albert described his role at Osborne as 'partly forester, partly builder, partly farmer and partly gardener'. Up at the castle, Philip too has extended his role to replan the east terrace and the south slopes. 'Although not strictly speaking anything to do with farming, the redesigning of gardens and landscapes is something that has to go on,' he says.

Through half closed eyes, on this succulent English summer's day, there is just stippled green shade below a cloudless sweep of blue. Queen and consort are dreaming up new names for the cattle.

Albert named the bulls on the Windsor farms after members of the royal family: Prince Alfred, after their second son; and a high-performing bull Fitzclarence in honour of an illegitimate son of William IV. The Queen may not take account of royal bastards, but she too shows a sense of history and a touch of wit. A famous purchase was Dream Jersey Lily – the pet name given to Edward VII's mistress Lillie Langtry. Another play on words came with Windsor Sparkler's Mandolin and Madeline – two prizewinning daughters sired by Browny's Louise Sparkler, a Royal Show male champion in 1966.

The bulls are mostly brought in from Jersey or New Zealand to strengthen

Pigman Tony Burton is also in charge of the Windsor farm turkeys which supply Christmas dinner for the royal tables.

The Large White/Landrace sows at Prince Consort Farm are weaned at three weeks into outdoor raised arks, and some still farrow in traditional pigsties.

'I like animals – I wouldn't be happy if I just had arable farming – I think that's very boring,' says the Queen. Her mud-on-the-boots farming is curtailed by her public duties, but she is actively involved in stock breeding. She is a conservationist in the traditional way that landowners preserve their heritage.

the bloodlines. But traffic also goes the other way when bulls and heifers from the Windsor Jersey herd go off to Brazil, Turkey, Iran or Oman. These days, the Brave New World of breeding includes embryo transfer, because, says Gibson, 'People can afford the cattle but the cost of transporting them is becoming prohibitive.'

When the Queen and her husband arrive at Shaw Farm, the manager is seeing to the turkeys, which are strutting about in the straw, but will soon start to be fattened up for royal Christmas tables. Later Gibson will go back down the dusty lane to Prince Consort Farm to select sows for slaughter, to check the controlled environment pens, the farrowing house and the pig litters. They are in traditional sties rather than crates, for Prince Philip, like his son Charles, is constantly evaluating the real cost of productivity achieved by more intensive methods. 'These have created their own problems of disease in livestock reared under intensive systems,' he says.

'There are too many chickens and farming is so intensive it increases the chance of infection,' said Charles during a scare over contaminated eggs.

The liquid golden light streaming down on the farmyard straw lends enchantment even to the piggery. The royal couple speak briefly to their farm manager before climbing into the Land-Rover to drive back to the Castle.

'If they are about the farm they will invariably stop and chat,' says Bill Gibson. 'And I'm always surprised at how up-to-date they are with what is going on.'

GOING ORGANIC AT HIGHGROVE

Little Boy Blue,
Come Blow your Horn,
The Sheep's in the Meadow,
The Cow's in the Corn

Traditional nursery rhyme

Highgrove is set in 100 acres (40 hectares) of parkland, fringed with woods with blocks of agricultural land that make up the Duchy of Cornwall Home Farm. The sheep graze close to the house.

BALES OF STRAW cushion the crash landings as William and Harry bounce through the barn. The straw rustles, scuffles, scratches, tickles. Wisps of it trickle down shirt collars, slide up sleeves and nest in the hair until William emerges looking more like Worzel Gummidge than England's future King.

Playing in the straw is in a fine tradition for royal children. 'The Prince turning somersaults on a haystack to show Bertie how to do it,' said Queen Victoria of her husband's romps in the country with his son.

Anne, the Princess Royal, remembers hours spent in the food store above the stable block at Balmoral, throwing bales 'down through the trap door' or playing amongst them. 'Something I don't encourage my children to do after the hours I have spent stacking bales at Gatcombe,' she says.

Straw is everywhere at the Prince and Princess of Wales's country home. Beyond the swimming pool at Highgrove are the stables with their stubby

74

pillars built of Cotswold brick. Diana is talking to the groom, both of them ankle-deep in bedding for the children's ponies: William's 12-hand Topaz, and Smokey, the Shetland pony passed on from Peter Phillips and soon to be inherited by Beatrice, daughter of the Yorks.

'The Princess does not like riding, but she has made a marvellous effort with the children,' says a member of the royal household. 'The boys do a lot of riding at Highgrove and they are pretty proficient.'

James Hewitt – a Major with the Life Guards whose friendship with the Princess of Wales was a subject of gossip in 1991 when he returned from the Gulf War – persuaded Diana back into the saddle, as well as teaching the children.

Diana has watched Harry since he first rode round the paddock, Smokey's head darting forward to take a mouthful of grass, the small rider pulling the pony back with a makeshift string running from bit to brow-band.

For the two princes playing in the barn, home life at Highgrove is also a traditional life down on the farm, with herds of beef and dairy cattle and the flock of 425 ewes that graze (now on organic grass) right up to the timber fences and drystone walls on the edge of the park. They know that two big bales of straw a day are used for the Ayrshire dairy herd when they are wintered at Broadfield Farm, beyond Tetbury; and that, during these summer months, hay is sent on from Highgrove to Windsor for their father's polo ponies.

Not all members of the royal family have been so close to rural life. 'So that's what hay looks like,' said the redoubtable Queen Mary, when she had her first taste of country life in old age, while staying with the Beauforts at Badminton during the war years. 'My mother loathed the country. She was a Londoner,' said the Duke of Windsor.

The Prince of Wales, like his mother, is a country person at heart. He even looks like a farmer as he works on the land, sleeves rolled up, face ruddy with heat and effort.

'Prince Charles with crab-apple-red cheeks and chin and nose, healthy, full of charm, and intelligent,' was Cecil Beaton's description. Today Charles is inspecting his pet project at Highgrove – thatching straw that has twice the roof life of conventional straw because it is organically grown.

'We've still got a few tonnes left,' says Highgrove's farm manager David Wilson, 'So anyone looking for superb organic thatching straw . . .'

Ah, organic farming! Prince Charles has been described as a crank and an eccentric for encouraging 'biologically sustainable and conservation-conscious farming', as the buffs call it.

'Many other farmers still look at organic farming as some kind of drop-out option for superannuated hippies,' complains the Prince. 'Most of us who want to farm organically do so because we want to produce food in a natural and sustainable way; to work with rather than against nature; and to rear and keep our animals economically in an extensive rather than an intensive manner.'

'Going organic' means giving up the fertilizers and crop sprays on which modern intensive farming relief to produce enormously high yields.

Prince Charles has become a spokesman for farmers, conservationists and naturalists who all express concern about modern agriculture. 'There is no doubt that, over the last few years, a growing anxiety has developed amongst all sections of the community about the consequences of modern intensive farming methods,' he says.

Prince Philip, who was 'green' before the word was invented, has spoken out publicly against over-exploitation of land. 'It may well be technically possible, but for a number of reasons it should be alarmingly clear that we cannot go on defying the laws of nature indefinitely,' he says.

As Duke of Cornwall, Prince Charles is a hands-on farmer. 'Many people are now four or more generations removed from anyone who has worked on the land,' he says.

The Cotswold stone stables at Highgrove house Charles's hunters and polo ponies in winter and the children's ponies. Both William and Harry (above) learned to ride on Smokey, the Shetland pony on loan from their cousin Peter Phillips. In turn, Beatrice and Eugenie of York learned to ride on Smokey during the Balmoral holiday.

At Highgrove, Wilson and his five-strong team have restored agriculture's traditional and natural cycle, mucking out the straw used for the cattle, creating narrow clamps of compost that are turned with the big yellow Matbro until the muck is well rotted so that the 'fym' (as farmyard manure is known) can be applied back on the land.

'We burn no straw here; fertilizer inputs have been cut in some areas – particularly nitrogen – and chemical inputs pared to the minimum,' says Terry Summers, the overall director of farm management at the Duchy of Cornwall's Home Farm at Highgrove.

Straw burning is another current controversy in agriculture. 'Stubble burning after the harvest reached sufficient proportions to bring protests about the pollution of the air,' says Prince Philip.

Highgrove House, bought in 1981, is set in 180 acres (73 hectares), the bulk of it parkland and woods, with two farm blocks of around 85 acres (35 hectares) at Beverston to the north and Westonbirt to the south. The home farm was made into a practical unit in 1985, when the Duchy bought the 420-acre (170 hectare) Broadfield Farm where David Wilson is based. More land at Upton Grove, 160 acres (64.7 hectares) adjoining Broadfield, was added in 1989. The stock and crops are divided between the five different blocks: the Ayrshire dairy herd at Broadfield; the Aberdeen Angus and Friesian beef herd at Highgrove, sharing permanent pasture with a flock of Masham and Mule sheep.

The Cotswold soil varies from clay to acid sandy loam, so there is a varied pattern of crops on the farms, which together grow winter wheat, winter barley, oats, spring beans, rape and maize.

Any idea that organic farming means a return to the picturesque haystacks

Diana, with Harry on Smokey. The Princess overcame her fear of riding to help her sons take to the saddle. All three were taught by James Hewitt, a Major with the Life Guards.

and stooks of the past is dispelled at Highgrove. At Broadfield, a new 1000-ton grain store stands out as a grey mass in a green landscape, even though a screen of trees softens its functional lines and two tow-haired figures – Prince William and his cousin Zara – are dodging around the high-tech barn.

'When Zara and William get together they are a precocious pair of rascals,' says a former member of the Highgrove staff.

Out in the fields, nature has returned to the landscape. At Westonbirt, undulating corn stippled with red poppies breaks against a horizon of trees. David Landale, the Duchy of Cornwall's Secretary and chief executive, is standing waist-high in the ripe wheat, the summer sun on his back.

'That's knotgrass and down there, look, is field pansy and then there's wild parsley, fumitory, fat hen, speedwell, chickweed . . .' He points out plants that might seem more suited to Highgrove's wild flower garden, devised by Charles's biologist and conservationist friend Dr Miriam Rothschild. She describes it as an 'alpine meadow', boasts of its 'nutritious highly-scented hay' and says that 'the Prince of Wales has planted several species of lilies, iris, daffodils, tulips, allium, gladioli, scilla and beargrass which do not in any way clash with the cowslips, oxlips, dandelions, lady's smock, ragged robin and yellow rattle'.

Why should any modern farmer want to encourage meadow herbs in acres devoted to commercial arable farming? There are sound conservationist reasons – not least the butterflies that flutter across the fields just as they did when Prince Albert told his Coburg relations, 'We are wholly given up to the enjoyment of the warm summer weather. The children catch butterflies, Victoria sits under the trees.'

'If you look around you here you will see all kinds of species of other plants,' says Landale. 'Those plants are producing seeds which, in turn, are feeding whole myriads of creatures.'

Prince Charles has set up a woodland butterfly sanctuary in Cornwall on Duchy land. He is a passionate conservationist. 'Large-scale soil erosion, the destruction of wildlife habitat and the excessive use of chemicals and unnatural substances are unacceptable and cannot continue unabated without ruining the countryside for future generations,' he says.

In 1985, the steering committee of the Duchy of Cornwall decided to convert to organic farming over a two-year period three blocks of land at Westonbirt, Beverston and Broadfield's Tetbury Common. For Charles, it was a chance to practise what he believes. 'It is now that farmers and policy-makers must be shown that organic farming is a viable approach to agriculture and that it is one means of dealing with the problems caused by modern intensive farming,' he said.

His advisors did not share his zeal, but are now increasingly enthusiastic. 'It needs a hard commercial approach and we feel confident that we can now take the next step to full organic status,' says Mr Summers. 'We have moved fairly cautiously so far while getting experience of organic farming. The Prince of Wales has wanted to go faster.'

Out of a total area of 900 acres (364 hectares), 30 acres (12 hectares) of wheat, 26 (10.5 hectares) of oats and 51 acres (21 hectares) of grassland are fully organic, with another 160 acres (65 hectares) under conversion. 'It is no secret that we are expanding that area bit by bit, going back to traditional farming methods,' David Wilson says.

'The greatest difficulties are experienced during the conversion period,' explains David Landale, who is an experienced landowner in South West Scotland. 'To qualify for the Soil Association symbol the land must be entirely free from artificial fertilizers for two years, during which time there is no compensation for the reduction in yield.'

Prince Charles sees that as a challenge to get government backing. 'The conversion period has to be regarded as an investment, and few farmers have anything left to invest,' he says. 'This is where the government should be prepared to offer help.'

The back-to-nature approach involves sowing a two-year red clover ley using a seed mixture of two or three red clovers and rye grasses, well dressed with compost. 'We always start with two years of a mixture of clover and grass which has actually given us quite a good yield of forage – not much less, in fact, than when we used artificial fertilizer,' says Landale.

At the end of the period, the ley is ploughed in and drilled with winter wheat in late September. The corners of fields are left wild as part of the conservationist philosophy, for the aim is not just to reverse the pattern of intense arable farming, but to protect the countryside. 'The Prince is environmentally friendly and is steering his farm in this direction,' says Mr Summers.

The only boost given to the wheat is seaweed concentrate. Weeds are controlled not with herbicides but by undersowing green catch crops such as trefoil between the rows of wheat and oats.

'There is definitely a balance of nature, it is not an old wives' tale,' says David Wilson. 'It seems to be that it's when you press too hard and try to extract more from the land than the soil is capable of producing that you get into trouble.'

FACING PAGE: As Duke of Cornwall, Prince Charles owns the largest English estate outside the crown lands – 126,000 acres (50,991 hectares) in the West Country and the Scilly Isles. His 'green' agricultural theories are put into practice at Highgrove.

In 1985, the Duchy of Cornwall expanded the Home Farm at Highgrove by investing in the 420-acre (170 hectares) Broadfield Farm near Tetbury. Five separate blocks of land, including Beverston and Westonbirt, make up the total.

ABOVE: *Terry Summers, overall director of the farms (left) with farm manager David Wilson in a field of rape which makes up 103 acres (41 hectares) of the crops.*

ABOVE RIGHT: *David Landale, the Duchy of Cornwall's secretary and chief executive, examining ears of Highgrove corn. The decision to 'go organic' was made in 1985. 'The greatest difficulties are experienced during the conversion period,' says Landale.*

His words echo what Prince Philip preaches: 'It is going to become much more difficult for agriculture to increase its output, not for lack of will or ingenuity, but simply because there is a limit to intensive methods and the earth's own natural resources.'

There is, of course, a price for 'going organic' – and one that it is easier to pay when you are Prince of Wales and Duke of Cornwall than if you are a small farmer struggling to break even. The yield on the organic areas is just one and a half tons of grain an acre.

'An East Anglian farmer growing wheat or barley is highly disappointed if he hasn't made four tons to the acre,' David Landale says. 'But then organic wheat is sold at a premium and costs far less to grow.'

'It's all down to the marketing,' says Mr Summers. 'And it hinges on premiums.'

Pushing up the yield by modern intensive methods means spraying crops at least eight times with a combination of pesticides and herbicides. 'One of the reasons that I became so closely involved with the conservation of nature was my first-hand experience of the devastating effects of the use of the very poisonous chemicals introduced into agriculture in the 1950s,' says Prince Philip.

David Landale, on the edge of the field, standing knee-high to trilling grasshoppers, knows what crop-spraying would have done to Westonbirt's wheat. 'When you looked at that field, there wouldn't have been a single foreign body, either plant or insect, which could have survived,' he says.

The first fruits of royal organic farming are already on the pine table for the boys' tea. The afternoon sunlight bathes the day nursery, lighting up the chalk drawing of Charles's labrador Harvey, picking out a crusty golden brown loaf. 'Highgrove Stoneground wholemeal bread made from Organic Flour' was the proud claim when the organic loaf went on sale at 23 Tesco supermarkets in July 1989. The 400-gramme loaf at 59p (Tesco donating 3p to the Duke of Cornwall's Benevolent Fund) was made from the wheat harvest of 40 tons sent directly to the Rank Hovis McDougall mill at Hull. 'It makes excellent bread – delicious,' says Mr Wilson. 'I eat it all the time.'

The Highgrove loaf was the first of several products – organic milk, beef and lamb are being considered – that may be offered for public sale. 'Consumers are increasingly showing an acceptance of organic farming as a positive solution to environmental problems by being willing to pay a premium for organic produce,' says Charles, although he admits that the 'high prices charged for organic produce continue to put it beyond the reach of many consumers.'

'What you are doing is producing something which is totally free from any unnatural substance,' says David Landale. 'And there are people who are prepared to pay a little bit more for food which was not produced at the expense of the environment.'

But it is not always easy to square the back-to-nature idyll with the realities of commerce. David Landale called the Tesco loaf 'an ideal opportunity to try to show that organic farming can produce financially profitable, good quality crops'. Alas, the Tesco loaf was discontinued because of an insufficient supply of grain. But in March 1991, the supermarket launched another Duchy of Cornwall product: 'Traditionally-reared prime Cornish lamb', produced under a new Duchy Code of Farming Practices regarding minimal use of fertilizers.

Highgrove has had other farming flops: harvesting seeds of the Rothschild wild flowers was not an economic proposition; nor was marketing cheese through Marks and Spencer food stores.

'We are learning as we go along,' says David Wilson. 'For example, couch completely took over our 1987 spring bean crop and we had to fallow and rotovate regularly to kill it before going back into wheat. We were a bit depressed and so was the Prince, but his attitude was "put it down to experience and start again" – so we did.'

The busy working farms are the best proof that organic farming is viable. 'The Prince's vision of what he wants to see has had an enormous impact already in the nine years he has been at Highgrove,' says Mr Summers.

For Charles, farming at Highgrove is more than a personal crusade – it is an opportunity to reverse what he calls a 'cultural crisis' about the identity of modern farming. 'Farming is not like any other business,' he insists. 'It is, or should be, a rather special way of life, and I believe most farmers recognize this. What makes farming different is the element of long-term stewardship of a precious natural resource. Farmers are at the very heart of rural life and without them we wouldn't have a countryside – at least not as we know it today.'

OVERLEAF: The Masham and Mule flock of 425 sheep shares the organic pasture with the beef herd. As part of an environmentally friendly policy, no hedgerows are grubbed up and drystone walls are repaired.

Prince Charles (inset) in front of Highgrove House. 'How long does it take to get out of organic farming if it doesn't work?' he asks. 'You can start fertilizing and spraying the next day if necessary.'

81

A caricature of the 'affable' George III and his wife Queen Charlotte down on the farm, by Gillray (1795). 'Farmer George' was the architect of modern farming methods at Windsor before being overtaken by bouts of insanity. 'He wasn't so mad,' says Prince Charles of his royal ancestor.

THE DUCHY OF CORNWALL

IN HIS SMALL, ground-floor study at Highgrove, looking out on the patio and from there to the peaceful park, Charles is deep in Duchy of Cornwall papers. Files stand to attention round his mahogany desk; farming journals, clippings and newspapers rise in mole heaps from the floor beside neater stacks of briefing boxes.

He is working under the eyes of Lord Mountbatten – a family photograph of his mentor – and those of 'Farmer George' – a pencil sketch by Sir William Beechey of George III, whose work he has studied in the archives kept in the round tower at Windsor Castle.

How and why has Prince Charles become such a dedicated farmer, with an absorbing interest in agriculture and a passionate belief in ecology? Is it the distant heritage of George III – the first monarch to want to be more than just a landowner, and to take an interest in the science of agriculture? The bluff, squirearchical Hanoverian monarch wrote in farming journals under the pseudonym Ralph Robinson and advocated a modified version of the age-old rotation of crops: the biblical method allowing fields to lie fallow. 'The most profitable plan of culture a farmer can follow is to examine which sort of Grain will pay him best and to vary his changes of Crops according to the demand of that particular kind of Grain,' he said.

George III was the architect of farming at Windsor, although he never made his imaginative efforts pay. 'I must confess myself surprised and mortified that instead of a surplus each farm should be a minus,' said Nathaniel Kent, the agriculturalist called in by the King. Kent's journal of Windsor Great Park, with his plans for improvement, is in the royal library.

Could it be that Prince Charles's farming bloodline has descended from the methodical, precise, bookish Prince Albert? His reforming zeal transformed not only the Windsor farms but also the ramshackle Duchy of Cornwall estates. Albert's model farms at Windsor and Osborne, and his enlightened attitude to crofters and tenants at Balmoral, laid the foundations of modern royal farming.

Or did Charles inherit a feel for farming from his mother, who worked with her hands on Windsor allotments during the war? Today the Queen will watch the powerful whining machines cut straight swathes through the corn at Sandringham. 'Sandringham is an escape place, but it is also a working place – and a commercially viable bit of England,' she says. Back in 1955, stacking barley by hand, her tiny platinum wrist-watch was lost. Army searchers with mine detectors, estate workers, Boy Scouts all searched in vain for the watch – the smallest in the world and a present to Princess Elizabeth in 1938 from President Lebrun of France for her twelfth birthday.

Princess Anne had childhood memories of the Sandringham harvest, when the royal children enjoyed 'threshing the straw and laughing at the corgis' inefficient attempts to kill rats that ran from the shrinking stacks'.

It was indisputably Prince Philip who planted the seeds of Charles's 'green' philosophy, although father and son may often be temperamentally out of sync. Indeed much of Prince Charles's belief in traditional farming and conservation may come from a romantic and emotional dislike of modern farming practices.

Charles admits the influence of his forthright father in his interest in ecology: 'It has occurred to me that my father has done more for conservation than almost anyone else. He started twenty-five years ago, but now many others have become concerned.' But, he argues: 'We need to get away from a sterile debate in which farmers accuse environmentalists of nostalgic hankering after the past, while environmentalists accuse farmers of a technocratic obsession with profit at all costs.'

In 1988 Prince Philip's speeches and writings over 25 years about the complex relationship of man with his environment were published in book form as *Down to Earth*. The following year he gave the BBC Richard Dimbleby Lecture 'Living off the Land', which discussed the theory and practice of modern agriculture. The texts reverberate with Charles's own thoughts and beliefs:

'Much of the increase in agricultural production and productivity has been achieved by more intensive methods . . .

'Competition has encouraged farmers to find more efficient ways of using their resources and more intensive means of production. Pharmaceutical companies have developed new pesticides, herbicides and fungicides . . .

'All this has had a dramatic effect on the output of food, but it has also had some dramatic side effects . . .

Charles has learned to work heavy machinery. At Highgrove, he has banned the burning of straw and instead converts it to farmyard manure which has to be mechanically turned and carted around Home Farm.

'The unpalatable fact is that agriculture has been the victim of its own success . . .

'The development of farming machinery of all kinds, based on an independent source of power in the form of the internal combustion engine, has completely changed the pattern of country life . . .

'Although food is the source of life, the fact is that modern civilized life is not just a matter of sufficient food for all. The land has to provide for all our needs.'

Prince Philip may be concerned about intensive farming and heavy machinery, yet he has accepted it on the Queen's Sandringham estates, where more than 150 tractors, lorries and a posse of combine harvesters service the 1,000 acres (445 hectares) devoted to spring and autumn wheat and the 675 acres (273 hectares) of barley and other crops.

'I don't think we can ever go out of grain,' said Sandringham's then estate manager Julian Lloyd in 1987. 'What else could we grow?'

Sandringham was bought by Queen Victoria for her eldest son with the money that Prince Albert made from efficient management of the Duchy of Cornwall – the heir to the throne's traditional source of revenue.

'Two-thirds of the Duke's income comes out of the udder of a cow,' said a Duchy of Cornwall Secretary in a reference to the dairy farming of the fertile West Country. The Duchy's income in 1990 was £2.9 million.

As Duke of Cornwall, Prince Charles owns the largest English estate outside the crown lands – about 126,000 acres (50,991 hectares) – with tenant farmers spread over Devon – 72,489 acres (29,336 hectares); Cornwall, Avon, Somerset, Wiltshire, Dorset and the Isles of Scilly. There, Charles, Diana and the boys have spent rare family holidays, bicycling along the narrow roads of Tresco, past the fields of daffodils that are Scilly's main cash crop.

Charles's relationship with the Duchy tenants puts him in a unique position to influence and encourage agricultural ideas in the farming community. He is determined to make his Duchy a model of a modern agricultural estate. 'It should provide an example of the best kind of stewardship of the land,' he says. 'This means acting responsibly and sympathetically towards all those directly and indirectly concerned with the Duchy and towards the environment; and it means taking initiatives to help solve problems in housing, farming and employment which are intensified in this time of change.'

Until Prince Albert's reforms the Duchy was run like a medieval fiefdom with no sense of direction from the top. He was appointed Lord Warden of the Stannaries – named for Cornwall's tin-mining areas – in 1842 and radically reformed his son's heritage over the next 19 years, taking advantage of the technical changes occurring in Victorian England, and investing in repairs and replacement. He also drained, levelled and fenced the land. New administration replaced feudal ideas with a modern corporate structure, enshrined in the Duchy of Cornwall Management Act of 1863, two years after Albert's premature death.

'The Duchy is above all a landed estate and will continue to be so,' says Charles. 'Its relationship with the people who work on the land is of paramount importance.'

Billingsmoor Farm at Butterleigh lies in the folds of the Devon hills at the heart of the English countryside, and John and Rosemary Berry are the Duchy of Cornwall's ideal conservation-minded tenant farmers.

'Your efforts coincide completely with my ideas,' said Prince Charles in October 1987 as he congratulated the Berrys on the Royal Association of British Dairy Farmers Conservation Award – one of ten different recognitions of their work.

'The Duchy is fair,' says John Berry. 'And it's in their interests to help tenants survive.'

Billingsmoor has 232 acres (94 hectares) – 190 acres (77 hectares) of pasture, 30 (12 hectares) arable and now 12 (4.8 hectares) devoted to wood and wetland. The fresh green fields with their bushy hedgerows and copses have been transformed since the Berrys took over the tenancy in 1979, after spending 13 years at the neighbouring Stout Farm. Their main business is now dairy farming, with a herd of 116 Friesian cows, lambs and pigs. They also harvest a forest of 1,500 Christmas trees and the 30 acres of organically grown cereals.

In the kitchen of the red brick farmhouse, Mrs Berry is looking after a premature calf in a makeshift pen. 'Prince Charles would be pleased to see she's being treated homeopathically,' she says.

On that score, Billingsmoor may even be in advance of Highgrove, where David Wilson says, 'It is much more difficult to make the switch [with animals] because of the veterinary medicine side.' Few vets are trained to use homeopathic remedies rather than fast-acting antibiotics.

Billingsmoor Farm is one of 13 on the 3,000-acre (1214-hectare) Bradninch estate in East Devon, near Exeter which has been part of the Duchy of Cornwall since it was established in 1337 by Edward III to provide a livelihood for the heir apparent.

'When we started farming in 1966, rents were woefully low, but the landlords did nothing,' says Rosemary Berry. 'Very shortly after that they caught up with the real world. Now the Duchy is much more hard-headed and businesslike. And there are no concessions for greenness.'

But the Prince of Wales is quite clear. 'He does not expect anyone to be forced into following him, or to feel themselves obliged to do so. He is giving a lead,' says Mr Landale.

This has traditionally been the Duchy's policy. 'It is for you to give only the impulse, to establish sound principles,' Albert's advisor Baron Stockmar told him when he first took over the Duchy.

The Berrys, like Prince Charles, are conservationists by conviction. When he followed his father at Stout Farm, John Berry transformed four acres of bogland into a nature reserve, creating three large ponds stocked with trout and coarse fish. 'You would be amazed at the wildlife we see now, kingfishers, dragonflies, swans and whole armies of toads,' he says.

At Highgrove, the Prince of Wales has been following the same ideas. Eight of the ponds scattered across the Prince's estate have been improved as part of a policy towards the environment. Hedges have been planted at Highgrove instead of grubbing them up to make larger and more economic arable areas.

'Big machines can reshape the landscape, remove hedges, drain wetlands, create dams and irrigation systems,' says Prince Philip of the dramatic changes that modern machinery has brought to the traditional English landscape.

'The intricacy of hedgerows,' Charles says. His romantic sentiments have been turned to practical support for Duchy tenants. Hedges no longer have to be cut square and symmetrical, and as long as they are stock-proof, hedges left untrimmed at the end of a tenancy do not now count as a dilapidation.

'When I came here in 1979, the hedges had all been given a short back and sides,' says John Berry. Now clumps of hardwood and mountain ash break out from the horizontal lines that trellis the Devon landscape.

Rosemary Verey, Charles's neighbour in Gloucestershire and a gardening expert, explains that 'most self-respecting animals use the hedgerows as a highway from one destination to another.'

'She makes gardening seem the easiest and most natural thing in the world,' says Charles.

To encourage wildlife at Billingsmoor, corners of fields, deep folds of land or impractical marshland are left as natural undergrowth. 'The Duchy gives us encouragement, rather than directives,' says Rosemary Berry. 'People respond to encouragement rather than being told, now that the era of touching the forelock is over. And we all have a tremendous respect for Prince Charles.'

'But we are still paying a full rent on the new conservation areas,' her husband adds. 'The Duchy may be green in outlook, but it isn't featherbedding tenants who are going green.' The farmers have to make their own hardheaded decisions about cropping and yields.

'There is no reason why organic farming shouldn't be very profitable,' says Terry Summers after his experience at Highgrove. But it is not so easy for tenants who have to cope with a reduced income during the transition period – and less land under cultivation if some is given over to conservation.

'Like most things, it's not just black and white,' says Rosemary Berry. 'Organic farming can be made to pay and work. But having said that, it would be difficult for someone with very high overheads. And we could not afford to convert the whole farm. But we made the decision before Prince Charles got into organic farming.'

'I reckon he took it from us!' says John Berry.

Prince Charles has run across from the Palace to the Duchy of Cornwall headquarters – a corner building bombed in the war, but reconstructed by 1950, No. 10, Buckingham Gate. There is a rush up the staircase, suit jacket flapping, and across the octagonal landing to the Council Chamber where his flushed face is reflected in the mahogany table.

Such informality caused a scandal when Edward VIII presided over the Council in the 1930s. 'Early in my reign I called a meeting of the Duchy Council,' he recalled. 'The afternoon was rainy; but, since it was only a two-minute walk from the Palace to the Duchy offices, I decided not to order the Daimler but to walk instead.'

'That umbrella!' said a distinguished Member of Parliament to Wallis Simpson after seeing a picture of the King walking in the rain in the newspaper. 'The monarchy must remain aloof from the commonplace. We can't have the King doing this kind of thing. He has the Daimler.'

At Buckingham Gate, Charles presides over a Duchy Council that includes his Secretary, a Lord Warden of the Stannaries and John Pugsley, an active farmer. The Duchy is divided into three districts – Eastern, Central and Western – with a land steward for each area as well as for the Isles of Scilly, the urban estates in Kennington, South London, and for other specialities such as woodlands and the Duchy's Penlyne Nursery at Lostwithiel in Cornwall. Each has to be considered separately.

'This is a period of rapid change,' says Charles. 'The Duchy is not immune from this and it has to take a businesslike approach to the management of its estates and assests.'

The Highgrove Home Farm has its own steering committee of Landale, his deputy Kevin Knott, the Duchy Eastern District Land Steward and his deputy, plus Terry Summers and David Wilson.

'This is where the farming policy is set, largely from the Prince's own ideas,' says Terry Summers. 'And he is concerned right down to the details. It's important to remember that he travels widely and sees far more new and interesting ideas than we ever do. He also has strong views of his own and there are plenty of new proposals to consider at each meeting.' These ideas can be controversial, for example Prince Charles's determination to discourage peat extraction on Duchy land because peatlands provide a unique but shrinking wildlife habitat.

Prince Philip was 'green' before the term was invented. His ecologically-sound ideas were founded 25 years ago. 'It occurs to me that my father has done more for conservation than almost anyone else,' says Charles.

Prince Philip was a vigorous steward of the Duchy in the 1950s and 60s before Prince Charles came of age in 1969. But Charles's agricultural inspiration was John Higgs, an agrarian economist whom he appointed as Duchy Secretary in 1981. He had a practical knowledge of farming and was also a university academic and visionary who had worked in the Food and Agriculture Organization of the United Nations. In him Charles found a soulmate and together they worked on policies that took account of conservation and rural employment, as well as looking benevolently upon the uneconomic Duchy areas on Dartmoor and Scilly.

'The major problem facing all landowners at the moment is that of reconciling competing demands on land, namely the need to make an economic return against social and other demands,' said Higgs, who died in June 1986 just after receiving a knighthood for his services.

Farmers find the Duchy fair, but firm. Charles, who has made discreet private visits to work on farms on Dartmoor and in Devon and Cornwall, might prefer the relationship to be closer. As Landale says, 'Personal relationships with tenants are valued above all and particularly by the Prince of Wales. Over the years he has visited every farm in the Duchy.'

'It is the farmer who is the backbone of the whole operation,' says Charles.

Out at Westonbirt on this sunny morning, a party of Duchy farmers is being shown round the areas devoted to organic farming. 'The Prince welcomes it; it's what he wants, exposing other people to organic farming,' Terry Summers says.

'His corn was nearly identical to mine, except that he was growing wheat and I grow oats,' said a Duchy farmer who had come up with a group from the West Country. 'He had got more red clover in his leys than I would like to grow. It must make the sileage heavy. It must be difficult to let the cows over it or they would bloat and fall over.'

The Aberdeen Angus beef herd, based at Highgrove, has been switched to organic production. The 110-strong Ayrshire dairy herd is based at Broadfield Farm. Where the skyline is lacking in trees, Prince Charles plants them.

The land agents' reports piled up on his desk are less convincing to Prince Charles than the evidence of his own eyes, here at Highgrove, where the stock is in fine shape, the organic corn is bringing in a good price and there is a sense that the landscape has been improved over just 10 years. The organic farming is now more than an experiment – it is a viable alternative, a genuine success, a beacon for the future.

'How long does it take to get out of organic farming if it doesn't work?' asks Prince Charles. 'You can start fertilizing and spraying the next day if necessary.'

The papers around him in his study include reports, documents and studies for future projects. 'Some ideas are discarded or postponed,' says Mr Summers, 'others are adopted or scheduled for future development. Usually we reach a very sensible conclusion for the benefit of the estate as a whole. But he is the boss and if he wants something in particular it is carried out.'

There is a note of defiance in Prince Charles's enthusiasm: 'If the Duchy of Cornwall can't have a go – who can?'

THE QUEEN MOTHER'S
SCOTTISH HILLTOP FARM

Lest any dare,
To say this land is bleak or bare –
Pray have a care, yea have a care,
For the eyes of a Queen have rested there –
And behold the land is forever fair.

From 'Caithness Makes her Curtsey' composed by
Scottish schoolchildren for the Queen Mother in 1956.

'LONG GOE FARM' say the white letters standing out against a sky wispy with wind-blown clouds. In one corner of the wrought-iron sign is a sturdy sheep with a brown wool fleece; in the other a dour, dark Aberdeen Angus cow with the sapphire sea behind; and on the top, a royal crown to prove that this far-distant Caithness farm is indeed the Scottish home of Her Majesty Queen Elizabeth, the Queen Mother.

The cattle graze right along the clifftop that leads from the Castle of Mey towards John O'Groats, on the north-east corner of the British Isles and just seven miles away.

'It must be saved,' said the newly-widowed Queen Mother when she first saw the stubby stone castle, its roof blown off by the whirling winds. She bought it in 1952, putting down again the Scottish roots planted during childhood years in her family's ancestral Castle of Glamis.

Long Goe Farm, bought in 1960 and linked to the Castle by the clifftop strip, now adds up in bits and pieces, called 'policies', of land to around 256 acres (104 hectares) including some good, heavy loam, and 86 acres (35 hectares) of a grazing and arable smallholding bought in 1990.

'This is good strong land for livestock,' says Donald McCarthy, farm manager at Long Goe.

On this calm August afternoon, the Queen Mother, in twinset, tweed skirt and floppy felt hat the colour of the aquamarine water lapping the shore, is taking a turn about the farm. 'Her Majesty loves walking and she's around the stock perhaps twice a week when she's in residence,' says Mr McCarthy.

She stops to look out to sea, to an elusive shadow on the horizon – the siren lure of the Orkney islands. 'I always look at the islands with pleasure,' she said on a visit to the Orkneys. 'And it is a great pleasure to set foot upon the land which has beckoned me so often.'

Hardly a ripple disturbs the Pentland Firth, where the waters, even in summer, can boil up with racing tides across the sweep of the sea and slap the coastline.

'It is either battered by gales or swathed in a damp mist,' Charles says of his grandmother's stronghold. 'Every now and then, as if by magic, the sun comes out and suddenly the fields become emerald green and the sea a sapphire blue. The scene is transformed into something peaceful and pastoral, but it is all very deceptive . . .'

This may be one of those nights when the streaks of purple, crimson, emerald and gold of the Northern Lights will be as bright as the firework displays marking a royal visit.

'Castle of Mey looks terribly impressive and we have lost our hearts to it from the start. We have had a glorious day,' the Queen signalled her mother on the first of many visits in August 1955 as she sailed off in the royal yacht

The farm sign at the Queen Mother's Caithness home depicts the royal crown and the stock: North Country Cheviot sheep and black Aberdeen Angus cattle.

OPPOSITE: *The Queen Mother has put down sturdy Scottish roots at the Castle of Mey. The clifftop farm overlooking the Pentland Firth and the Orkneys is the most northerly farm on the British mainland.*

The Queen calls in to see her mother at Mey on the Britannia's *Western Isles cruise that traditionally starts the royal family's Scottish holiday in August. 'We have lost our hearts to it from the start,' she radioed from the ship.*

Britannia, past the illuminated castle and its pyrotechnic display.

With one's back to the sea, the smell is a sweet, dry mix of sileage and clover. The fields on the estate are no longer dotted with the pointed haycocks so typical of the area. Instead, the round hay bales are bagged up in black plastic near the handling pens. 'The weather rules our lives here,' says Mr McCarthy.

'The uncertainties of our intractable climate,' says the Queen Mother, who spent one memorable birthday on 4 August 1962 huddled in a raincoat and hood, buffeted by driving rain from a north-westerly wind, at Caithness's Agricultural Show in Wick, 20 miles away. With royal panache, she emptied the water out of the trophies before handing them over.

Three of her North Country Cheviot sheep won awards, and her bull, Invader of Durran, squelched away with the first prize. Recognition also went to the stock of Sir Ralph Anstruther, her good friend, her household treasurer and neighbouring Scottish landowner at Watten Mains.

Sir Ralph, and Lady Fermoy, join her now to look at the Aberdeen Angus herd – founded in 1964 – now 35-odd breeding cows but with the accent on bulls. Cannon Ball of Peebles – Long Goe Farm's stock bull – won the supreme beef championship at the Caithness County Show in 1976 and 1977. The Queen Mother's heifers won the Inter-Breed Cattle Trophy in 1986 and 1989.

'They need that almost indefinable asset called breed character, which the older stockmen know so well,' says Martin Leslie, the factor of the Balmoral estate. He makes a monthly visit to Long Goe.

Down south at Balmoral, Queen Victoria founded a herd of Aberdeen Angus after visiting the cattle-breeder William M'Combie in 1881. The distinctive black breed is no longer found in Balmoral's Highland fold, but

Prince Charles took two of his grandmother's heifers as foundation stock for his farm at Highgrove.

The Queen Mother is asking about the results of stock-breeding that used insemination from Canadian bulls – scientific methods for a modern age. 'She takes an active interest in the farm,' says Martin Leslie. 'I report to Her Majesty by telephone after every visit or if Her Majesty is at Birkhall I go and see her there.'

The bulls are bedded down in sand, rather than the traditional straw, which is at a premium on the cold north coast. The storm-grey Caithness slates that are used as windbreaks out in the fields also tile the roof of the cattle house. They are part of the traditional outbuildings that the Queen Mother wants to preserve, just as, down at Highgrove, Prince Charles has painstakingly restored slate roofs, renovated an old stone fold yard and rebuilt 548 metres of drystone wall round the estate.

'The Prince considers this as much part of the countryside picture as trees and hedges,' his farm manager David Wilson explains.

The wind is getting up, draughts and eddies of pure air gusting across the cliff. 'That will blow the cobwebs away,' says the Queen Mother.

'The air remarkably pure and light,' was Prince Albert's comment, when he discovered Scotland.

The winds often overwhelm the Queen Mother's elderly friends who are invited to stay at Mey (with overflow guests at Seaview House on her land) during the three-week August holiday or a brief October visit. The royal family admit that the Castle is an indulgence, but with the acquisition of additional policies in the area, the farm is a going concern.

Woolly brown fleeces coat the flock of 100 North Country Cheviot sheep that was founded in 1960. They are also prize-winning livestock, bringing in big money at the pedigree sales at the nearby town of Thurso. Her Majesty's ewes and tups carry off awards at the local Caithness County Show and at the Royal Highland Agricultural Show in Edinburgh. In 1977 she had a breed champion at the Royal Highland and again in 1990.

Sheep do not feature greatly on the royal estates. At Balmoral, there were the Soay sheep, a prehistoric breed which survived for centuries on the island of Soay, in the St Kilda group of islands. They were kept not for selling on, but to supply meat for the royal tables. But perhaps the most famous royal sheep were the Spanish merinos introduced to Britain by George III, who carried out a cloak-and-dagger conspiracy to smuggle the animals out of Spain via Portugal to Windsor Great Park, where they were bred for their fine wool and used to strengthen other stock.

The Aberdeen Angus herd has come in from the clifftop and is nuzzling against the fence by the castle walls. 'We try to organize the grazing so that she can look out and see them or wander round them at will,' Mr McCarthy says.

'The peace and tranquillity of an open and uncrowded countryside with the rugged glory of a magnificent coastline,' is the Queen Mother's description of her remote part of Scotland.

As the sun slips down, the Hills of Hoy are etched in a sharp blue, the 1,000-foot cliffs of the island a bright red.

It is a long time since that June, four months after the King's death, when she was staying with Commander and Lady Vyner at their House of the Northern Gate at Dunnet Head, and saw Barrogill Castle (as it was then called) for the first time.

Built by the Earls of Caithness in 1566 on the site of a bishop's stone house and before that a Viking stronghold, it had 'been up for sale for months', as Lady Vyner said.

'Stop the car a moment, please,' said her royal guest.

Princess Margaret disembarking at Scrabster en route to the Castle of Mey. Her first visit in August 1955 was at the height of her romance with Group Captain Peter Townsend, whom she publicly renounced because he was divorced.

The Queen Mother with Long Goe farm manager Donald McCarthy in front of the Castle of Mey, which she bought as a roofless ruin in 1952 after George VI's premature death. The Aberdeen Angus herd was founded in 1964 and the pedigree stock has won prizes at the Caithness and Perth shows.

TOP: *The flock of ewes with the traditional farm buildings.*

Lady Fermoy, Diana's grandmother, entertains Mey's guests on the piano.

Then came a visit to Dunnet Head lighthouse to see the sun set over the Atlantic from the most northerly point of mainland Britain; and then, as she was leaving for Balmoral on 18 June, the school children of Wick singing 'Will ye no' come back again.'

The Queen Mother bought the ruined castle, changed its name to Mey and started the major restoration.

The first royal visitor was Princess Margaret, who flew up with her mother to Inverness and came on by train to stay with the Vyners and look at the progress at the castle in August 1955. It was just before Margaret's 25th birthday on 21 August, when she was technically free to marry the man of her choice. She finally and publicly renounced the divorced Group Captain Peter Townsend that October.

The wind is starting its wild whistling round the tower where the castle's ghost traditionally walks – the Primrose Lady, an earl's daughter who fell unsuitably in love and jumped to her death on the stones below.

Now that the mist has come down, it will mean a cosy evening in. 'Ruth Fermoy on the piano and *Dad's Army* on the telly,' says a house guest of staying with the Queen Mother.

Outside, the stock huddle against slate slabs. 'If you can farm in Caithness,' says Donald McCarthy, 'you can farm anywhere.'

SHORT HORNS AND TALL PINES

Mon beau sapin
Roi des forêts
Que j'aime ta verdure

Traditional French children's carol

THE SCOTS pine trees reach straight for the sky. Their dense branches close overhead, shutting out the fine rain and casting an eerie blue light. The thick carpet of pine needles muffles the sound of approaching boots.

'It is impossible not to feel awed by the beauty of the forest, by its immensity, by the sense of a history spanning millions of years,' said Charles after visiting the rainforests of South America. He calls this Ballochbuie Forest, on the west of the Balmoral estate, 'one of the most precious and almost sacred parts of the countryside'.

The trees here go back, perhaps, 250 years – to well before Queen Victoria bought the land in 1878 to preserve these stately Caledonian pines, swaying and creaking on their slim trunks. 'The bonniest plaid in Scotland,' she said on a commemorative plaque, because legend claims that the forest had originally changed hands for a tartan plaid.

'The fact that this part of it still exists at Balmoral is entirely due to the intervention of my great-great-grandmother Queen Victoria,' says Charles, who in 1985 got volunteers to put up a windmill-driven electric deer-proof fence round a woodland site at Balmoral.

Now the Duke of Edinburgh is walking round 50 acres of fenced-in forest, with the chap from the Forestry Commission and a fell pony weighed down not with the usual stag, but with two fallen branches to be taken back for study.

'Tough, extremely willing with plenty of speed. If anything, a bit dour in character, but the good ones are quite unflappable,' says the Duke of Edinburgh of the sturdy ponies he uses for four-in-hand carriage driving, as well as stalking, timber extraction and pony trekking on the estate.

The forests cover 7,200 acres (2,915 hectares) of the Queen's 50,000-acre (20,000-hectare) Scottish estate where the land is mostly granite-hard heather-clad hills. The farming takes place in pockets of fertile land – only 380 arable acres (154 hectares) – along the south bank of the Dee and the north west of the River Muick at Birkhall. 'Land strung out like this, plus the climate, has always made it a problem to farm,' admitted Balmoral's factor Martin Leslie in 1987.

To add to the difficulties, there are the marauding deer, so that the cropped fields and the tree nursery down by the South Deeside road require six-foot fences to keep stags at bay.

Prince Philip has come to Ballochbuie this moist September day to inspect his conservation project: a trial plot of forest fenced in and planted with pine and rowan seedlings. He, like other Scottish landowners, knows that conservation does not mean leaving the land to the balance of nature. Instead the deer have to be kept out, before they strip the bark from mature trees, devour the seedlings and finally destroy an entire landscape, as witness the Mar Lodge estate down the road.

There, bad management has turned the great 77,000-acre (31,161-hectare)

99

Quoich Water on the Mar Lodge estate
where mismanagement of the deer
population has ravaged the terrain.
In the background, land fenced off from
the marauding deer shows regeneration
of the forest.

Prince Philip is head of Balmoral's
management structure, although the resident
factor Martin Leslie runs the estate,
according to policy laid down by the
Queen and her husband.

Balmoral Castle was bought by Victoria and Albert in 1848 and completely rebuilt in Scottish baronial style in 1855. The original eagle fountain given by the King of Prussia was replaced by the chamois statue and fountain during the First World War, because of anti-German sentiment.

sporting estate stretching up to the Cairngorms into a wilderness of starving deer and broken trees. Mar Lodge itself, which Charles described as a 'vast and incongruous Swiss Cottage style of a house', was destroyed by fire in 1990, apart from its antler-filled ballroom. The lodge was originally built for Queen Victoria's daughter and was acquired by a Swiss industrialist on the death of Princess Arthur of Connaught in 1963. Over the years, the deer population increased far beyond what the land could support. In 1989, Mar was sold again to the American billionaire John Kluge for £3 million. His wife Patricia, a former soft porn model and Baghdad belly dancer, hoped in vain to be invited to Balmoral.

In the eyes of the people of Braemar, the free-spending Kluges could do no wrong – apart from changing the traditional heather-purple and pink shades of the Mar tweed for a green check 'like something you'd put on a poodle on a wet day'. But the Kluges' separation and imminent divorce left Mar an environmental wasteland.

Plans were formed for a consortium of the Worldwide Fund for Nature, the Royal Society for the Protection of Birds and the Chris Brasher Trust to put up half the £10 million needed to buy the estate. It would then be managed by the Scottish Natural Heritage Agency (an amalgam of two other conservation agencies headed by Magnus Magnusson from April 1992). This scheme had the support of Prince Charles, who also wanted to involve the Crown Estates. But the locals remain sceptical.

'That'll be an absolute ruination,' says a former estate worker. 'I'd be far happier if it was bought by somebody else like Mr Kluge, instead of these people who want to chase the bloody deer all over the place.'

But the nearby Ballochbuie experiment proves that a forest can regenerate

Albert upset Victoria by taking pot shots at the deer from the castle windows. Today, a culling policy is decided by the East Grampian Deer Management Group.

naturally when the seedlings are not destroyed. The red deer are fed a supplement of grass and proteins instead.

In Victorian times, a Queen could do as she damn well pleased with her own estate, and Prince Albert (when he wasn't taking pot shots at the deer from the castle windows) replanned the entire area and started several afforestation schemes. 'The planting and replanting of trees is such an amusement to him,' said Queen Victoria.

Now both deer and forest have become a business of officialdom and paperwork. The deer are counted each February and reported to the Red Deer Commission; then the East Grampian Deer Management Group (comprising the estates in the Braemar area) decides on a culling policy before the stalking season begins.

Trees grown in the tree nursery are not planted on a royal whim, but have to measure up to official Forestry Commission requirements and are used to replace trees from Prince Albert's plantations that have reached maturity and been felled. Wood is processed at Balmoral's sawmill, where Charles and Anne would play as children on an improvised see-saw made out of a plank of wood balanced on a log.

At Sandringham, Philip expanded and modernized the estate's sawmill in 1988, so that softwood can be turned commercially into fencing posts and gates. The situation there is different from Balmoral, with its designated forest land. In Norfolk, trees are often viewed as a hindrance to modern farming. As Prince Philip says, 'The massive oak trees are a great feature in the landscape but highly inconvenient from a practical point of view.'

Now at Balmoral Castle, he attends a forestry meeting in the estate office in the stable block. The Duke of Edinburgh is head of Balmoral's complex management structure, Martin Leslie, the resident factor, under him. Between them they oversee seven other departments, including forestry, game, farms and the Wildlife Trust, and look after all the different areas of land. Even repairing the miles of drystone walls on the Balmoral estate is a complicated business, and in 1992 the Queen gave Norman Haddow of Tirlin Pin Dyhers, Perthshire, a Royal Warrant.

The Queen – a cluster of seven corgis at her heels – is in the middle of a brisk walk which has taken her by the river and now back towards the castle, past the dogs' graveyard, where the statue of 'Noble, for 15 years the favourite collie and dear and faithful companion of Queen Victoria', sits on its marble plinth; up towards the rose garden by the granite steps which Queen Victoria so admired when they were completed in 1857, two years after the castle itself. 'Very fine and such splendid workmanship,' she said. Generations of the royal family have been photographed on these steps, dressed in plaid right down to the tartan sling that Charles wore when he broke his arm in 1990.

The Queen's walk skirts the castle's west front and goes round the water-garden bordered with flowering plants; past Garden Cottage, where Queen Victoria would have breakfast on the covered verandah; through the pergola towards the conservatory, with its mass of bright azaleas; across the kitchen garden, filled with formal plantings of vegetables and fruit in cages; and a quick trot across the main drive back to the stable block where Philip and the Range-Rover are waiting to tour the farms.

At Invergelder home farm, once the heart of the estate, turnips – 'neeps', the factor calls them – are piled like cannonballs in the yard. There are no cattle in Prince Albert's dairy complex – the monument to his farming expertise that Victoria insisted on completing after his death. It saw just a century of service before the herd of Ayrshires was dispersed in 1965. Now Invergelder's 96 acres (39 hectares) of arable land are used for growing winter feed for the livestock – hay and big bale silage, barley and the turnips, while an estate worker uses the dairy to produce honey, which is a favourite with the royal family.

'Did you bring the honey?' Prince Charles would ask his valet on any royal trip. 'He was paranoid about the honey,' says Stephen Barry. 'If there was half a spoonful left, it still had to be gathered up.'

The farm grieve is walking the Queen through her most picturesque livestock: the fold of Highland cattle. With their shaggy ginger hides and wide-set horns, the Highlanders look like a last survival of the Celtic age. In fact, the beasts were introduced to Balmoral by Philip only in the 1950s with in-calf females and stock bulls, but the Queen has now become a show winner and Patron of the Highland Cattle Society. There are currently 20 breeding cows and the fine bulls they produce command high prices at the Oban sales, although the best are kept for stock: Angus MacDomhnull of Easton, the Great Yorkshire Highland champion in 1983; the splendid Tearloch of Camerory; and the imperious, autocratic Gille Ruadh of Glenforsa. This last 'had a habit of rounding up all his "wives" like a red deer stag after they were moved to a new field,' says Martin Leslie. 'He kept them in a tight bunch until he was satisfied with the accommodation and general situation.' This ladies' man of a bull came to a sad end. He hurt his back after serving a cow and had to be put down. The Highland fold has produced more champion bulls at the Oban spring sales in three consecutive years, 1988, 1989 and 1990, as well as the female champion in 1990.

By bringing commercial beef cattle to Balmoral, Prince Philip has been the prime mover in the stock changes during the Queen's reign. 'It was largely as a consequence of the Highland cattle,' he says, 'which I introduced to Balmoral

Balmoral's herd or 'fold' of Highland cattle was founded in 1953 and there are currently 20 breeding cows.

in 1954, that we later went in for the then newly developing Luing cattle as they are derived from Highland shorthorn cross.'

The Luing breed, established by the Cadzow brothers on the island of Luing in Argyllshire, was brought to Invergelder in 1966, when cross-breeding experiments were started to get the best beef calves. The most spectacular was the purchase from Sandringham in 1973 of a Blonde d'Aquitaine bull – a breed from South West France. But Philip did not entirely approve of what he called 'Blondes at Balmoral'. 'In all forms of "double-cross" beef production,' he says, 'I have always maintained that the bigger British beef breeds are just as successful as the more fashionable exotics. But I do not always win.'

At Gatcombe, Princess Anne and her husband, before they separated, cross-bred their beef herd: upgrading shorthorns to Charolais, crossing Hereford with Friesians and blue-greys.

'Heinz 57 – a really mixed lot!' Mark Phillips used to say.

In 1971 there was a plan to intermix the livestock on the different royal estates by breeding blue-grey heifers for sale to Sandringham from a herd of Balmoral Galloway cattle established at Knock Farm. But 'sadly my plan to combine the beef operations on the two estates had to be abandoned for various, but what I still maintain were not convincing, reasons,' says Phillip. The suckler herd was dispersed in 1986.

All the changes have been part of a wider scheme to make Balmoral a self-supporting business. In response to the changing agricultural scene, Philip wanted to establish stock that is less labour-intensive and can command premium prices in the Scottish markets.

The Queen is Patron of the Highland Cattle Society. The Highlanders live out all year, protected by their shaggy hides. Females are bulled at three years to calve in the spring, with the calves weaned in December.

Reform has been a continuing process on the royal farms. Edward VIII asked his brother – the future George VI – to produce a report on updating Sandringham, something the two had discussed before his accession.

In the end he sold the private estates to his brother after the Abdication, but not before Edward VIII had instigated unpopular cut-backs at Balmoral without consulting his brother, who complained to their mother, Queen Mary: 'He arranged it all with the official people up there.'

The new King defended himself by claiming that the estates had to move with the times. 'I was, after all, the first British King of the twentieth century who had not spent at least half his life under the strict authority of Queen Victoria,' he said.

Now Prince Philip is using his crook to point out a likely steer as he and the Queen discuss with the factor which beast will be finished for the royal table, one of two that provide Balmoral beef during the year.

'We are hoping to develop an outlet for our steers with a local butcher,' says Mr Leslie. The Royal Warrants for supplying poultry to the Queen, the Queen Mother and the Prince of Wales are held by H. M. Sheridan in Bridge Street, Ballater – a traditional local butcher with striped blinds shading the windows and striped aprons on the butcher's boys. At Balmoral's tea rooms there is an innovation: 'venison burgers' are on sale to the public.

On the hills the mist has closed in again and the Highlanders are now just bulky shadows against the coarse grass. As Prince Philip says, 'The management of land is a very long-term business, and the best results can only be achieved if there is confidence in continuity.'

OF CABBAGES AND KINGS

'The time has come,' the Walrus said,
'To talk of many things:
Of shoes – and ships – and sealing wax –
Of cabbages – and kings – '

From *Alice Through the Looking Glass*
by LEWIS CARROLL (1832–98)

PRINCE CHARLES is proposing a toast:
'Our coal production figures may have been exceeded, the tonnage of our shipping may have been overtaken, but there remains one area where we still reign supreme – blackcurrants,' he said at a 1977 Farmer's Club Dinner Dance. 'It is a little known fact that Britain still leads the world in the production of blackcurrants. We are still, believe it or not, self-sufficient in blackcurrants. There are no imports to disturb our trade figures in this particular soft fruit field, no foreign price rises to threaten our blackcurrant market. The wind still blows through ten thousand acres of British blackcurrants, and quite a lot of them, if I may say, ladies and gentlemen, reside at Sandringham.

'Very few people know all this, but perhaps they will ponder on this rare glory as they sip their next Ribena.'

The reality of Sandringham's fruit farm is not as romantic as Prince Charles suggests. A mechanical stripper – a Smallford Twin Hydrapick – straddles a row of blackcurrant bushes, taking sprigs of currants by vibration, sorting berries from leaves and tipping them onto wooden trays. The fruit will then, indeed, be processed under contract by the Ribena drinks company. This

mechanized picking and the irrigation system that can sprinkle the blackcurrants for frost protection, is a long way from the sturdy Norfolk yokels with
a row of hoes that were still part of Sandringham at the onset of the Queen's
reign.

'Gangs of female labour were contracted to lift the vegetable crops,' Prince
Philip remembers. 'Sugar-beet was topped and toed by hand, and produce in
general was bought and sold in markets, a pattern not much changed in two-
hundred years.'

Anne outlines the changes since her childhood as that 'Suffolk Punches no
longer work in the fields' and also that the stubble once replaced by plough is
now going back to grass for sheep. 'Yes, the tractors have grown, as have the
sugar-beet lorries,' she says.

At Sandringham's Appleton Farm, 183 acres (74 hectares) are devoted to
fruit, mostly, as the name implies, apples. Here in the orchards the fruit is
picked by hand – 3,000 pairs of hands on peak weekends in September and
October. Markets used to sell the apples in wrappers marked with a triangle
and circle and the word 'Royal fruit farms Sandringham'. But 'pick-your-
own' was tried out on the royal farm in the early 1970s, and now almost the
entire crop is sold to these people who are standing in the orchards filling
plastic bags with the small, rosy Cox's Orange Pippins.

But alongside the mechanized fruit farming and the pick-your-own there is
another kind of royal fruit farming: gnarled apple trees heavy with small,
succulent apples; sunset yellow nectarines splayed against old stone walls; fat
strawberries pushing against spiders' webs of netting; beans, raspberries,
marrows mixed with lupins and hollyhocks.

Prince Charles has a bond with his grandmother that is tied with garden
twine. For both the Queen Mother and Charles are by nature royal kitchen
gardeners, and there is a striking similarity. In his garden, Charles has leeks
and cabbages, roses, fruit trees and a herb garden within a geometric frame-
work: a horticultural mix that is the hallmark of the Queen Mother's gardens.

'A square of gladioli faces a rolling line of sea-green cabbages,' says the
Queen Mother's friend Lady Salisbury, describing the walled garden at the
Castle of Mey where two and a half acres are tucked away from the whip of
the wind behind 15-foot rose-pink granite walls. 'The only place anything
will grow, because of the shelter,' Prince Charles says.

The Queen Mother will sit in this walled garden on a wooden bench, her
feet crunching on a seashell path, drinking in the mingled scents of honeysuckle, clematis and climbing rose.

'I must have scent here, Rosemary, can we possibly add honeysuckle?'
Prince Charles asked Rosemary Verey as they walked round the garden he has
created in his grandmother's spirit at Highgrove.

At Mey, the kitchen garden is divided by thick hedges into snug compartments – broad beans and globe artichokes, currants and cauliflowers. Among
them are sweet peas, their pale, papery petals tremulous in a wind that has
been known to uproot cabbages and hurl them over the wall.

'The Queen Mother loves this manner of growing plants,' says Lady
Salisbury of the intermingled fruits, flowers and vegetables. 'It is, too, another
nostalgic reminder of the homes of her childhood, where the plantings were
similarly planned.'

'They shared a place with radishes and one rose,' says the Queen Mother,
describing her ideal planting for nasturtiums.

'We loved the sloping garden full of fruit and sweet peas,' said Princess
Alice of Athlone, Queen Victoria's granddaughter, of the garden at Birkhall
where the Queen Mother today grows a mass of fruit and blooms in a bell-
shaped bed.

*Prince Philip in the conservatory at
Balmoral. At Sandringham, the historic
teak glasshouses have been replaced by
modern aluminium-framed structures which
are given over to carnations and pot plants
for commercial sales.*

The Queen Mother's walled garden at
Mey mixes fruit, flowers and vegetables
in the traditional Scottish style. The wind
can be strong enough to blow cabbages
over the wall.

The cottage garden style is born of the Queen Mother's Scottish roots, and a
legacy of her childhood homes: the plant-filled country garden at St Paul's
Waldenbury and the formal, Italianate Glamis Castle garden cultivated by her
mother, the green-fingered Lady Strathmore.

From his upbringing, or from innate instinct, Charles wanted to create
mixed plantings at Highgrove. 'I had always rather wanted to grow fruit,
flowers and vegetables in one place with box borders,' he says. 'And one of the
great things was that as a wedding present we were given a complete set of
fruit trees by the Fruiterer's Company, and, believe it or not, a herb garden by
the Sussex branch of the Women's Institute.'

'When I first saw this walled garden I did rather fall in love with it,' he adds
as he walks through the arched gate towards the central fountain from which
symmetrical squares radiate, each with a rose arbour clambered over by
wistaria and clematis. Geraniums in a terracotta urn add colour to the cool
green shade, while vegetables sprout in neatly hedged compartments. Sunlight skitters on brick paths that lead under arches trailed with sweet peas and
runner beans. ('It's rather fun because you can then walk down the tunnel
picking the beans and the flowers,' he says.)

Just as, at Mey, Lady Salisbury will meet the sous-chef 'in checked trousers,
white apron and knotted kerchief, carrying a large bowl to collect redcurrants
for the kitchen', so Charles will walk Highgrove's chef round the gardens,

watching him pull rhubarb and encouraging him to try cooking with new herbs.

'Lovage makes interesting soup,' says Charles. 'I rather like cold soups and you can make very good ones that way.'

The 'rather basic' garden at Highgrove was redesigned for the Prince and Princess of Wales by the Marchioness of Salisbury, a garden expert and historian who also created a Wilderness Garden for the Romseys at Broadlands and wrote a survey of the Queen Mother's gardens in 1988. Charles has now adapted, on his own initiative, the original scheme.

'The layout of the walled vegetable garden was based on Lady Salisbury's plan but now it is teeming with his own ideas,' says Rosemary Verey. 'The runner beans are supported by nut branches, tied at the top to make a Gothic arch. Hellebores and polyanthus underplant the apple tunnel in the spring, and brilliant nasturtiums make a carpet throughout the summer.'

'Two apple tunnels,' says Charles, 'which in about ten years will look marvellous when they grow completely over.'

Charles the conservationist feels passionately about the English apple in all its varieties, compared to the 'boring homogeneity' available in shops. When the Government-funded experimental fruit station at Brogdale near Faversham, Kent, was threatened with closure in April 1989, the Prince of Wales intervened to save the national apple collection that includes the Decio species eaten in Roman Britain, saying, 'It is virtually impossible to exaggerate their importance, I believe, for if they disappear, a heritage goes with them.'

They are also part of Charles's childhood memory. In the royal gardens at Windsor, the gardening expert Dr Shewell-Cooper noticed, when Charles was just four years old, a variety of unusual apples. 'I saw Sunset, for instance, and Tower of Glamis (named after the Queen Mother's old home). There were No Surrender, Blenheim Orange, the Duke of Devonshire, Cornish Aromatic and Arthur Turner,' he said. All the apple trees were grown in grass so that the mown clippings served as a mulch for the trees.

A dislike of chemical fertilizers is another thing that Prince Charles shares with his grandmother. 'No chemical fertilizers are used in the gardens at all, as Queen Elizabeth does not like them on the flowers or vegetables,' Lady Salisbury says of Birkhall and Mey.

'Nobody likes them,' the Queen Mother claims.

Prince Charles made the walled garden at Highgrove in the image of his grandmother's garden. Beans and sweet peas are trained over nut branches to create a tunnel, which Charles finds 'rather fun'.

Charles finds weeding 'very therapeutic' and keeps a torch on hand in winter to finish working as the light falls.

FACING PAGE: *The Marchioness of Salisbury, the gardening expert, among foxgloves and roses in the west parterre of Hatfield House. Charles's gardening mentor and good friend, Mollie Salisbury designed the garden at Highgrove and gave the Prince his Jack Russell, Tigger, as a puppy in 1986.*

Thirty years before Prince Charles took up organic farming, George VI and Queen Elizabeth had already espoused the cause. 'In the midst of the great controversy of organic versus inorganic "manures" it is interesting to report that, just like many of our biggest and most successful market growers, the royal gardens do not use artificial fertilizers at all, except very occasionally as a tonic,' Dr Shewell-Cooper said.

The roses at Birkhall are dressed with well-rotted farmyard manure, just as Rosemary Verey describes Charles planting at Highgrove 'with a barrow of well-rotted manure standing by to give them a promising start'.

This in the royal tradition. Until April 1991 twenty tons of steaming horse manure were sent weekly from Windsor barracks and the Royal Mews to turn muck into money in the mushroom sheds at Windsor and Sandringham. Now however this arrangement has ceased and the Palace is obliged to pay for shifting the manure heap created by the 40 horses in the Royal Mews.

Today's royal farms are commercial, and that is why the old-fashioned or uneconomic crops, however picturesque, have become an endangered species on the estates.

'It's a disgrace – a tragedy even – that the royal family has allowed its advisers to bulldoze away part of the heritage in the name of economy,' says a gardening expert who was appalled to find that the quinces, pears, peaches and nectarines that used to cling to Windsor's sun-baked stone walls have gone, and that an orchard of Cox's Orange Pippins has been ploughed.

Similarly, at Sandringham, the magnificent teak glasshouses were once filled with unusual and exotic fruits: peaches, apricots, grapes and figs. 'We had to go over 14 acres of *jardin potager* and visit royal farms and dairies,' said Disraeli of a visit to Sandringham in 1875. 'The glasshouses are striking; one of them containing a grove of banana trees weighed down with clustering fruit, remarkable.'

Now the original glasshouses have recently been demolished and replaced with modern aluminium-framed greenhouses in which carnations, roses and pot plants are produced for sale wholesale to local florists or in the souvenir shop. The last of the fruit trees in the 17 acres of walled gardens have been replaced with pick-your-own raspberries.

Charles went to the owner of London's Neal Street restaurant to buy the

Thirteen-year-old Princess Elizabeth (left) and 10-year-old Princess Margaret living up to the wartime slogan 'dig for victory' in April 1940 in the gardens of Royal Lodge, Windsor, where they had their own garden plots.

ABOVE RIGHT: *The same wheelbarrow became a favourite toy for Prince Charles and Princess Anne when they visited their grandmother.*

FACING PAGE: *Prince Charles with Harry. He wants to encourage his own children to garden. 'If you have got your own little garden, you learn that way,' he says.*

hamper of truffles, aubergines and bottled fruits that he gave to his father for his 70th birthday present. But private royal kitchen gardens are still used to supply green treats for the royal tables.

'Our Queen Mother, as Queen, insisted on all crops being picked on the young side and arriving at the kitchen beautifully fresh, if possible with the dew still on them,' Shewell-Cooper said. He listed the likes and dislikes in the gardens created by George VI and his wife: French beans rather than runners, pink potatoes, no parsnips, carrots pulled when young, petite cauliflower heads, green marrows, not white, and a variety of cabbages from Durham Early to Greyhound and January King.

'What about growing some unusual vegetable and then sending it to the kitchen to see whether the chef knows what it is?' Queen Elizabeth suggested to the head gardener at Balmoral.

Lady Salisbury has inspected all the Queen Mother's vegetables growing today at Birkhall and Mey: 'cabbages rolling in precise military lines'; 'the brilliant emerald of the curly kale; a small field of carrots, neat rows of leeks, beetroot with red fringed leaves and a goodly patch of the humble potato, besides onions and the clotted heads of cauliflower.'

There are also globe artichokes, mulched with manure from the royal farms, turnip, parsnips, swedes, leeks and early potatoes called 'Duke of York.'

Prince Charles too has a taste for country vegetables. 'I was also thinking of trying to grow some wonderful old-fashioned vegetables like coloured cabbage,' he says, going back to the roots planted by his grandmother in her royal plot.

MOTHER NATURE

'And I do believe, Your Majesty takes no scorn
to wear the leek upon Saint Tavy's day.'

Henry V by WILLIAM SHAKESPEARE (1564–1616)

PRINCE HARRY is watching, solemn-faced, as Charles plants shrubs in deep, wide holes. 'I've yet to see which child takes to gardening,' says his father. 'Sometimes children – if a parent is keen on something – one of them likes doing it as well.'

In the summer of 1951, Prince Charles, aged two and a half, created his first garden at Royal Lodge, Windsor: a path of miniature bricks, and a bowl to form a pool.

Creating a garden is part of royal childhood. Charles's mother and Princess Margaret had their own plots at Royal Lodge, separated by a stone pedestal. 'The two princesses used to have their gardens, with their own sets of tools, a little tool house, a seat and a barrow, where they would grow rock plants, aubrietia and the other simple cottage garden flowers that children love,' says Lady Salisbury.

'I noticed the Princess's tidy seed boxes were labelled by the owner

113

"parsley", "parsnips",' said the royal photographer Lisa Sheridan, who captured the two girls during their wartime evacuation at Windsor 'digging for victory' in the royal allotments: hoeing carrots, planting strawberries and gathering beans.

'The Princess showed me how she had outwitted the sparrows by netting a few strawberry plants, so that she had been able to serve her own fruit at her parents' dinner table,' Lisa Sheridan said. 'She had planted lettuces between the strawberry plants and was delighted to see that some of them were ready for the table that day.'

Generations of royal children have played gardener since Victoria and Albert's offspring had their own miniature tools and personal patches of earth in the gardens at Osborne House. The Queen Mother, as four-year-old Lady Elizabeth Bowes Lyon, fought with her brother David over a toy wheelbarrow. A mischievous Princess Margaret hid the gardeners' brooms. A playful Prince Andrew clutched a watering can with Prince Edward as a toddler in Buckingham Palace gardens.

William and Harry are helping their father draw up the earth in a bed of leeks, scattering the soil around the sprouting green tops.

'What I want to do when they are a little older perhaps, is to set aside a little area for them to garden,' says Charles. 'If you have got your own little garden, you learn that way.'

As they grow up, gardening becomes for some of the royal family an escape from duty and formality, a chance to create something of their own, and an opportunity for quiet contemplation in the country air. 'And while it is growing, he is able to polish, to cut up and carve, to fill up here and there, to hope, and to love,' said Prince Albert, describing his passion for creating a garden to his eldest daughter Vicky.

In the Edwardian era, the monarch was involved only in the garden's grand design. George VI and his brother the Duke of Windsor were the royal family's first 'dirt gardeners'. 'He was an absolute slave-driver, hacking, sawing, pulling out dead wood,' says Marion Crawford of George VI creating the garden at Royal Lodge.

The Duke of Windsor, who had dragooned his smart friends into creating a garden at Fort Belvedere, his country home at Windsor, took his passion with him into exile in France after the Abdication. 'It is a very tranquil place where one can garden, as one should, in old clothes, with one's hands, among familiar plants,' he said of the country home The Mill that he and his wife established outside Paris, and added, 'I now love, it is true, to stay quietly at our two homes in France, endeavouring to cultivate my garden.'

As the light fails Prince Charles is working fanatically at Highgrove. 'Everything has to be done properly with no corners cut,' says Rosemary Verey. 'And when evening comes on in winter there is a torch to hand to finish the last tidy-up.'

'Very therapeutic, weeding,' says Charles. 'And it's marvellous if you can do enough to see the effect.' His hoe, in the half light of early evening, moves rhythmically through the soil among the leeks – symbolic for a Prince of Wales.

'A daffodil!' Garter King of Arms expostulated to the royal couturier Norman Hartnell. 'On no account will I give you a daffodil. I will give you the correct emblem of Wales, which is the leek.'

The court dressmaker was researching for the Queen's coronation dress, and he found inspiration in the soil at Windsor.

'I went out to the vegetable garden, pulled up a leek and suddenly remembered the cap badge of the Welsh guards,' said Hartnell. 'In the end, by using lovely silks and sprinkling it with the dew of diamonds, we were able to

*The wild garden at Highgrove which
contains lilies, iris, daffodils, tulips, allium,
gladioli, scilla and beargrass, as well as the
'common-or-garden' cowslips, oxlips,
dandelions, lady's smock, ragged robin and
yellow rattle. Biologist and conservationist
Dr Miriam Rothschild says that 'the whole
effect is reminiscent of an Alpine meadow'.*

transform the earthly leek into a vision of Cinderella charm.'

'Her pink hands are folded meekly on the elaborate grandeur of her
encrusted skirt,' said Cecil Beaton as he watched the 25-year-old Queen walk
down the aisle of Westminster Abbey on 2 June 1953 – diamond dewdrops
lighting up the pale green leaves of the leek.

In Gloucestershire Charles is working on a new idea, inspired by Rosemary
Verey, to extract plant oils and make Highgrove fragrances and soaps. He
might even create a phial of oil that could be used on that distant, future day
when he himself is crowned and anointed in Westminster Abbey by the
Archbishop of Canterbury in the ancient ritual: 'Be thy hands anointed with
holy oil, be thy breast anointed with holy oil, be thy head anointed with holy
oil as King, Priests, and Prophet were anointed.'

Right now, the walled garden at Highgrove is Charles's kingdom, the
beanstalks his aisle, his vaulted roof the open sky. 'I put my heart and soul into
this,' he says.

Dr Armand Hammer, the late philanthropist and one of the Prince's
confidants, recalled a visit to Charles at Highgrove. 'When we were about to
leave, Prince Charles suddenly disappeared and returned to present us with
several boxes of the plump, sweet strawberries which he had picked himself as
a present to us,' Hammer said. 'I think his pleasure in those strawberries tells
you all you need to know about him. He was more delighted to give us berries
he had grown, and picked with his own hands, than if they had been jewels
from the family vault.'

HORSES

*Stud farms, carriage driving
and steeplechasing are private
royal passions*

The Queen at the Sandringham stud which
was established, with nearby Wolferton, by
the future Edward VII in 1886. The
Queen has 18 brood mares, with three
stallions standing. Stud manager Michael
Oswald is in charge of bloodstock.

RIGHT: *The bronze statue of Persimmon
in front of the stud. King Edward VII's
stallion won the Derby in 1896, the Ascot
Gold Cup, Eclipse Stakes and St Leger.*

PRECEDING PAGES: *Prince Philip
driving four-in-hand at Windsor.*

CHAPTER 4

A Kingdom for a Horse

'A horse, a horse. My kingdom for a horse!'

Richard III by WILLIAM SHAKESPEARE (1564–1616)

RACING DEMONS

THE QUEEN is pacing the turf in front of the red brick and cobblestoned stud farm. She is as taut with anticipation as those thousands – millions – of dignitaries who over the years have waited for her royal visit, mouth sandpaper dry, palms damp.

The motorcade that is already on the Fakenham road, about to turn off towards Sandringham, consists of two Land-Rovers and an olive green horse box, bringing a stallion to cover the pick of Sandringham's 18 brood mares. It is for the Queen another hope, a fading dream now that Sheikh Hamdan Al-Maktoum and his brothers have moved so deeply into racing, that she could breed – at last – from her own stud, from bloodlines she has developed, a Derby winner to run in her own scarlet and purple colours.

'My philosophy about racing is simple,' she says. 'I enjoy breeding a horse that is faster than other people's, and to me that is a gamble from a long way back. I enjoy going racing, but I suppose basically I love horses, and the thoroughbred epitomizes a really good horse to me; and my particular hope for the future – like all breeders of horses – is to breed the winner of the Derby.'

In front of her, the mighty head, heavy flanks and streaming tail of Persimmon are silhouetted in greeny bronze against the wide open Norfolk sky. The statue of her great-great-grandfather's horse, the triumphant Derby winner of 1896, dominates the Sandringham stud.

'One of my earliest memories, although for years I'm not sure I knew what he had done to have been turned into statue,' says Anne, the Princess Royal. 'That's not altogether too surprising, considering I first saw it from my pram!'

The horse stands four-square on its plinth, a splattering of bright red tulips round the base, in front of the main offices of the royal stud where the EIIR insignia is now worked into the local stone. Persimmon, 'out of Perdita II by St Simon', the Queen will recite.

'Both descendants from Feola,' she will suddenly observe while studying her horses; or 'a typical daughter of Hyperion.'

'A complete expert in this field,' says her racing manager and close personal friend, Henry, 7th Earl of Carnarvon, formerly Lord Porchester.

One of the Queen's favourite conversation pieces with house guests is to ask for help with the crossword complexities of naming a new foal: Hiawatha's Song (Soprano and Dancing Brave); Deadly Serious (Queen's Hussar and Joking Apart); Highlight (Borealis and Hypericum).

It is a new twist to Queen Mary's passion for the ramifications of family history. 'Genealogies, historical and dynastic, were very interesting to children,' Queen Mary claimed when reviewing the educational curriculum of the two Princesses. 'Was Arithmetic really more valuable – for them – than History?' she asked their governess.

Persimmon is part of royal racing history – the crowning glory of years of investment and enjoyment by the future Edward VII. The Duke of Windsor remembered from his childhood the royal Sunday afternoon promenade that 'always culminated at the stud farm', its 'commodious loose boxes' filled with his grandfather's stallions. 'There was a special building for the two stallions of the stud that had won the Derby,' he said. 'One large box was for the great Persimmon, a fine bay foaled at Sandringham.'

In the collection of royal jewels is the Cartier stickpin made for the future Edward VII (his trainer Richard Marsh had another) to commemorate that magnificent day on Epsom Downs in 1896 when Persimmon battled past the winning post while the crowds cheered themselves hoarse for the royal owner.

'Nothing ever pleased him so much as winning a race, and receiving the congratulations of his people afterwards,' the future King's friend Lord Marcus Beresford told Dick Marsh. Marsh received a cheque for £1,000 for training the royal owner's other Derby winner Diamond Jubilee, a temperamental colt which galloped in to wild public enthusiasm in 1900.

The Queen has her own memories of the cheers that greeted Highclere's win in 1978 at the French racecourse of Chantilly. She had decided to run the filly in the Prix de Diane – the French equivalent of the Oaks – after Highclere had won the 1,000 Guineas.

'It seemed that she had a good chance and I'd never been racing in France when I'd had a horse running,' she says. 'Well, it was a lovely outing for me – the President was of course very kind and made it very easy for me to get to Chantilly.' President Giscard d'Estaing even sent the Queen a bouquet of red roses, and the French racing fraternity cheered her on.

'The crowd was tremendously friendly, and even after the race when Highclere had won they seemed even more friendly,' she says.

The win was followed by an impromptu celebration dinner at Windsor with Prince Philip, the Queen Mother and Princess Anne, Lord Mountbatten, the Porchesters, the royal stud manager Michael Oswald, the trainer Dick Hern and jockey Joe Mercer and his wife, who called it 'the greatest day of our lives'.

The Queen may have mares in foal in France, but she does not have many opportunities to go racing there. 'If it were not for my Archbishop of Canterbury, I should be off in my plane to Longchamp every Sunday!' she says.

But there are private trips to the French studs, with 'Young Porchie' as Lord Carnarvon is sometimes still called, even though he inherited the senior title from his father in 1987 and a new young Lord Porchester (the Queen's godson) is installed with his wife Jayne in a cottage in the grounds of the ancestral home at Highclere Castle in Berkshire.

Porchester (whose grandfather the 5th Earl of Carnarvon discovered Tutankhamun's tomb) was appointed to a new post as the Queen's Racing Manager in 1970. At the same time, Oswald became Stud Manager, and the two have co-existed for over twenty years, with Her Majesty making the final decisions.

The French racing circle – the Baron Guy de Rothschild, the Duc de Noailles, the Duc d'Audrifret-Pasquier – admire the Queen's prowess and welcome her discreet visits. 'If you seat her next to the right person, she is so

Henry, 7th Earl of Carnarvon, was appointed the Queen's racing manager in 1970. The former Lord Porchester (and known as 'Porchie'), he is a close friend of the Queen.

animated, like a young girl,' says one of her hosts in Normandy. 'She is really, really knowledgeable about horses, the bloodstock and the form. She would do it professionally, if she weren't Queen. It is a real passion, and you can see that when she touches the horses and feeds them sugar lumps. But it is not the same for Prince Philip, you know. He gets very bored with it all.'

The stable boys are leading out the brood mares, groomed to a high gleam. The Queen caresses a nose. Only Anne, of all her children, shares that communion with a horse, the pleasure in looking after it, the agony at the moment of departure.

The Queen opens a hand and proffers an apple. Aureole, the magnificent chestnut with three white socks, the bright star at the beginning of her reign, would always refuse an apple – unless it was very sweet, and demand instead sugar lumps or the carrots dispensed at Sandringham in Edwardian times. 'While my grandfather discoursed in detail on the pedigrees and performances of each one, Queen Alexandra dispensed carrots to the thoroughbreds from a basket,' the Duke of Windsor remembered.

Princess Elizabeth's love affair with horses started in the nursery, where she would harness her governess in a pair of red reins with bells and demand that she paw the ground 'like a proper horse'. She and Margaret looked after the 30-odd toy horses on wheels, removing their saddles, cleaning their tack and feeding and watering them each night. When their father succeeded to the throne, the royal sisters supervised the move of their toy stables to Buckingham Palace in 1937, and the horses were still lined up there on Lilibet's wedding day.

'Is all well, ma'am?' a lady-in-waiting asked on the morning of the Queen's coronation in 1953.

'Oh yes, the Captain has just rung up to say Aureole went really well,' the Queen said, referring to royal trainer Captain Cecil Boyd-Rochfort and to the colt which so nearly won the Derby for her that summer.

'I won't put you in the Tower this time,' she joked to winning jockey Gordon Richards when he pipped Aureole to the post on Pinza. 'One couldn't really be sad not to win because Gordon had at last won a Derby,' she said.

When Aureole was retired to stud at Sandringham in 1954 he was given royal treatment – his own high-walled yard, a personal covered exercise area and a paddock. 'With quite the grandest field barn I've ever seen, with a thatched roof, if you please,' recalls Princess Anne.

When did the Queen's girlish enthusiasm, for riding, for reading *Black Beauty* and for marking 'all the horsey books' in the Christmas catalogues, turn into an adult passion for racing and breeding?

'I suppose I first became interested in racing during the war when my father had leased Big Game and Sun Chariot from the National Stud; when my father took me down to Beckhampton to see them working, which I had never seen before, and I was able to put them in the stable afterwards,' she says.

After touching Big Game (the colt which had won the 2,000 Guineas in 1942) in the Beckhampton yard of trainer Fred Darling, she did not want to wash her hands. 'I'd never felt the satiny softness of a thoroughbred before – it was a wonderful feeling,' she said. For horse lovers, touching has a mystical effect. When the highly strung Aureole was being treated by the neurologist Dr Charles Brook in 1953, he would put one hand on the colt's withers and the other on his girth to calm him.

'Well, Aureole was always an independent and frankly naughty character,' the Queen admitted. 'He was often loose at Newmarket when he was in training, which I think was why it didn't disturb him when he got loose at Ascot before he won the King George VI that year.' After that win at the King George VI and Queen Elizabeth Stakes at Ascot in July 1954, the young Queen ran in high excitement into the unsaddling enclosure, her racing manager Captain Charles Moore trailing behind her.

Her knowledge and understanding of breeding were developed by visits to the Hampton Court Stud to see Charles Moore, who laid the foundation of the successes achieved in the early part of her reign. He had managed the Royal Stud since 1937, and had guided George VI when he so unexpectedly came to the throne and took over the royal stables.

'I shall take a great interest in racing, but of course at the moment I know nothing about breeding or anything else,' the new King admitted in 1936.

'In my father's time, he left the breeding policy to the manager Charles

The Queen watching horses in training at Alec Head's stud in Normandy. She first visited the National Stud as a child with her father, and she is now an experienced judge of form, setting breeding policy and following the progress of her foals and yearlings.

Moore and then when I succeeded I came in for all the successes of that policy rather unfairly,' the Queen admits.

Changing with modern times has meant trying to inject a bit more speed into the staying blood of Captain Moore's era – especially by sending mares to stallions in America. It has been the Queen's policy that the resident royal stallions (currently Belmez, Bustino and Shirley Heights) standing at Sandringham and Wolferton should be syndicated. She remains a majority shareholder, while others take a share – usually 1/40th – in return for the right to send a mare to be covered. In her turn, the Queen may invest in a stallion – as in 1979, when she invested £180,000 in a 1/40th share in the Weinstock/Sobell syndication of Troy, a convincing Derby winner in 1979, when he trounced her own colt Milford. 'It isn't a profitable venture at the moment because the

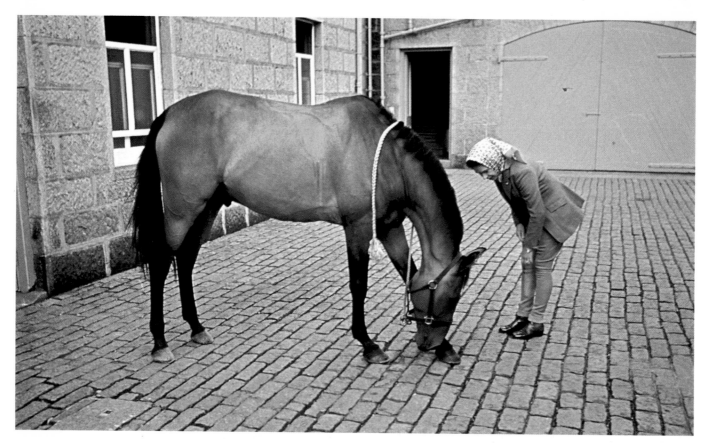

The Queen is fascinated by 'the satiny softness of a thoroughbred', and frequently visits the stables. She has been obliged to reduce the number of horses in training from 36 to 25 as a cost-cutting measure.

problems of racing are so very great,' admits the Queen. 'But I think that as a human being one always has hope – and one always has perhaps the gambling instinct that one's horse is going to be better than the next man's horse – and that's why one goes on doing it.'

In the recent past, things were easier and cheaper, for George VI would lease horses from the National Stud, founded in Ireland but moved to England during the war and run by the Ministry of Agriculture. The National Stud was moved to Newmarket in the early 1960s, and the special royal arrangement ceased at that time.

Both the Queen and her mother get twice-weekly progress reports from stud farms and stables.

'Our conversations go on for a long time,' admitted a royal trainer.

The arrival of stud manager Michael Oswald causes a flurry of activity at Sandringham as the brood mares are led out for a 'team photograph'. In the royal archives is a memorable picture of brood mares visiting Shirley Heights at Sandringham in 1986: each stable lad, with crested pocket and flat cap, holding one of the six mares, the Queen herself leading Dunfermline, so difficult to get into foal, so much missed since her death in 1989, such a brilliant winner of the Oaks in Jubilee year 1977.

'Because Prince Andrew had returned that morning from Canada, I didn't go to the Oaks, but of course we watched the race on TV,' says the Queen. 'At first it didn't seem to us that Dunfermline was going to be even placed. It was Andrew who suddenly spotted how fast she was going, and then of course it was excitement all the way.'

Probably the only thing that would have kept the Queen from the racecourse that day was the homecoming of her favourite son.

'Princess Margaret once showed me round Balmoral when everyone was at church,' says a friend. 'In private, the Queen surrounds herself with photo-graphs of Andrew – it's an obsession.'

After Dunfermline's win, the Queen Mother phoned from Epsom to share the excitement and accepted the trophy. Dunfermline and her jockey Willie Carson went on to win the St Leger and take a crack at the Arc before she was retired as a brood mare. Although the Queen Mother's emotional involve-ment is with National Hunt racing, she still enjoys the Flat.

'It is always interesting with the Queen's runners and the breeding side which is so interesting,' she says.

He's here! The horse box containing its precious cargo comes to a halt in front of the main offices. Photographs are taken, and when the excitement is done, the Queen is off (with her camera) to the Wolferton stud over by Sandringham parish church. Apart from these few days in April, and the longer New Year visit to Norfolk, the Queen has so little time to spend at the studs.

'Being there in January, if we were lucky, one or two of the mares might have foaled before we had to leave, and that was a real treat,' says Anne. 'My children aren't so fortunate because they have to go back to school much earlier than I did.'

The Queen likes to watch the entire progress of the foals as they are bitted, lunged, long-reined and, finally, ridden.

'Well, I thought it was one of the most interesting aspects of breeding horses – to see them . . . and learn their character and their temperament, and you see exactly how they'll move and how they're going to go on,' she says.

The foals are usually weaned at Sandringham and then sent on to the Polhampton stud on the chalk downs of Hampshire ('so good for teaching animals to use themselves'). Polhampton, bought by the Queen in 1972, is near both Kingsclere and West Ilsley where her trainers operate, and is used for the yearlings or for resting injured horses or those that are out of training.

The Queen had 13 yearlings in 1992. She rarely buys yearlings 'except to get a new family', although she has vivid memories of going to the Doncaster sales with Charles Moore and Lord Porchester and 'falling in love' with a filly who became the dam of Canisbay, winner of the Eclipse in 1965. Canisbay is named after the parish round the Queen Mother's Castle of Mey.

On her trips to America, where she has horses in training in Kentucky, the Queen will stay with the American breeder Will Farish and his wife Sarah, and may visit the family of Lord Carnarvon's wife in Wyoming. The Queen sees the foals she has bred, evaluating their good and bad points and noting especially the wayward family blood that can produce 'an absolute devil'. 'Temperament one has to watch very carefully when one's planning and breeding,' she says.

Owner and trainer will watch a young filly given a turn round the paddock while the early judgments are made: 'going very nicely'; or 'joints a little bit stiff'; or 'this one seems very awkward'; or 'big and backward, she'll have to be taken rather slowly'.

Here at Wolferton, in fitful sunlight, the Queen is taking swift snapshots of the future champions and disappointments on the Flat.

On her first visit to Beckhampton, Fred Darling was amazed to see her picking out horses for her father. 'Princess Elizabeth must have a natural eye for a horse,' Darling told the jockey Gordon Richards.

'I've quite a good memory, but I've always taken pictures of the foals, especially since the days when they used to go to Ireland and once came back without names on their headcollars,' the Queen says. 'I was able to identify Doutelle from Agreement as yearlings. It turned out to be rather an important difference!' Doutelle went on to win six races and to sire Canisbay.

Anne, the Princess Royal, shares with her mother a passion for riding that extends to tacking up and grooming. Saddlemakers W. & H. Gidden hold the Royal Warrant.

The royal insignia is a prominent feature in flat racing, even for horse blankets. The Queen inherited her racing colours – purple body with gold braid, scarlet sleeves and gilt-fringed black velvet cap – from Edward VII and George IV.

There is nothing but pleasure to be had from standing here with the smell of damp earth, photographing the gangly colt ('he's got a mind of his own') careering across the grass, his head picked out against the straight squares of white fence.

The decision to cut down the horses in training from 36 to 25 did not come easily. 'Rationalization', it is called, and it is a matter of policy, of making the royal racing business pay for itself by a combination of shrewd sales, stud fees and prize money. There have not been enough winners in recent years, since the Arabs have invested unfathomable amounts of money in bloodstock, regardless of profit.

'For most of the racing period the Queen has made it pay, but not in some years and particularly since the arrival of the big opposition,' said Lord Carnarvon, as he announced in May 1991 the plan to improve the quality of the Queen's Flat runners and cut back to 'about 20' brood mares. She had 14 brood mares at stud in England at the beginning of 1992.

'The Queen has been unlucky with her racing manager, not her horses,' says a racing colleague. 'There have been some terrible blunders, like selling Height of Fashion which would have gone on to give the Queen her Derby winner. All the racing in England is designed to test the stock, so that the thoroughbred owners can decide which horses to retire to stud. Porchester's all for breeding and selling on, which may be good commercially, but not what one expects of royal racing.' Height of Fashion, a bay filly sired by the Queen's fertile stallion Bustino, went on to produce Nashwan, a Derby winner for Sheikh Hamdan Al-Maktoum in 1989.

Lord Carnarvon justifies the cuts, which include four brood mares from the Sandringham and Wolferton studs. 'This is a commercial decision at the same time as being a sensible one which fits in with the assets in terms of studs and stallions,' he claimed. The Queen might also reduce by half the 36 horses in training at the start of 1991. In 1992 there were six with Ian Balding at Kingsclere and 25 with his brother-in-law the Earl of Huntingdon at the Queen's own West Ilsley stables set in the heart of the Berkshire Downs, 12 miles north of Newbury. These were bought from Sir Michael Sobell and his son-in-law Lord Weinstock of GEC for £800,000 in 1982 – using part of the £1.25 million paid for Height of Fashion by H. Maktoum, son of the ruler of Dubai and the country's finance minister.

'Porchester's a bit of a spiv, but he and Oswald do what they are told, and it is HM who makes the decisions,' said a member of the Jockey Club. 'The thing is that she mustn't be seen by the public to be spending too much or to be making big prize money, whereas the stud fees she earns for her investment in a syndicated stallion are more or less private. Height of Fashion was sold because she wanted to buy West Ilsley and here was this Gulf sheikh offering her a million pounds for a horse the public thinks cost HM nothing to breed. It was all a public relations exercise.' In another discreet move in January 1992, Carnarvon arranged a 'swap' of two of the Queen's fillies for two colts in training with Sheikh Al-Maktoum – without any money changing hands.

A potentially damaging event in the public's eyes was the departure of

Daredevil Prince William tries rodeo riding as he leaps over the head of his pony Trigger during the Easter holiday 1991.

The Queen and Sarah, Duchess of York at Sandringham hacking out. Riding was a bond between the two during Sarah's marriage to Andrew.

Major Dick Hern, the Queen's trainer for 23 years, whose lease at West Ilsley was not renewed in 1989, in spite of the fact that the Major, at 69, had made heroic efforts to overcome his 1984 hunting accident and subsequent heart problems. He had vocal support from the racing fraternity, including the jockey Willie Carson. The lease was given to William Hastings-Bass (now Lord Huntingdon), who is Lord Carnarvon's godson.

The row reverberated for three months after the decision was announced from Buckingham Palace in May 1989, and it was one of the rare occasions when the Queen and her mother had words. However, the Queen decided, uncharacteristically, that regardless of sentiment and loyalty, a practical decision had to be taken about the future of West Ilsley in the 1990s.

Royal racing has always been a costly business. Edward VII spent so much on his horses that his mistress Lillie Langtry had to bail him out with a loan so that he could keep his training stables at Egerton House near Newmarket, where the mile-and-a-quarter moss gallops helped to train winners.

The Queen knows that she herself shares both credit and blame for her racing career, and that success on the turf is a mixture of skill at thoroughbred breeding and pure luck. 'From my experience of racing and breeding I think one obviously has to aim to breed a classic horse either in the first or second generation,' she says. 'My racing manager and I have argued how important is the breeding and the influence of the past over many years' acquaintance, and we've had a lot of fun out of it.'

Prince Charles, like his father, is not involved in the Queen's passion and folly. 'Whenever I back one of my mother's horses, it is always a total disaster,' he once said. 'I keep well out of that and I advise you to do the same thing.'

The Queen absorbed as a child the pleasures and dashed hopes of the Turf. She and her sister listened on the radio when Big Game ran – and was beaten – in the Derby at Newmarket, where the race was run throughout the Second World War.

'Isn't it a shame,' said 12-year-old Princess Margaret.

'Not at all, Margaret,' Princess Elizabeth replied. 'It's just horse-racing.'

OVER THE STICKS

If you can meet with Triumph and Disaster
And treat those two imposters just the same . . .

'If – ' by RUDYARD KIPLING (1865–1936)

THE ARGONAUT is safely over, but Roscoe Harvey has unseated jockey Charlie Lane at the first fence. The Argonaut and San Ovac are over the next, but Canon Class – Princess Anne's favourite mount – has unseated his rider. Now Bob Tisdall is out. OUT! The favourite gone at only the second fence! Erins Dancer is pulled up at the next. At the sixth Kevin Evans unseats his rider. What a chapter of accidents! Just seven runners left with sixteen fences to go. San Ovac is still in the lead, but The Argonaut is well in touch. On into the second circuit, and now, seven fences from home, Gerald Oxley, in the Queen Mother's blue and buff colours, takes The Argonaut to the front. Into the back straight: up and over; again; again. And safely over the water. Now the last quick 'railway' fences: one-two-three. And The Argonaut is leading by a distance into the home straight – 14 or 15 lengths clear! Two pairs of binoculars and four royal eyes are fixed on the finish as mother and daughter watch The Argonaut romp home.

A win! *Another* win for jump racing's favourite owner in the Grand Military Gold Cup here at Sandown Park. 'Always a great favourite with everyone. A wonderful course to see . . . there is always a thrill somehow,' says the Queen Mother of the National Hunt racecourse lodged in its grass-green amphitheatre near Esher in Surrey.

Here 'Queen Elizabeth' – as the world of racing knows her – comes right through the winter months, whatever the weather, in her plump, polished Daimler. To sustain her through the afternoon's racing, she has a pair of sheepskin ankle boots, a sturdy coat, a couple of glasses of Dubonnet and a little something from the seafood bar.

This dull March day in 1990 is special. It is the 150th anniversary of the Grand Military – 'the soldiers' Grand National', they call it – and the Queen has come with her mother to walk around among the army folk and to inspect the regimental band of the Royal Hussars playing on the terrace outside the members' bar. Together they have watched The Argonaut carry to victory the Strathmore colours – brought back to life by the Queen Mother fifty years

Prince Charles and Princess Anne were taken to horse trials and racing as children, but both grew up to be active participants in steeplechasing rather than spectators.

after they were worn by her great-uncle, Lord Strathmore, a keen amateur rider.

'Not quite royal blue,' the Queen Mother says of the turquoise sweater with buff-striped body and plain sleeves that is worn with a distinctive gold-tasselled black velvet cap.

The first steeplechaser to carry Queen Elizabeth's colours was Manicou, jumping to victory through the 1950 winter season, especially the bold win in the George VI chase, when the then Queen left the family Christmas to drive to Kempton Park on Boxing Day and watch him win by three lengths at five to one.

'I've always loved it,' says the Queen Mother about the thrills she gets from National Hunt racing. 'I think I always wanted a horse for steeplechasing, and because the Queen is very keen on the Flat, I thought I'd have a horse and see. And of course I got hooked.'

'Her real passion in life,' claims the royal stud manager, Michael Oswald, who organizes a breeding routine for the Queen Mother's brood mares and their foals in Norfolk.

'Why do you keep half of my mother's mares at Sandringham and the other half at Wolferton?' the Queen once asked Oswald.

'Well, if I didn't, Ma'am, one groom would think he hadn't had his fair share,' Oswald replied.

'Yes, that's the effect Mummy seems to have on people,' replied the Queen.

Mother and daughter were originally joint owners. The first steeplechasing memory goes back to the summer of 1949, when they each took a half share in Monaveen after a chance conversation over the dinner table at Windsor with Lord Mildmay – a family friend and champion amateur jump jockey. His good friend Peter Cazalet became the royal jumping trainer, and on Mildmay's death by drowning, inherited his horses – including Manicou.

The thrill and tragedy of steeplechasing were encapsulated in that first year: the pride at Monaveen's wins at Fontwell, Sandown and Hurst Park; the excitement of the visit to Hurst Park on New Year's Day 1951; the terrible fall on twisted legs at the water jump; jockey Tony Grantham knocked uncon-

The Queen Mother dressed for warmth at the Badminton Horse Trials. She is a frequent visitor to Sandown Park, Cheltenham and other National Hunt racecourses. Although she has had many winners, her first chaser, Monaveen, owned jointly with Princess Elizabeth, was killed at Hurst Park in 1951.

scious; the decision to put Monaveen out of his agony; the urgent request to the commentator Raymond Glendenning not to give out the news of the horse's death on radio in case Princess Elizabeth, abroad in Malta, picked up the broadcast.

'It's terribly sad, isn't it,' Queen Elizabeth said to the crowds who pushed her car out of the mud at the course. 'This has been a very sad day.'

Today at Sandown is a moment of pure pleasure and family pride as the Queen presents her mother with the Grand Military Gold Cup in front of the winners' enclosure. The two Queens, in shades of blue, beam across the

The Queen presents the Horse and Hound *cup to her mother after The Argonaut's win at the Grand Military Gold Cup Chase at Sandown Park in March 1990.*

trophy given by *Horse and Hound* – sponsors of the Grand Military since 1976 – as the crowd applauds a popular win, a fourth for the jockey Gerald Oxley of the 9th/12th lancers in this particular steeplechase for amateur riders. He brought the royal owner a hat-trick of winners with Special Cargo in 1984, '85 and again in '86, when the news of his grandmother's winning day was relayed to Prince Charles out hunting with the Belvoir. Five years before, in 1981, the Queen Mother had watched her grandson compete – and, alas! fall – in the Grand Military during his steeplechasing days.

'If people could just understand the real thrill, the challenge of steeplechasing,' said Charles. 'It's part of the great British way of life, and none of the other sports I've done bears any comparison.'

The Argonaut's win at Sandown is also a joy – one of his final triumphs – for the trainer Fulke Walwyn, mourned by the racing community as 'the greatest jumping trainer of all time' when he died the following January.

High on the Queen Mother's list of delicious outings is tea at Saxon House with Walwyn's widow Cath, who took over the training yard at Lambourne, Kent after her husband's death. She had half a dozen horses in training – two or three home bred – for the Queen Mother in 1991. Fulke Walwyn was a Sandhurst man who had turned professional after winning the Grand National in 1936, during the fleeting reign of Edward VIII – himself a keen steeplechaser. The partnership with the Queen Mother started when Walwyn was sent her horses in 1973 on the death of Peter Cazalet. He was appointed Commander of the Victorian Order – the most private royal honour – in 1983.

'I am so pleased to give you this. I hope you will show it around the yard to the lads,' the Queen Mother said as she handed over the honour in person.

Together the royal owner and her ruddy-faced trainer shared the sorrows of

'the sticks'. 'I suppose there must be about eighty per cent disappointment, or more,' the Queen Mother admits. 'But that makes up when you do get a winner. I think it is well worth it.'

'She loves racing so dearly,' said Sir Martin Gilliat, her Private Secretary, after Sunyboy won the Fernbank hurdle at Ascot in 1976. 'There have been days of pain, as when her fine horse Three No Trumps had to be put down at Sandown. So it is nice to see her enjoying moments like today.'

Sir Martin, her good friend, faithful servant and unofficial racing manager, ('But ma'am is the expert') has also met the triumphs and disasters of 40 years in racing. He marks on the Racing Calendar where Queen Elizabeth's horses have been entered, and he slots the racing in with official engagements.

'And he bets like smoke,' says a racing friend.

At Clarence House, 'The Blower' – the racecourse commentary service relayed to betting shops – was rigged up in 1965, although that has now been superceded by modern electronics. 'My Scottish logic,' the Queen Mother calls it when she has a little flutter and picks a winner. 'I read *The Sporting Life* and get my day-to-day news and a little bit of gossip which is always great fun,' she says. 'One likes to keep in touch and I do all through the Flat season as well.'

The Queen Mother has an eye for a horse, inspecting The Rip – son of Manicou and a useful three-mile steeplechaser – on the lawn of a pub, the Red Cat at Wooton Marshes in Norfolk, and buying him for 400 guineas.

Racing folk insist it is her expertise that brings the winners. As Jack O'Donaghue, the Irish trainer at Reigate, put it: 'She won't run a horse if the going's not suitable. And she knows what courses suit them. She knows plenty she does, by gosh she does.'

Fulke Walwyn (left), the Queen Mother's late trainer, with Michael Oswald, the Queen's stud manager. Since Walwyn's retirement in 1990 and death the following year, the Queen Mother's horses are in training with his widow Catherine at Lambourne, Kent.

Prince Harry delighted his mother by winning two trophies and a rosette in the show jumping competition at a gymkhana near Highgrove in June 1991.

In the smell of mud, turf and tack here at Sandown, there is also a whiff of fierce, if friendly, competition. There was a genteel contest through the 1960s between the Queen Mother and Anne, Duchess of Westminster (owner of the legendary Arkle) to see who could have the greater number of winners in the owners' table.

'We must get her century up,' Michael Oswald will say about the Queen Mother's racing when one of the 'magic' numbers is approaching. 'She's had eighty-something winners and we're trying to get her up to a hundred this year.'

There was a party in the Savoy River Room to celebrate the 200th win, in January 1970, after Master Daniel won at Worcester. The 300th win came up in 1976 with six-year-old Sunyboy, bought from Lady Beaverbrook who had originally trained the horse for the Flat.

'Keep Columbus away from her!' was the royal family's joke, when Princess Anne was training on the big grey gelding which might well have suited her grandmother as a steeplechaser. Now it is the other way about: the Queen and other members of the royal family ride out on 'granny's' jumpers that have been retired.

At the end of 1991 there were 380 winners under National Hunt rules according to Sir Martin. Each horse, each race, each win is recorded in his detailed reports, hefty volumes filled with photographs of all her 'darling boys'. 'I've always loved them, ever since I was a little girl,' she says. 'Probably one gets too fond of them. Sometimes you hate to see anything happen to them.'

The 13 runners are parading round the ring before the next race – the Whisky Hurdles. Even with no horse entered, there is pleasure in seeing the big chasers taking Sandown's fences – especially the last three on the back straight beside the Waterloo line where so many riders have been unseated – not least Prince Charles. In 1981 he pitched out of Good Prospect's saddle at the eighteenth fence.

'It happens to everyone,' said the racing expert Lord Oaksey, 'and the only thing that varies is the time you take to learn to avoid it by racing differently.'

Prince Charles was bitten by what Oaksey calls 'the highly infectious bug of riding over fences at speed.' He was excited especially by the prospect of the Grand National, 'the indescribable, tingling thrill of seeing those gallant horses fly over a series of astonishing obstacles . . . A glorious, and somewhat eccentric, part of our heritage,' he said.

Charles took up both steeplechasing and cross-country team-chasing in the late 1970s. Steeplechasing (originally named after the dash from one church spire to another) was a natural extension of his enthusiasm for hunting, as it had been for the future Edward VIII.

'Talking to people out hunting I got rather excited by the idea of trying race riding – and also overcoming my anxiety about jumping at speed,' Charles admitted.

When things went wrong and he joined the list of unseated riders at Sandown and at Cheltenham, it was splashed over the newspapers. 'They were headline news,' said Oaksey of these falls. 'But Prince Charles is far too accustomed to the pitiless spotlight in which his family lives to waste his time complaining.'

Prince Charles's first race over the sticks at the age of 32 was a celebrity contest at Plumpton in Sussex in March 1980. He came second and already had dreams of glory, outlining his ambitions on the eve of his wedding in 1981: 'To ride a winner of course – and I'll do it too.' But within a year he had stopped National Hunt racing.

'He yearns to ride in the Grand National, but the weight of opposition is too great,' Stephen Barry said at that time. 'I doubt if it will ever happen. When he came off his own horse Good Prospect, in 1981 at a steeplechase meeting at Sandown, that probably finished his chances of having a crack at the National.'

It was then, to that Grand Military at Sandown, that the Queen Mother and Princess Margaret brought a nervous Lady Diana Spencer, peeping shyly from under a brown felt hat to watch Charles in action. The royal jockey, in scarlet colours with royal blue sleeves and black cap, rode Good Prospect well – until he misjudged the stride at the eighteenth fence.

Charles was more angry than hurt. 'All he did was bruise his back and his ego,' Barry said.

Lord Oaksey found it quite normal that the inexperienced Prince Charles did not 'immediately ride in triumph into the winner's enclosure, behaving like a joint reincarnation of Lester Piggott, John Francome and Fred Archer.' 'For any ordinary amateur rider having only his third and fourth rides over fences, the Prince's two "unseated riders" at Sandown and Cheltenham would have been minor, unimportant setbacks, significant only for the lessons they taught,' he said.

But Charles realized that the spectators both cheered him on and doubted his prowess. 'It is a funny sort of mixture. People half *want* you to make a fool of yourself and half assume that you should, somehow, be good at everything and almost automatically succeed,' he said.

Privately he cursed himself for picking the wrong horse in Good Prospect. According to Barry, 'The horse, he insisted, had no shoulders. He said grumpily "It's going". And it went.'

Good Prospect had been taken on at short notice after the sudden death of cherished Allibar, when Charles was exercising him at the trainer Nick Gaselee's yard in Kent. Lady Diana Spencer, watching from a Land-Rover with Nick's wife Judy, saw Allibar sink to his knees, keel over and die.

'The awful, awful tragedy of Allibar,' says Charles. He had developed a special relationship with the brown gelding, brought over by Gaselee from Ireland and sold to the Prince for £15,000.

The death of a horse is a bond shared by all riders.

'I cried and I cried,' said Mark Phillips of the death of his horse Rock On in 1972. 'Even now, just talking about him gives me a funny feeling . . . He was the bravest horse I ever knew, and you have to admire pure courage in a horse. He'd look at you with big, wide, brown eyes and I'd think . . . Why should you be so brave, so courageous?'

'Quite the most ghastly experience of my entire life,' says Anne of being told by the vet that her chestnut gelding Doublet had to be put down after breaking a leg in May 1974.

Princess Anne also discovered the thrill of National Hunt racing, which, she says, 'has given me as much satisfaction as anything I have ever done'. Anne was 35 when she took up racing at a celebrity benefit for Riding for the Disabled in 1985. Jump racing followed the Flat, and Anne has now had 38 rides over fences, including the Grand Military at Sandown in 1988 with her family gathered to watch. Although her real success has been in eventing, she says that she has enjoyed her races 'over the sticks'.

'Nothing quite compares with that final commitment of being "upsides going to the last" and the excitement of a horse going as fast as it can to beat another horse,' she says.

Her grandmother says that she needed a couple of stiff gins before watching her grandchildren in the racing saddle.

The Queen Mother has had her own heartsick memories, going right back

Prince Charles checking out the course before competing in the Quorn Hunt cross-country event.

Walking the course to become familiar with the terrain and obstacles is part of the preparation for cross-country events. Charles took up steeplechasing and team-chasing in the late 1970s, but like a previous Prince of Wales (the future Edward VIII), Charles was criticized for indulging in a dangerous sport.

to Monaveen's death on New Year's Day 1951. Then there was National Hunt's great racing mystery – the sudden, inexplicable stop of her gelding Devon Loch in the 1956 Grand National, when he was so near the winning post and the cheers of the crowd faded into silence.

'Well. That's racing,' said Devon Loch's jockey Dick Francis, whose racing thrillers his royal patron now devours.

'Please don't be upset. There will be another time,' the Queen Mother said to console him.

'She was always the same whether we had won or lost. She would have a kind word for me and for the horse's lad and her knowledge of racing was quite incredible,' said the royal jockey Terry Biddlecombe. The burly

'Biddles', son of a Gloucestershire farmer, rode seven winners for the Queen Mother before becoming Central TV's racing correspondent.

The next race is about to start – the Duke of Gloucester Memorial Hunters' Steeple Chase – the prize a silver statuette presented by Princess Alice in memory of her late husband who was a chairman of the Grand Military Race Committee.

It's de Pluvinel and Father Brady in a two-horse race; the favourite Dromin Joker is nowhere near as they come down the back straight; de Pluvinel in front at the water jump; now Father Brady just inching ahead; and Father Brady it is from game old de Pluvinel.

Prince Charles nearly lost his seat as he took a fence in the Fernie cross-country team event. He pitched out of the saddle under the eyes of his fiancée Lady Diana Spencer when he rode in the Grand Military at Sandown Park in 1981.

The Queen Mother is asking after Major Charlie Lane, being treated for concussion after a nasty kick in the head when Roscoe Harvey unseated him in the big race. The dangers of steeplechasing are ever present – the reason why the public, according to Lord Oaksey, often consider it 'a nasty, dangerous pastime to the risk of which an heir to the throne should not in any circumstances be exposed'.

Edward VIII, when Prince of Wales, was beseeched by his parents to give up as he crashed and dashed from point to point; yet he was determined to carry on jumping. 'My father's letters became equally forcible in their insistence that I should, in the interests of my safety, give up riding in point-to-point races,' he said. 'I eventually – and reluctantly – bowed to his wishes.'

After the heir to the throne was knocked out for half an hour in an army point-to-point, both his father and Prime Minister Ramsay MacDonald insisted that he should abandon the thrill of speed.

'The very strong opinion of Mama and myself that you should not expose yourself to unnecessary risks,' wrote King George V on 30 March 1924. 'You have shown great courage and horsemanship . . . but the time has come when I must ask you to give up riding in the future in steeplechases and point-to-point races . . .'

Racing over fences proved a siren lure for Prince Charles, who has risked his neck at team-chasing and jump racing. 'I enjoyed the whole atmosphere of the weighing room,' he admits. 'The jockeys really made me feel welcome and, like hunting, it is a whole new world you can never know unless you share just a few of the risks they take.'

The Queen Mother, making her farewells to friends and getting into the

Princess Anne took up racing in 1985 and enjoyed going 'over the sticks', but her real success has been in eventing.

Daimler for home, shares vicariously with her grandson the sense of excitement and escape, the pleasure in fresh air in open countryside, that a day at 'the sticks' can bring.

'Racing is perhaps her favourite hobby,' says Sir Martin. 'Perhaps it is at the course that she relaxes most.'

In a revealing television interview with Terry Biddlecombe in 1987, the Queen Mother opened her heart about the joys of racing. 'It's the one sport that's left to us,' she said. 'A bit of danger and a bit of excitement . . . and the horses, which are the best thing in the world.'

FOUR-IN-HAND

'Do you usually drive in bed?' I asked.
'I mostly go once or twice round the park before I go to sleep, you know,' she said.
'It exercises my horses.'

From *The Little Princesses* by MARION CRAWFORD, 1950

The Queen regards the annual Windsor Horse Show as a gymkhana in her back yard. She comes down from the castle every day to watch events in the ring and showground.

T HE QUEEN's house guests have come down from the Castle to watch the International Driving Grand Prix in Windsor's showground. Through budding branches down by the river, a carriage with spanking yellow wheels is thundering to the end of the 26-kilometre marathon. The team leaders are two black Cumberland cobs, Tinker and Baby, ears pricked above yellow bridles as they catapult the carriage forward. George Bowman, driving his team, seems to have sprung straight from Wells Fargo in his ten-gallon hat.

'It was easier than last year,' announces Bowman with characteristic bravado.

The Duke of Edinburgh, like his son Charles, enjoys the chance of mixing with what he will call 'ordinary blokes', and Bowman is one of driving's more colourful characters. 'Prince Philip knows I'm a scrap merchant,' he says. 'It makes no difference. Backgrounds don't come into our sport.'

'Geordie' Bowman played clown to the Queen during the Sandringham trials by training his horses to bend into a royal curtsy.

'They are getting better at it!' said the Queen.

For her, the Harrods Grand Prix in May 1991 has produced a lot of fun: watching Prince Philip drive the royal team of fells through the hazards; then dashing back to see Pippa Thomas race her tiny team of blacks with Pippa's husband 'jumping' the carriage so it would not hit the gateposts. Out had come the Queen's camera to record the trickier moments of this feat.

And finally there is the pleasure of knowing that Philip himself has won the newly instigated Duke of Edinburgh's Trophy for ponies, for which he will receive a bumper Harrods hamper.

'I am not sure whether she was chuffed about Philip – or whether it was because it was her ponies that had won,' said a guest who had tea with the Queen after the event.

The Queen – so closely associated with horse and carriage for all royal pomp and ceremony – is a keen whip herself. Here at Windsor in 1943, at the age of 17, she took first prize in the Private Driving Turnout in a wartime Utility vehicle and driving a fell pony called Gypsy.

Her interest now – as with racing – is in the breeding. Earlier in the day she scored a personal success in the Mountain and Moorland Championship with her Highland pony Balmoral Dee – a 10-year-old grey dun stallion, 14.1 hands 'out of Dewdrop of Whitfield by McNair of Denmill'. The National Pony Society judge Daphne Peddie had picked Balmoral Dee as winner, and the cup was collected by the former Crown Equerry Sir John Miller – so much associated with the Windsor Horse Show, even though Prince Philip has now taken over from him as President.

'A very keen driving man,' said Philip of Sir John, who introduced him to driving when he gave up polo. The former Crown Equerry has been a frequent four-in-hand competitor, driving the Queen's team of Windsor greys – the team which is famous for leading out the landaus at Royal Ascot.

Now Sir John is sitting behind the Queen in the stand at the Windsor show ring, tipping forward, his upright back stooped, to whisper snippets of information in HM's ear.

It was Sir John who played the hunting-horn to serenade the Prince and Princess of Wales at Balmoral in the summer of their marriage in 1981. He and Prince Philip had staged an informal carriage event to encourage driving in Scotland, and on the evening of the second day, all the competitors were invited 'to see the Prince and Princess of Wales home from their honeymoon'. Estate workers pulled the newly-weds in a heather-decked landau to the skirl of bagpipes.

The Queen has memories of driving round Balmoral in the war years, when petrol rationing had sent the royal family back to traditional transport and she and Margaret would harness up Jock and Gypsy. Her enthusiasm for driving goes right back to her early childhood. Crawfie's first sight of five-year-old Princess Elizabeth, when the royal governess had just arrived in London, was of 'a small figure with a mop of curls, sitting up in bed in the night nursery at the family home at 145 Piccadilly.

'She had tied the cords of her dressing-gown to the knobs of the old-fashioned bed and was busy driving her team,' Crawfie said.

King George VI used to hear the creaking of rocking horses outside his study door and called his elder daughter 'a horse fiend'. Princess Elizabeth's 'first love' was Owen, the groom who taught her to ride.

'Don't ask me, ask Owen,' George VI would say. 'Who am I to make suggestions?'

A testimony to Princess Elizabeth's early passion for riding is written on a photograph of Jock, the bronze-coloured half-Highland pony that she would ride on the long Balmoral holidays.

'Jock, who taught me more than any other horse,' she wrote.

Today Balmoral's coach house, that once held Queen Victoria's 'own dear Scottish sociable', an open carriage with facing side seats and Balmoral tartan

When Philip competes in carriage driving, the Queen is cheering both for her husband and for the horses, which come from the Royal Mews and are used also for formal carriage processions.

ABOVE RIGHT: *The apron is designed to keep the ends of the reins from rubbing the trousers. It comes from short to ankle-length and is traditionally buckled with straps, but Philip finds a Velcro fastening more convenient.*

upholstery, has been converted into a recreation room for the staff. But pony traps and game carts are still kept in the stables. Prince Andrew ultimately gave up on horses, yet as a child he loved his miniature Shetland pony Valkyrie, which would be freighted to Balmoral to trundle the Prince around in a barouche originally made for Queen Victoria's children.

Prince Philip's first attempts at competitive driving – soon after he took it up at the age of 50 – included an outing for the Balmoral dogcart at Windsor in 1973 for the European Championship. 'A splendidly old-fashioned vehicle,' he says of the wooden-framed carriage with its small front and larger-diameter back wheels, spindly axles and sturdy leather box seat. But he admits that 'In present-day conditions it would be hopelessly unsuitable.'

The Duke learned the perils of the flimsy dogcart when he competed at the Lowther Castle trials in Westmorland. The inside front wheel caught on the roots around a stump that was one of the course hazards. 'Over we went with quite an impressive splintering crash, and the horses were gone, breaking traces and wooden swingle-trees like cotton and matchwood, and the carriage was out of action for months,' he said, and soon switched to the modern metal-framed carriage he uses today. He still does a lot of four-in-hand driving with the fell ponies at Balmoral and takes part in driving events at the local agricultural show at Tarland near Aberdeen.

How did carriage driving develop from a royal pastime for touring the estates to a lively international sport celebrated by Prince Philip in his book *Competition Carriage Driving*, published in 1982? The spur was the Duke of Edinburgh's decision to give up polo in 1970 because of the arthritis in his right wrist which is still such a curse on his shooting. 'I reckoned that fifty was quite old enough for that game,' he said.

The other catalyst was Sir John Miller, who was as influential in persuading Prince Philip to 'take up the ribbons' as he was in getting Prince Charles into the hunting saddle. Later a more delicate task – responding to a request from Princess Michael of Kent to learn to ride side-saddle as the Queen did until recently at the Trooping of the Colour – was taken up by Sir John's niece Sylvia Stanier. Princess Michael, who was brought up in the saddle, even courted her husband on horseback in Richmond Park.

'As luck and Cupid would have it, my beautiful dancing Anglo-Arab steed fell madly in love with this other rather churlish animal,' she claimed, 'and from miles away would whinny and gallop up to him.' At the time Prince Michael was riding a horse borrowed from the Mounted Police, who use his sister Princess Alexandra's stables at Thatched Lodge in Richmond Park.

As Crown Equerry Sir John Miller was in charge of the Royal Mews from 1962 for 25 years, until his role was taken over by Lieutenant-Colonel Seymour Gilbart-Denham. Sir John had taken up four-in-hand driving himself, and soon convinced Prince Philip that 'this driving business' might be 'just the thing' – a new sport which could make use of the royal pool of horsemen, carriages and grooms. Thus two mares from the four-in-hand team appeared at Prince Charles's wedding in 1981, drawing Philip and Diana's mother, Frances Shand Kydd, in the state landau, while the royal greys drew the Prince of Wales himself down the Mall to St Paul's Cathedral and back to the palace with his bride.

A century earlier, when coaching clubs were fashionable, the four-in-hand driving parades in Hyde Park were attended by Princess Alexandra and the future Edward VII, who would occasionally take the box-seat himself. But by the time the Duke of Edinburgh was made President of the Fédération

Presentation and dressage are part of the competition rules established by the International Equestrian Federation in the 1970s, under the guidance of Prince Philip as President. The appropriate dressage turnout for four-in-hand carriage driving under the 'English' neck-collar harness includes a grey or black top hat.

The Queen watching Philip compete at Windsor. When she is nervous, she twists round her engagement ring, designed by Philip using diamonds from a tiara that belonged to his mother, Princess Andrew of Greece.

ABOVE RIGHT: *Prince Philip negotiating the water hazard during the International Driving Grand Prix in Windsor Great Park in 1978. Now that he has turned 70, Philip has stopped racing four-in-hand, but he still competes with teams of ponies.*

Equestre Internationale (FEI) in 1964, carriage driving in England had dwindled to a genteel pastime. Its few enthusiasts still hold the British Driving Society meet in Windsor's showring, where Prince Michael, impeccably turned out, bowls around the ring looking like some reincarnation of a former time.

Prince Philip prefers carriage driving in the tradition of continental Europe, where he – and Princess Michael – have family roots. She has a penchant for dressage and equestrian elegance, as well as memories of driving horse-drawn sleighs through the Austrian winter, just as German-born Prince Albert drove Queen Victoria on a royal sledge. 'It went delightfully . . . the horses with their handsome red harness and many bells . . . a charming effect,' Queen Victoria recorded in her journal.

In 1971 Philip went to Budapest to watch Sir John and the Queen's grey Oldenburgs compete in the first European Championship for Carriage Driving. He witnessed demonstrations of precise training, orderly efficiency, controlled energy and fierce competition in Austria and at Aachen and

Hamburg in Germany. As FEI President, he spearheaded a campaign to make dressage and cross-country driving internationally recognized elements of a competitive sport.

Later, when the Duke himself competed in Hungary, he had a spectacular crash that left him flat on his back on the open plain, clinging to the reins. The cause of the upset was the appearance of imposing Hungarian cattle 'with horns as long as Highlanders', that startled the leader. 'I am sure they were bulls, but I didn't have time to look,' Philip recalled of the moment when he found the whole carriage turning over.

'People often say to me "I hear you are doing this dangerous carriage driving thing,"' admits Philip. But he insists that it is not a risky sport. 'Exciting, yes; rewarding, yes; but dangerous, no,' he claims. His carriage driving is now part of the rhythm of the royal year, using both horses and ponies as available. 'Let no one believe that ponies are easier to drive than horses,' he says. 'What ponies lack in size they make up for in independence and speed of reaction.'

Prince Charles as a child played in a toy pony and cart and grew up to be a competent carriage driver.

As a child, the Queen tied dressing-gown cords to bed-knobs to 'drive her team' before going to sleep. She became a keen pony-and-cart driver, taking a young Prince Andrew in a pony chaise at Windsor in 1962.

At the end of the 1980s, Philip, faced with his 70th birthday, stopped racing four-in-hand; but he continues to drive competitively with teams of ponies. For him driving is both a competitive sport and a pleasant country pursuit. At Balmoral, he uses the fell and Haflinger stalking ponies and puts a team together to compete locally at Scone in Perthshire or at Floors Castle, Kelso. The grooms are not so amused to find themselves harnessing up the sturdy shooting ponies to a converted milk float to take tourists clip-clopping down the main drive at Balmoral.

When the Kluges took over Mar Lodge, Patricia Kluge made a big thing of carriage driving and had hopes of taking a turn about the Balmoral estate with the Duke.

'She was a lovely lady,' declares a Braemar local. 'Although there was no chance that the Queen would go down and see her, they do say that the Duke of Edinburgh's head man came up to help her with her four-in-hand, which we loved to see being driven through the village.'

John Kluge also became a major sponsor of the Windsor Horse Show, whose committee membership is a roster of crisp military titles with royal family connections, from Charles's good friend Brigadier Andrew Parker Bowles to Sarah's father Major Ronald Ferguson.

Prince Philip's competition horses (plus one in reserve) are kept at Windsor, and the Easter break is spent on training practice. For the royal Christmas celebrations, held at Sandringham nowadays while Windsor is being extensively refurbished, they come with him to Norfolk, where he taught his daughter-in-law Sarah to drive four-in-hand. The Duchess of York used to roar round Windsor Great Park in a black Victoria, driving with the sort of gusto her mother and her late stepfather Hector Barrantes would display riding out on their ranch in Argentina. She took up carriage driving when she was expecting her first baby Beatrice and was advised not to ride. Although she is now outside the royal circle, she used to hack with the Queen at Balmoral and at Sandringham, and enjoyed driving on her own or with her father-in-law.

It was at Sandringham in the New Year of 1973 that Philip (who had been

experimenting with pairs and then four-in-hand at Balmoral) started serious training, with the help of Major 'Tommy' Thompson, former riding master of the Household Cavalry and a member of the Royal Mews until he retired in 1979. Prince Philip took a tumble when he tried to teach the palace horses, used to London streets, to get their feet wet fording a Norfolk ditch. The wheels got stuck in the mud, the horses broke their traces, and Philip finished up on the ground.

Prince Philip is not 'a horse fiend' like his wife, but he has a special affinity with the horses he drives, bridled with the royal insignia, for competitions, or for recreational driving on the country estates.

'As luck would have it, coming the other way was a very surprised daughter on a young event horse, who gallantly rode to father's rescue,' Philip said.

Anne's enthusiasm was for the three-day events on which her father based the rules for competitive carriage driving. She and her former husband Mark Phillips were originally drawn together by eventing and shared an understanding of the different qualities needed by both horse and rider. The same applies to driving. Dressage requires obedience from the horse and accuracy from the driver; strength and quick reactions are needed for the marathon; discipline and calm for the cone obstacles; and always 'that essential bond of trust and confidence' between horse and driver.

Philip insists that 'it does not follow that the more animals you drive, the more difficult things become'. 'I believe that a competent driver can produce a better dressage test with a team than he can with a pair or single,' he says. 'Provided the team is physically and temperamentally well matched, they tend to even out the minor discrepancies and turn in a more flowing performance.'

Now Prince Philip is driving back across Home Park, the apron tucked over his lap fastened with velcro. Along this same path, he took Nancy Reagan on a formal drive in 1982. And here too Charles once drove Davina Sheffield in a coach and pair when in the days of his bachelorhood she seemed a likely bride and future Queen.

'The art of handling horses,' claims Philip, 'is very similar to the art of handling children as it depends almost entirely on the ability to sense what is going on in their minds, to anticipate their reactions to situations and to treat them accordingly.'

BALMORAL

*Walking or stalking, sketching
and fishing are holiday pleasures at Queen
Victoria's Scottish castle*

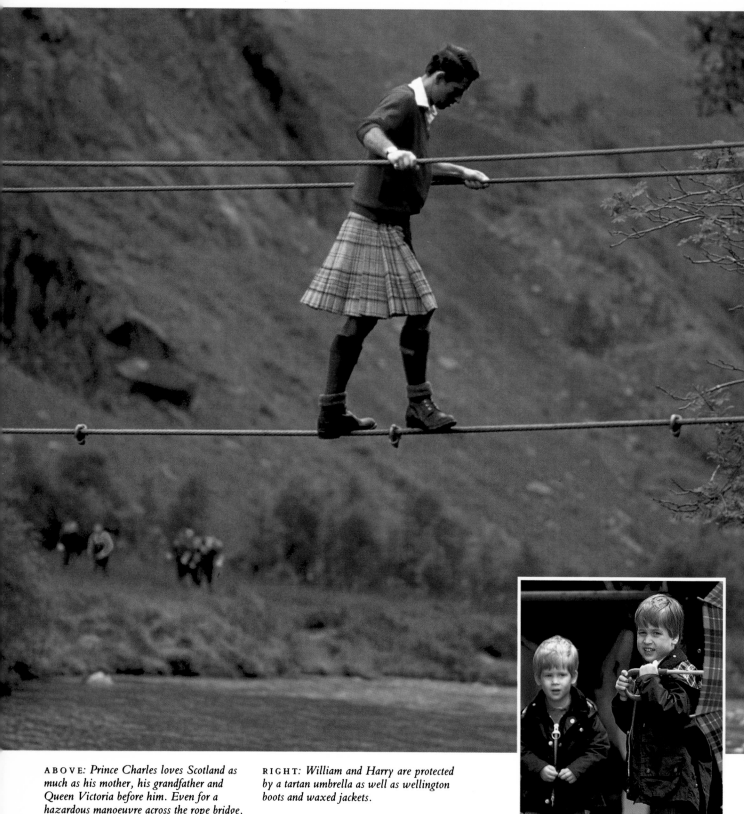

ABOVE: *Prince Charles loves Scotland as much as his mother, his grandfather and Queen Victoria before him. Even for a hazardous manoeuvre across the rope bridge, he wears a kilt in the granite-grey and heather-coloured Balmoral tartan, designed by Prince Albert.*

RIGHT: *William and Harry are protected by a tartan umbrella as well as wellington boots and waxed jackets.*

PRECEDING PAGES: *A view from above of Balmoral Castle – the royal family's Scottish holiday retreat.*

CHAPTER 5

Balmoral's Outside Days

So it was that the old man failed to reach London. Secretly he was rather pleased, for he hated leaving his cave and his friends who lived in the hills around him. The stories he had heard from the picnickers were all he needed to know about London. He couldn't think of anywhere more special to be than to be living at the foot of Lochnagar.

From *The Old Man of Lochnagar* by
HRH PRINCE CHARLES, 1980

SCOTCH EGGS

THE ROYAL picnic is taking place on tartan rugs spread out under the thin, tall pines at the farthest curve of Loch Muick.

'Means pigs, *not* a pretty name,' complained Queen Victoria of the austere Scottish lake – a teardrop of glassy grey water between dark mountain cliffs.

This picnic spot is picturesque enough – among the forest of pines fringing the Glas-allt-Shiel – the granite lodge used by Queen Victoria as a rustic hideaway. 'A truly sylvan abode,' she called it after she had rebuilt the simple cottage with mullioned windows into gabled grandeur.

'Dreadfully remote,' complained the keeper's wife.

The distance from gawping tourists is the charm of the Glas-allt for the Queen and her family, who are protected from the hikers by a couple of policemen and a sign encouraging a detour up through the trees and across the rickety wooden bridge over the Glas-allt waterfall.

'The Queen likes her picnics and especially in Glen Muick,' says an estate worker. 'They don't like being disturbed, and it's all open to the public, but there is always a policeman to keep people away.'

It is not, in truth, picnic weather. 'One of those cold, grey and increasingly gloomy afternoons,' says Prince Charles. His wife Diana, in a defiantly bright pink sweater, keeps glancing balefully at the overcast sky.

'It is a marvellous life and Balmoral is one of the best places in the world,' a euphoric Princess of Wales had announced on her honeymoon. She now prefers to spend at least part of the family holiday in Mediterranean sunshine.

The rest of the group, conspicuously Scottish in plaid and tweed, seem impervious to the dank chill. 'The whole family goes out in weather that most people would think mad,' says a veteran of Balmoral summer holidays. The future Queen Alexandra once painted the family at Lock Muick clustered around a warming fire.

'Come along and get wet with me,' George VI would say to his head stalker on a soaking Scottish day.

This gathering of the Windsor clan includes, exceptionally, all the close family, except Andrew who is away at sea. Princess Margaret sits with the Queen and Queen Mother, just as they did as children with their parents on Balmoral holidays long past. Lady Sarah Armstrong-Jones is playing with the

Diana does not like the cold and damp weather in the Scottish Highlands. The Waleses now take a Mediterranean sunshine holiday before arriving at Balmoral in mid-August.

Prince Edward shares with his mother an enthusiasm for the freedom and fresh air of Scotland.

Loch Muick, the glassy lake between granite cliffs, has been a favourite royal picnic spot since Victoria and Albert's time. Bonnie Prince Charlie's men crossed the glen in 1745 on the way to the Battle of Culloden. In 1974 the Balmoral estate, in conjunction with the Scottish Wildlife Trust, established the Loch Muick and Lochnagar Wildlife Reserve to protect the unique environment.

Duchess of York's daughter Eugenie, while her brother David Linley and Prince Edward are keeping the more boisterous boys under control.

The treat for them all is eating without any ceremony in the open air. 'Picnics to a royal are as banquets to the rest of us,' Barry said. 'We like picnics and we like the open air,' says the Queen. 'As the holidays are very short, you live them to the full.'

Unpacking the picnic is women's work. A barbecue, held in a more accessible spot, would have been left to the royal males, although Princess Elizabeth once pleaded for her sister to be allowed to join in the fun with the Girl Guides. 'She loves getting dirty, don't you, Margaret, and how she would love to cook sausages on sticks.'

Today Princess Margaret, in quilted body-warmer over a cashmere twin-set, is passing on a Tupperware box labelled in felt pen 'HRH Prince Charles'.

'Plain chicken or white meat and that special bread – he's very fussy about sandwiches,' says a guest who has seen Charles bring his cook along on a house party visit to make him baked potatoes.

Here, the royal family dispense not only with protocol, but with the staff, who may still come out on shooting days, using a custom-built trailer with a hot-plate and an ice box. 'Prince Philip designed this trailer and had it specially made. The food and drinks are kept in sections, some of which are refrigerated,' Barry said. He sometimes found himself lurking, with the other servants, on a Scottish hillside during stalking or grouse shooting. 'At lunch the royals sit on their section of the moorland, while the staff sit a respectable distance away on their bit of territory,' he said.

When Princess Elizabeth was first taken out stalking, the ghillies would treat her with more deference than Queen Victoria received from her brusque Scottish favourite, the ghillie John Brown. 'They would find a big boulder at lunchtime, put her on one side of it with her lunch, and themselves retire to the other side,' explained Crawfie of Lilibet's days out on the moor.

Victoria loved eating outside, and would even take her breakfast on the terrace of Garden Cottage in the grounds of Balmoral, looking towards the pepper-pot castle turrets across a green lawn now used as the royal helicopter pad. She and Albert enjoyed many picnics together, but in her old age she frowned on such informality for her court.

'Once when a picnic was arranged, by the members of the Household, the Queen was asked if the Maids of Honour might go,' said her Assistant Private Secretary Sir Frederick Ponsonby. 'She replied that they might, although she did not altogether approve of the ladies "junketing" with the gentlemen.'

Sarah, Duchess of York and Edward are larking about, staging a juggling act with the Scotch eggs, until one rolls off down the slope, gathering speed as it tosses over the ground until it is just a brown speck hurtling towards the loch.

Picnic standards have slipped since the Earl of Strathmore – the Queen Mother's grandfather – took out a simple lunch at Glamis: 'Rabbit and beefsteak; mutton pies; 2 chickens; shoulder of lamb in pastry – and Prince Albert pudding,' read the menu for 1866.

The next Lord Strathmore, grandfather at Glamis Castle to the two princesses, 'ate plum pudding for lunch every day of his life', according to Marion Crawford. 'He was a countryman through and through,' she said. 'He timed all his movements by country things – the coming of the migrants, the wild geese on the river, the rising of the sap.' This gave a sense of being 'much nearer to reality and nature there than at any other place'.

There is now a bottled Strathmore water, bearing the legend 'as pure as the day it was born' and a drawing of Glamis Castle on its silver, gold and green label.

Philip and Anne cooking on a barbecue that is transported to inaccessible spots on a custom-built trailer designed by Philip. He and Charles wage a vendetta against litter and insist that every last scrap has to be cleared up.

The Queen Mother, sitting on a rug folded over a tree stump, smiles benignly under her felt hat, ignoring the veil of drizzle from the low clouds screening the mountains. She inherited from her Strathmore parents a passion for al fresco eating, and still gives grand picnics in the family tradition when she, Lady Fermoy and the Queen's senior lady-in-waiting the Duchess of Grafton will decant from Edwardian picnic hampers, wines and pies, porcelain, silverware and glasses.

Today's more homely family picnic is glimpsed only by a few hikers in their bright waterproofs, making the circuit of Loch Muick from the Spittal of Glenmuick – now a nature centre – over Capel Mount and round the still water in the shadow of the granite cliffs.

'Countless feet, both human and animal, must have trodden the path in days gone by,' says Charles of the days when people drove cattle and sheep south from summer pastures to more sheltered wintering grounds and the Spittal of Glenmuick was the resting place – as well as 'a major entrepôt in the illicit whisky business'.

'There must have been some great characters in those days,' says Charles. 'Real individuals who understood the wiles and whims of nature and had been brought up in an unforgiving environment.'

The annual royal family Balmoral holiday – from August right through to the autumn – follows a pattern set by Queen Victoria and Prince Albert who first escaped to the Highlands in 1842, staying with the Duke and Duchess of Buccleuch and other landowners. On one of their earliest expeditions in September 1844, while staying at Blair Castle, Victoria, wearing a shepherd-plaid apron, and her entourage, with an enormous luncheon box strapped onto a moor pony, made their zig-zag way up the mountain path. 'Just like a Highland sketch of Landseer's,' said Lady Canning, one of Queen Victoria's ladies-in-waiting.

The German painter Carl Haag captured in misty water-colours the arche-typal Balmoral picnic – Queen Victoria sitting on a tartan rug, Prince Albert in deerstalker cape and hat cutting a game pie; the mountains in heather-covered folds, sloping down to the water. The picture still hangs below the stags' heads on the wall of the Balmoral ballroom.

A century later, during the reign of George VI after the war, the picnic tradition continued. 'The luncheon baskets were deposited in some favourite situation, plaid rugs would be spread about the heather and bog-myrtle,' said a visitor to Balmoral in the early 1950s.

And here are the tartan rugs laid out again today under the trees that encircle the shuttered house. Prince Philip is dressed not as Sherlock Holmes but in the grey plaid criss-crossed with purple checks adapted from the Royal Stuart to Prince Albert's design, the colouring inspired by stones and heather. 'At Balmoral the royals wore the Balmoral tweed, a dull grey matching the colour of the moors,' said John Dean, the Duke of Edinburgh's former valet.

The Queen, who has a penchant for the Fair Isle sweaters sold in the knitwear shops in Ballater, is wearing under a thick quilted jacket, a patterned slipover to match her Balmoral tweed skirt.

'Wearing an old-friend Burberry macintosh, a headscarf, muddy rubber boots, and wrapped up against the rarely kind Scottish weather,' said Barry of the Queen's country clothes.

Philip wears an oatmeal sweater with his kilt; Charles a burgundy one. Prince Albert introduced the 'German kilt', 'so decently long as almost to cover the knees', said the Duke of Windsor, whose own collection of Highland dress was taken on his death by Prince Charles for William and Harry.

The two princes, like their mother, are in jeans, and when Diana does dress the boys in full Scottish fig, she gives them ordinary knee-high socks and moccasins, rather than the traditional thick stockings and ghillie brogues that Anne's son Peter Phillips is wearing as he squats on his haunches eating a bridge roll.

'The Balmoral shooting lunch is always the same: a stuffed roll, a slice of plum pudding, an apple,' said Crawfie. 'The war-time plum pudding never had any plums in it, but anything tastes good eaten out of doors in the sunshine among the heather.'

The Queen takes the same down-to-earth view about picnics, although chicken drumsticks, crisps, ginger biscuits and chocolate bars are now added to the inevitable sandwiches. Or there may be flaky envelopes of sausage roll and mince pies – indeterminate grey meat inside a round, raised pastry case – that are made by George Leith, the baker by royal appointment in Church Square, Ballater.

Mrs McKee made a list of suggestions in her recipe book for sandwich fillings: 'Hard-boiled egg, chopped and seasoned with peeled, thinly-sliced tomatoes; grated cheese and shredded lettuce; minced ham and mayonnaise, mixed to a smooth cream with sliced tomato and watercress; thinly sliced cucumber rolled up in brown bread and butter.'

Prince Charles invented more imaginative fare in the story he made up for his younger brothers about the Old Man of Lochnagar – named after the mountain lake and its granite cliff that can just be seen from the Glas-allt landing stage by climbing on top of the upturned blue rowing boat and peering over the trees.

'The old man was so big and fat after many years of living on grouse pâté and blaeberry pie,' Charles said of the wizened little creature living in a cave on the mountain that rises up 3,789 feet (1,155m) into the clouds.

'The jewel of all the mountains here,' Queen Victoria said of Lochnagar.

The name means literally 'loch of the goats' or the 'rough loch', and the swelling mountain now takes its title from its hidden lake, although it was originally known to the locals more graphically as 'Beinn Ciochan' – the mountain of the breasts.

The Scottish names – Lochnagar, Creag Lurachain, Allt-na-guibhsaich, Glas-allt-Shiel – have a swishing, harsh rhythm of their own. 'Making wild work with the names of the mountains,' said Albert of Victoria's efforts to pronounce the Gaelic. He and Victoria earnestly studied a Gaelic dictionary and even made Gaelic lessons available to estate workers.

The sheer scale and presence of the Lochnagar massif is daunting – a solid slab with jagged crowns, the sides steep, sheer, dark. Right now, in this flowering season, the heather clinging to the rock face looks like wine trickling through the corries.

A royal picnic in the formal style with Prince Albert in deerstalker tweeds. 'Luncheon at Carn Lochan' by Carl Haag, painted in 1865 after Albert's death, still hangs in Balmoral's ballroom.

The Glas-allt-Shiel in its forest of pines fringing Loch Muick. Queen Victoria expanded the remote croft into a granite lodge and called it 'a truly sylvan abode'.

'Like all mountains it has a variety of moods,' says Charles. 'It becomes fierce and brooding, even sinister on occasions. It is a mountain that needs to be treated with great respect.'

Lunch over, plates, cups, Thermoses and plastic boxes are all stowed neatly away. 'A busy repacking would begin, rather on the lines of happy families, one collecting plates, another knives and forks, and a third coffee cups, until at last the straps were fastened once again,' a 1955 Balmoral visitor reported to Lord Buxton.

In the clearing in front of the Glas-allt-Shiel, Prince Philip and Charles are marshalling the children for their war against litter, 'the curse of the countryside', claims Charles.

'What astonishes me is that so many people continue to ignore the possibility that anyone else might like to use the site after them,' Philip says.

Since 1974 this noble, savage area of countryside has been officially designated the Glenmuick and Lochnagar Wildlife Reserve. With the help of the Countryside Commission for Scotland, a Ranger/naturalist is employed to feed the deer during winter and to run the Visitors' Centre, where a photographic display and an explanatory booklet describe the local flora and fauna and their habitat.

'The beauty of the Glenmuick landscape is immediately apparent to every visitor; what is not so apparent is the geological and natural history of the area,' says Philip, who was instrumental in setting up the reserve. Now he is telling William and Peter why the antlers they have found on the ground should be left for the stags to nibble at; and how deer antlers follow a natural cycle – cast each spring and re-grown in a soft velvet skin through the summer to be honed for the fights in the autumn rutting season.

'When October came, we could hear the stags roaring in the hills,' said Crawfie. 'Sometimes, from afar, we watched them fighting. We were always horrified at the faithlessness of the females, who stood meekly round to see who won, and then lined up behind the winner.'

For those with eyes and ears open, Glenmuick is teeming with wildlife – not just the red deer, wallowing in the peat bogs at the end of the loch – but the gold-ringed fox moth caterpillar on the heather and shoals of whirligig beetles in the peat pools.

Prince Philip is passionate about protecting the countryside from the human element. 'People complain about the filthy environment, but that does not stop them throwing cigarette packets out of their car windows. This must be one of the dirtiest countries in Europe,' he complains. 'Judging by the amount of rubbish of all kinds which the average citizen chucks out of his car or dumps on every available parking, camping or picnic site, he is unlikely to feel any concern for pollution on a grander scale.'

At the foothills of Lochnagar, the problem at the end of the summer holiday season is all too evident. William is careering ahead, a black plastic garbage sack flapping behind him like the wings of a crow. From this small area alone, the flat-floored valley that crosses from the car park at the Spittal to the Lochnagar ascent, the sack will be one quarter full.

'You spend the afternoon hauling all the plastic and muck together and burning it. But by the following year it's just as bad,' says Philip about clearing the cans and plastic bottles from this area.

'It is wonderful that they all love and appreciate the grandeur and the wildness of the country,' Charles says. 'What I cannot understand is why so many people should then show scant regard for other travellers, and for the area as a whole, by mindlessly scattering rubbish wherever they go . . . You would be appalled by how much there is.'

Charles had inherited his father's personal vendetta against litter. When he was staying in Sicily with the Marchesa Fiamma di San Giuliano Ferragamo in May 1990, the house party took a stroll in a favourite local beauty spot, following a track through dusty olive groves. 'This is appalling – and I'm going to do something about it,' said Prince Charles when he saw the tide of rubbish left by tourists after the long May Day weekend. An embarrassed argument went on at dinner that night as to how to clear the mess without insulting the pride of the local mayor or involving the party's hosts.

'But Prince Charles wasn't having any of that,' says a fellow guest. 'He just walked off to his room after dinner saying that he would be out there at 6 the next morning and anyone was welcome to join him. I didn't go, but I heard all about it.

'They stopped in the local village to buy leather gardening gloves and rubbish sacks. Then the Prince led the party up the hill, with the British officials looking sheepish and the Italian police furious because they were ruining their smart leather shoes. The Prince was absolutely manic. He filled about five bags himself – and all that before a full day's programme. The only one who seemed to enjoy it was Inès de la Fressange, who even peeled off her jeans to wade into the water and collect all the plastic bottles floating about.'

'Inès, you are my heroine,' Charles said to the droll, vivacious, aristocratic model who was staying in Sicily with her Italian husband.

In Glenmuick, the royal dilemma is part of a general problem facing all private landowners, who agonize over the problem of public access to land that is often a last reserve of wildlife – and a way of life. 'All Britain now contends with the pressure of numbers as a more mobile and aware public takes its pleasures even farther and wider,' said the Duke of Westminster, setting out his 'green' philosophy in *The Field* in 1991. He insists that the country must not be fossilized but respond to change, because 'conservation and prosperity have to go hand in hand'.

'I have been fortunate that those who walk and appreciate the countryside are well-mapped, dressed correctly and understand the Country Code,' he says.

A sudden break in the clouds transforms the loch, reflecting a light blue sky and turning the leaden water silver as the wind ruffles it. 'Scudding clouds,'

The Queen Mother walking through the pines near her Scottish fishing lodge. She is almost as inveterate a walker as Queen Victoria.

Prince Charles said when he was painting Glenmuick Glen, 'their shadows racing on the peat hags below.' Way above the loch, a bird with a wide wingspan swoops between the mountains.

'There is a lack of perception about Nature's demand,' says the Duke of Westminster. The public, so used to urban colonizers – pigeon, sparrow, starling, crow and the urban fox – have no concept of how much peace Nature needs elsewhere, especially our hawk life which requires hunting grounds extending to many square miles, only surviving if the food chain is undisturbed.'

The Duke of Edinburgh conducts a heated debate – both within the family and in his official role with the World Wide Fund for Nature – over how to balance the different demands on the land.

'Modern civilized life is not just a matter of sufficient food for all. The land has to provide for all our needs,' he insists. 'We all know the value of food, but it seems that economists have no way of putting a value on such things as 'natural beauty' or 'amenity'. Yet the fact is that the principal motive for looking after the natural environment is for the use and pleasure of the human population.'

The public has year-round access to the Loch Muick area – except within rifle shot during the stalking season. Yet Albert and Victoria were drawn to the Highlands in the first place because of its remoteness from sightseers, who had intruded into the Queen's privacy at Windsor and even at Osborne House. 'Let the Queen of Great Britain be able to sit down to her piano or sketch-book with the same security against intrusion as any other lady in the land,' thundered *The Times* in 1849.

Now tourists must be actively encouraged to come to Scotland, for they bring money to the area and to the royal estate. (The gardens and grounds of Balmoral are open to the public during the midsummer months.) But Lochnagar has serious problems of soil erosion from the tramping of tourist feet, and the Ranger asks volunteers from the Scottish Wildlife Trust to help with repairs.

'It is a hideous problem, and it's very difficult to know what to do,' says Philip. 'If you try to limit numbers, you are accused of restricting access. If you don't, you create erosion and destruction.'

Queen Victoria thought she had an answer. Lord Bryce tried in 1892 to bring in an Access to Mountains Bill that did not reach the Statute Book. Victoria suggested that the royal family ought to have a protected season, like the game on the estates.

'A *close* time of *six weeks against tourists*,' she begged.

George VI climbed the Lochnagar path with boys from the summer camps he set up when Duke of York in the 1920s. As his health failed, a trace round his waist, pulled by a pony, would help him uphill.

LEGGING IT UP LOCHNAGAR

When they had reached a great height the old man looked down and saw Balmoral far below him, looking like a small toy.

The Old Man of Lochnagar

PRINCE CHARLES is leading the walking party aiming for the top of Lochnagar; his mother has already announced that she and Sarah will go only part of the way; Princess Margaret has aligned herself with the smaller children and is heading for the Land-Rovers and home.

'She doesn't even own a pair of walking shoes,' claims the Duchess of

Prince Charles with Harvey in the Highlands. His enthusiasm for Scotland was conveyed in the story about the Old Man of Lochnagar that he wrote for his younger brothers in 1980.

Devonshire. In fact, Margaret's battered brogues would get her at least up the first incline, and her sister has claimed of her that she had 'a very fine pair of hiking legs', but Margaret did not grow up with the family passion for long walks in a cold climate.

The hikers are divided into the nimble-footed and the sheep straggling behind. 'The Prince goes up mountains like a goat – not so easy for those of us who aren't so fit,' Barry said of the athletic Charles, who is striding on ahead in his stud-soled walking boots.

Although the Queen Mother has opted out of this climb, she too is an inveterate walker, as though Queen Victoria's legendary energy had touched all the royal family. 'I seldom walk for less than 4 hours a day & when I come in I feel as if I want to go out again,' Victoria said after an invigorating Scottish holiday. 'Even her family seemed to treat her as a perambulating legend,' says Charles.

The Queen is climbing steadily, her muscles toned by walking up the coverts with the gun dogs or by more domestic exercise with the corgis. 'When Her Majesty first arrives at Balmoral she may look tired and pale,' said a former head stalker. 'But within a few days, spending many hours in her hills, I see the rose and the tan come into her cheeks.'

Guests, and even staff, are often overwhelmed by the royal family's physical energy. 'My God, I was stiff after the first few days!' said Barry. 'Muscles I didn't know I had were hurting.'

'Can you keep up?' Charles will ask visitors.

'Go that way, it's quicker and less painful,' he says.

This solicitude does not extend to his children, who are being shouted at to get moving, unless they want to be left behind.

The Queen is pushing William uphill, one hand in the small of his back. Her own father, in his declining years, had a long trace fastened round his waist, attached to a pony which helped him uphill.

'I've only got to *move* my legs without having to exert myself at all,' George VI would explain. Just in case the horse bolted off with the King of England, a quick-release mechanism as on a parachute was fitted to the trace.

There are vivid memories of George VI on this Lochnagar path, dressed in kilt, tweed jacket, open-necked cricket shirt, long stockings supporting the traditional skean-dhu Gaelic dagger, climbing energetically up with boys from the Duke of York's summer camps. These were set up as a social experiment in 1921 to encourage working-class lads to 'chum-up' with boys from public schools. George VI's attempts to help the disadvantaged were the forerunners of Philip's Duke of Edinburgh's Award Scheme, launched in 1956 'as an introduction to leisure-time activities, a challenge to the individual to personal achievement about the development of our future citizens'. His father-in-law's boys' camps were a more modest, personal effort.

'One thing in particular stuck me,' said a boy who was at the Balmoral camp in 1939. 'The King was intensely aware of everything around him. He pointed out birds and animals and views, never growing tired of answering all our questions.'

Today's walk is the easy tourist route, well-worn by hikers, not the perpendicular ascent from the pines above the Glas-allt-Shiel, where you can watch the ptarmigan – the snow grouse – rising like a silent helicopter up the vertical cliffs.

'Arrived at the Glassalt, we started on the steep climb up to the ptarmigan world,' said John Elphinstone of an expedition up Lochnagar with George VI. 'It was a cloudless and very hot day, and before we had gone far we were discarding our coats and ties, and wondering whether we should ever make the top.'

Today a grey film separates off the departing party looking up from the squat grey stone boat house, where once Albert and Victoria would set off round the loch until the wail of the bagpipes at dusk called them home. The Loch Muick boat from that Victorian era is back at Balmoral – refurbished in 1982 by the Royal Naval Engineering School at Rosyth.

The Queen Mother, Margaret, Diana and the small children are watching from below: the walkers look like ants scrabbling their way up the huge, brown concave bowl of mountainside.

For the climbers, there is nothing in view but stone stained peat-brown and tufts of heather, as the track winds up. The sheer grind of the climb, the physical effort involved in keeping up, the absolute silence apart from the rattle of dislodged scree, all bring an extraordinary sense of peace.

'Complete mountain solitude,' Prince Albert said.

Here at Balmoral, above all other royal residences, it seems possible to break away from royal conventions and constraints, to blow the invigorating air of freedom through stuffy court life.

'It seemed to offer a reward for many months of unceasing engagements, and for weeks before the departure from London really arrived, release must have danced entrancingly before the imagination,' said a Balmoral guest.

'I'm exhausted. I can't wait to get to Balmoral,' Charles will say throughout the early summer months. 'I suppose Balmoral is a place one looks forward to very much as the summer goes on,' says the Queen. 'I think it has an atmosphere of its own. It's rather nice to hibernate for a bit.'

As they emerge from the rocky cleft, the full romantic beauty of the Highlands unfurls – gothic crags rising from deep black gullies; low clouds cushioning the loch; festoons of mist from the grey mass draped across a duck-egg blue sky. And illuminated by a bright shaft on the horizon, the donkey-brown Cairngorms, which an early mountaineer described as a 'countless herd of hills tossing shining muzzles in the sun'.

'The grandest, wildest scenery imaginable,' said Victoria. 'The scenery all around is the finest I have seen anywhere,' she told her Uncle Leopold. 'It is very wild and solitary.'

'This place is a sort of paradise,' Victoria's Foreign Secretary Lord Clarendon said of a visit to Balmoral.

For Albert and Victoria, Balmoral meant more than escape to a Ruritanian idyll. The wild mountains and straight, upstanding trees stirred childhood memories in Albert, who had been torn from his roots in Coburg at the age of 20 to become the Queen of England's consort. His thoughts went especially to The Rosenau, the royal hunting lodge where he had been born, looking 'like a little squirrel with a pair of large black eyes', and to which his fevered imagination returned in delirium on his deathbed.

'The paradise of our childhood,' he called the enchanted Schloss enfolded in the branches of a green forest.

'Beautiful wooded hills, which reminded us very much of the Thüringer-wald,' Victoria wrote after their first visit to Balmoral. Albert had taken her to visit Coburg in the autumn of 1845. 'If I were not who I am – *this* would have been my real home, but I shall always consider it my 2nd one,' she said of The Rosenau.

Their Scottish home was her safe haven in troubled times. Balmoral was purchased in September 1848 – towards the end of the 'Year of Revolutions' that blew a tornado through the kingdoms of Europe – hurling the French royal family into exile, shaking the Empire of Austria, and thrones in Hanover, Bavaria, Prussia and Naples. In England, the Chartist riots on London's Kennington Common in April sent Albert and Victoria fleeing to Osborne. Scotland was a practical bolthole, as well as the spiritual escape it has remained.

For Queen Victoria, it was always a wrench to leave this place where she seemed 'to enter a better world'. 'I was *quite* miserable to leave those fine, wild mountains, that pure air, – & I had become quite attached to it & accustomed to our simple life there,' said Victoria.

Prince Charles, who will snatch just a few days in Scotland whenever he can, feels the same way. 'She hated leaving, much as I hate to leave this marvellous place,' he says.

A Victorian climbing party painted in misty blue water-colours in Richard Leitch's 'View of Carn Lochan' looking towards Perth in 1862.

OPPOSITE: *A modern-day walking party: Sarah, Duchess of York, with her daughters Beatrice and Eugenie on piggyback in 1992, shortly before the break-up of the Yorks' marriage was made public.*

Each member of the royal family has a private memory tucked in the wrinkled hills, where Charles walked day after September day in 1979 after Lord Mountbatten's assassination, cementing a friendship with Norton Knatchbull (later Lord Romsey) in the anguish of shared grief.

Here George VI was picnicking on a vile day of low mist and chill east wind in August 1942, when his brother George, Duke of Kent, was killed in a plane crash in poor visibility. The Duke was in a Sunderland flying boat on the way to inspect RAF installations in Iceland when it went down in Scotland. His Duchess, Princess Marina, who had posed for official engagement photographs at Balmoral only eight years before, came back to Scotland to grieve. 'On foot she made her pilgrimage to the spot, and sat for a little while on a boulder, alone,' Marion Crawford wrote.

Like Queen Victoria, Prince Charles has heard the distant rumble of revolution. When President Sadat of Egypt was assassinated Charles was on

honeymoon at Craigowan Lodge – ten minutes' walk away from the castle – which the Prince has used as a holiday home both before and after his marriage. Sadat's assassination was a personal shock because the Egyptian President and his wife had been guests of Charles and Diana on the royal yacht *Britannia* during the earlier part of their honeymoon.

Charles has also known in Scotland moments of absolute contentment and peace, when he escaped to the Hebrides to live the life of a crofter in 1982 and again in 1991. He defends these moments of solitude, for a spiritual breathing space from royal life, with self-mocking irony. 'As far as I can make out, I'm about to become a Buddhist monk, or live halfway up a mountain, or only eat grass,' he says. 'I'm not quite so bad as that.'

For the Queen, the hills are resonant with childhood happiness. There was the annual anticipation of the Scottish holiday, described by a courtier during George VI's reign: 'Then at last, from the descending lift, first a cascade of

dogs . . . then the Princesses, dancing down the steps, and behind them the King and Queen, radiating goodwill in the anticipation of their well-earned and lovely holiday.'

There are echoes of the crisp autumn days, hardening into winter, when she and her sister stayed on in Scotland after war was declared in 1939; and, when peace finally came, sweet memories of days out stalking with her father; and of family picnics frying onions and washing up in the burn.

Scotland is also linked in family memory to the people who have given long service to the court: Margaret 'Bobo' Macdonald who was born just north of Inverness in 1904 and who came into the royal household as nursery maid or under-nanny in 1926 when Princess Elizabeth was a few months old. She was still sleeping in the bedroom of 11-year-old Princess Elizabeth on George VI's Coronation day, and brought in the early morning tea when Lilibet herself was crowned. She stayed for a lifetime as a steadfast and outspoken personal maid and dresser, and became a unique critic and sounding board.

Bred from the same forthright, hard-drinking Scottish stock was John Brown, Queen Victoria's ghillie and favourite, around whom scandal swirled. 'Whether there was any quite unconscious sexual feeling in the Queen's regard for her faithful servant I am unable to say,' says Ponsonby. 'I am quite convinced that if such a feeling did exist, it was quite unconscious on both sides.'

Victoria's romantic view of the Scots as loyal servants was shared by her husband. 'The people are more natural, & marked by that honesty & simplicity which <u>always</u> distinguishes the inhabitants of mountainous countries, who are far from towns,' said Albert.

'Scotch air, Scotch people, Scotch hills, Scotch rivers and Scotch woods all far preferable to those of any nation in or out of this world,' was Queen Victoria's opinion, claimed royal governess Lady Lyttelton, whose letters were published in 1912.

Today's enduring recruitment of palace staff from Scotland – for Buckingham Palace and all the royal homes – owes more to rural unemployment, a useful network of contacts, and a sense that the Scots know their place, than to any idealized view of the noble Scottish peasant.

'You can't imagine how feudal it is still at Balmoral,' says a house guest of today. 'All those grieves and ghillies – it's like going back a century or more in England. And although the royal family is always saying that the younger generation isn't prepared to come into service any more, there seems to be an endless supply of star-struck local women to work at the castle. Then there is a New Zealand mafia who come up every summer and muck in at the souvenir shops or with the horses. It's the staff brought up from London who get bolshy, complain that the country is boring and get drunk.'

Hard drinking at Balmoral is nothing new. Queen Victoria would describe the inebriated Highlanders tactfully as 'in great ecstasy'. 'The footmen smell of whisky and are never prompt to answer the bell,' complained a Woman of the Bedchamber during the failing Queen Victoria's final visit to Balmoral in the autumn of 1900.

London lackeys have never enjoyed life at the Scottish hideaway. 'For the staff this summer "isolation" seemed a long time, for although the Highland scenery is magnificent there is not much to do in off-duty hours,' said Dean. But the library of video tapes, as well as the films screened in the evenings, are open to staff as well as the royal family.

The walking party stops on a mountain ridge where the Queen, Sarah, Duchess of York, Sarah Armstrong-Jones, Zara Phillips and Prince Harry will all start back.

OPPOSITE: *The Queen's fierce love of Scotland is infused with sweet memories of her late father on family holidays in the Highlands. Philip understands her yearning for freedom and escape from the court ritual. 'Nothing disturbs the privacy, barely even the visit from the Prime Minister,' says an aide.*

Prince Charles in the wide-open freedom of Scotland at the age of 24, playing with Princess Margaret's daughter Lady Sarah Armstrong-Jones, who has become a painting companion for her cousin.

Looking down from here, the path cuts a broad slash through the heather, a scar on the Highland landscape.

'As I know from experience at Balmoral, many public paths are simply inadequate for the numbers who want to walk them today,' says Philip. 'The path up one local mountain is now fifty yards wide. The vegetation is gone. You can see it from miles away. Eventually we put a Land-Rover track part way up, and that has concentrated the walkers. It means we've got to repair it the whole time, but at least people don't wander.'

The climbers press on, single file as the path narrows. Only Anne, the Princess Royal, is left among the men, large and small, aiming for the top, still more than an hour and a stiff climb away.

'I went to Balmoral for about a week and did as much walking as I could up and down the hills,' says Anne of her way of recuperating after a small operation.

The air is now thin and rare; breaths are shallow gulps; an aching thread of muscle pulls up the calf from heel to the back of the knee; feet stumble towards the rocky plateau at the summit. 'The jumbled chaos of rocks and stones which runs round the top of the whole Lochnagar massif,' the Master of Elphinstone described Balmoral's famous summit.

When Victoria and Albert first made their royal progress up the mountain, they hit the sudden bad weather that boils up round the plateau and makes Philip insist that everyone should come out properly equipped, at the very least with a compass and windproof cagoule. 'When we had nearly reached the top of Loch-na-gar the mist drifted in thick clouds so as to hide everything not within one hundred yards of us,' Victoria said.

Today, although clouds still pad the valley, the bright ring of mountains piercing through the mist is spectacular: there the peak of Ben Nevis thrown up to the west; to the north, the summits of Sutherland; Ben Lomond due south; the Cheviots just visible on the border.

Prince Charles waits for William to scramble first up to the boulder that commands the panoramic view ahead. England's future Kings stand side by side as the young Prince screeches into the misty valley below that he is King of the Castle.

Across the century and a half is the reverberating echo of another royal Prince – the eight-year-old son of Albert and Victoria on their Highland holiday in 1850.

'I am first,' he shouted from the mountain. 'I am at the top.'

STAG AT BAY

It was a splendid affair and he was rightly very proud of it. It had a finely carved stone door and a lock made of a stag's horn. The seat was upholstered in leather made from a stag's skin . . .'

The Old Man of Lochnagar

ANTLERS sprout from the walls of the long gallery like ghostly branches of invisible trees. Glassy eyes from the stags' heads stare reproachfully at the man who brought them down from 'the hill'. Prince Albert stands in the stairwell – a lifesize marble statue of the Prince Consort 'in full Highland dress, complete with dog and gun' . . . and 'with a patient and slightly martyred expression, as though he was getting a little tired of waiting around,' said Marion Crawford.

Edward VIII, who filled Balmoral with a house party of sophisticated friends during the autumn of 1936, had a different explanation for Prince Albert's stern expression. 'My Saxe-Coburg great-grandfather seemed to register disapproval whenever the tray of cocktails was carried into the drawing room before dinner,' he said.

The Queen and Philip are walking down the blood-red carpet of the gallery to wait for the start of the day's stalking. It is the morning after the ghillies' ball, and the previous night's celebrations will make it a struggle for some guests to get up on time.

'Bloody hard work,' is how one visitor describes Balmoral's demanding sporting schedule: 08.30 for gentlemen shooting or fishing; ladies out with the Queen riding at 10.00, or following the shoot. 'You can go out for miles and never see anyone,' says the Queen. 'You can walk or ride. It has endless possibilities'.

'You never really see the Queen until 12.30, for drinks before lunch, although you might spot her riding or walking the dogs, and she may join the guns at lunch,' says another guest. 'The exception is stalking, because that is the one sport she is really keen on.'

The Queen is looking at the *Scotsman*, laid out on a table in the drawing room, which now has almost no trace – apart from one plaid chair – of the 'tartanitis' of Queen Victoria's Balmoral, when everything was in a different plaid and, as her Foreign Secretary, Lord Clarendon put it, 'thistles are in such abundance that they would gladden the heart of a donkey'.

'This tartan has got to go,' said Wallis Simpson when Edward VIII took her to play hostess at his great-grandmother's home in 1936.

The drawing-room carpet and curtains are now a soothing pale green; the chintzy chair covers and the bay window seat where Philip is sitting are sprigged with fern. On the wall is one of Landseer's heroic paintings of Prince Albert, gun on one shoulder, a dead royal stag in the foreground and Queen Victoria with John Brown behind.

Stags' heads line the walls not just of the main hall and the upper landing, but also of the ballroom, where the Queen was dancing to the Jack Sinclair band – the Eightsome Reel and the Duke of Perth are her favourites – until nearly midnight last night.

'I was enchanted by one thing more than all else – the ghillies' ball,' said Princess Marina, who was taught to dance the reels by the Queen Mother, then her young Scottish sister-in-law. 'There the servants dance with the royal family without any sense of familiarity but with the utmost good friendship.'

Diana has been known to fling herself so energetically into the reels that she ripped the hem of her dress. Ghosts of past revelries include the young Princess Margaret, a Stuart tartan sash across her tulle ball gown, the centre of a social whirl on Deeside in the 1950s.

In Queen Victoria's time, the festivities were closely linked to the sporting and gaming. 'The amount of whisky consumed by the servants was truly stupendous,' said Fritz Ponsonby of the nights when the stags shot were laid out each evening beside the game larders and illuminated by the ghillies' torches.

'The Queen came out after dinner and dancing took place, all of which was very pretty,' he said, 'But after she left it became an orgy of drink.' Balmoral's circular game larder with its frieze of stags' antlers still stands, like a giant nursery-rhyme toadstool, in the castle grounds.

Prince Philip moves into the entrance hall, where the turreted castle seems more like a local hunting lodge, with its 'stalactitic sort of chimneypiece', its interlaced Jacobean ceiling and the inevitable stags' heads.

Princess Alice of Athlone remembered with nostalgia the 'special smell' of Balmoral's hall: 'a smell of wood fire, stags' heads, rugs and leather, and it was delicious in a way I can't describe,' she said.

Prince Albert even sent the antlers of stags he had shot to Frankfurt to have them made into furniture for Osborne House and mounted deers' teeth as a necklace for his wife. She, in her turn, had Balmoral writing paper engraved with roebuck. 'I hope you will admire my paper – Landseer designed it,' Victoria wrote to her Uncle Leopold of Belgium in September 1851.

The lugubrious decor of Balmoral was gently sent up by Prince Charles in the stories he told his young brothers.

When the Old Man of Lochnagar went to the lavatory ('always a good thing to do after breakfast'), Charles described its seat as 'stuffed with finest down and feathers from several grouse. The actual mechanism of the loo was very cunning. The old man had found an antique pair of bagpipes and rigged them up so that . . . it not only flushed the lavatory, but played his favourite Scottish tune as well.'

There is a bustle in the hall as the housekeeper Patricia Halsey checks off against the guns the waterproof shoulder pouches containing a 'shooting lunch': a roll stuffed with cold meat and a plum pudding. The Balmoral kitchen remains faithful to tradition in spite of Wallis Simpson's efforts to pep things up.

'My contribution to the traditional grandeur of Balmoral was the introduction of the three-decker toasted sandwich,' she said, admitting that this innovation 'hardly endeared the new reign to the household staff'.

Tradition is all, here at Balmoral, which is one reason Diana always pulls a wry face and raises her eyebrows when the Scottish stronghold is mentioned among friends.

The old Victorian game larder at Balmoral is decorated with stags' antlers. It has slits in the walls and a louvered lantern to provide ventilation. It stands near the ice house and the stables, which have mostly been turned into garages for the fleet of four-wheel drive vehicles.

The Queen and Philip in the library where stags' heads stare from the walls. The 'tartanitis' of Balmoral has been swept away, and the jumble of fishing rods, nets and waders testifies to the holiday atmosphere of the Scottish castle.

'There is, I suppose, a certain fascination in keeping the place as Queen Victoria had it,' says the Queen. 'Nothing much has changed. And I think luckily all the children like it. All the grandchildren like it. They sense the freedom.'

The trophies on the walls of the castle – the 'royal' stags whose antlers have twelve points, the trio at the highest point 'large and deep enough to hold a glass of wine' – have hung at Balmoral for more than a century, with the addition of a couple of Philip's royals.

After Albert's death, Queen Victoria forbade any stags to be removed or added to the upper and lower corridors, although in the hall and ballroom they 'might be sparingly added'.

'The Queen does not wish any but extraordinarily fine heads (something quite peculiar, not ordinary royal ones) to be stuffed in future, if shot by the Princes,' the edict said. 'Tangible signs proclaiming her dedication to the dead,' the future Duke of Windsor called Queen Victoria's 'private memories' immortalized at Balmoral.

Princess Elizabeth fell in love with stalking when she shot her first stag with her father in 1945 at the age of 16 and 'promised to become a good shot'. Since then, as Queen, she has brought down many monarchs of the glen, including a royal in 1959, and one of the best heads in Scotland (an eleven-pointer) the previous year.

'In the evening we talked of nothing but stalking and antlers and points,' says Crawfie of the year when Princess Elizabeth learned to shoot. 'We had to retrace with her, in mind, every exciting inch of the day.'

Princess Anne also has a vivid memory of 'my first day's experience of the art of stalking red deer in what felt to me like the vast expanses of the Highlands. I was following my brother – never again,' she said. 'I very nearly didn't make it back to the car as my legs seemed to have gone on strike.'

Since stalking is one of the few sports where women are encouraged to go out with the guns, even the young Lady Diana Spencer joined in. 'D. Spencer' says the label on the small deer's head hung proudly on the wall of the night nursery at Althorp, although by the time the future Princess of Wales was invited up to Birkhall in October 1980, she preferred to stay at home working on her needlepoint.

When Diana did go stalking with Charles on honeymoon, it caused a furore. 'She was absolutely furious about the story that she had shot a deer, not killed it properly and fainted,' said Barry. 'She had merely been out for the day with a ghillie, and as a country girl, she is quite used to blood sports.'

In the royal family albums there are photographs of royal children at their first blooding – the future Edward VIII standing with one foot on a downed stag at Balmoral in 1910, his brother beside him.

Albert's trophy stags were recorded by the court painters – with artistic licence. On canvas the Prince Consort stands proudly over a royal stag or surveys its dead weight borne down the mountain, but the reality was rather different. 'Was he *proud* to have shot a beast of five or six pounds?' asks Duff Hart-Davis, a historian of deer-stalking, after studying the Balmoral game books.

Albert was forced to admit that he was not much of a shot with a rifle. 'I, naughty man, have also been crawling after harmless stags,' he said. 'I shot two roe deer, at least I hope so, for they are not to be found.' To the derision of the local keepers, Albert introduced the Teutonic concept of The Ditch – a four-foot-deep trench half a mile long to help him stalk upright, rather than crawl.

He even shot tame stags out of Balmoral's drawing room window, in an incident that upset his wife and 'made her shake and be very uncomfortable'. Yet when five stags appeared at night outside the house in 1857, Albert, moved by their beauty, let them go.

The Queen and Prince Philip are neither bloodthirsty nor sentimental about the deer in their back yard. The talk at Balmoral now is of 'culling' and 'reclamation' – about the experiment of sending 19 hinds down from Balmoral to re-stock Windsor park; of the fate of the starving deer on the overstocked Mar Lodge estate.

The royal stalking party sets off, as four generations have done before them: a ghillie slung about with telescope – to scan the enormous distances – binoculars and rifles, and the 'pony boy' (in fact an elderly retired ghillie) with one of the

Haflinger ponies to cart the carcass down the mountainside to the road.

These little deer ponies are tough and resilient, living rough through the hardest weather. Prince Philip lists the characteristics of the estate's game workhorses: 'Very clever, in fact they can be too clever by half and are easily bored, although they respond to a challenge. Great independence of character.'

As they work up the slopes of the glen, the Queen herself, sharp-eyed, is the first to spot a herd of deer at the foot of a ravine. She and Philip drop down immediately, wriggling forward across rugged terrain to behind a boulder, where they train binoculars on two fine stags among the deer. The tweed shooting suits blend so perfectly into heather and rocks, that from even the next ridge it would be hard to spot the Queen of England's camouflage.

It is wise, on this inhospitable terrain, to wear something old and sturdy. When Edward VII's friend Sir Derek Keppel tried to break his new shooting suit in gently, the Balmoral keeper told him off for crawling with his behind up in the air.

'It is such durable material that I doubt if I shall ever wear it out,' said John Dean of the Balmoral tweed suit he was given to accompany Prince Philip on his earliest expeditions.

After the war, when clothes were still rationed, the royal family had to make do with well-worn tweeds. 'In the end, Lilibet wore the plus-four trousers of one of her father's suits,' said Crawfie. 'It is a nice neutral shade that merges easily into the background on a moor. The King had it specially woven for him.'

The problem on this blowy day is to move downwind of the deer. After a quick whispered conference, the royal couple start to climb down the corrie, ready to manoeuvre across the base of the ravine to where heather will provide camouflage and cover.

In the deceptive way of moor and mountain, the detour proves far longer

'Evening at Balmoral', painted by Carl Haag in 1854, was an idealized vision of the orgies of drinking by the ghillies when the stags were laid out by the game larders each evening. In spite of his heroic posturing, Prince Albert was not much of a shot.

Two future Kings – Edward VIII and his brother Bertie, who became George VI – standing over a stalking trophy at Balmoral in 1910.

than the naked eye would judge. Two hours later, they are still toiling up the last rise, splashing through peaty streams, and then dropping down to the ground where wiry tufts of heather provide cover.

'Crawling on hands and knees dressed entirely in grey,' said Albert of stag shooting.

'Such sport in the Highlands has special difficulties,' said the future Kaiser Wilhelm II when he stayed at Balmoral at the age of 19 and went out stalking on the cliffs of Lochnagar. 'The Scottish sportsman is . . . equipped with binoculars with which . . . he scans the horizon, lying flat for the purpose. I

The stalking target at Balmoral. The Queen, who shot her first stag at the age of 16, is described by a former head stalker as 'a dead shot'.

could hardly see the deer we were to shoot; it may have been three miles off, yet we had to take full cover. After three hours' exhausting chase . . . we had to negotiate a series of bog holes which would have taken us over our heads, and do the last part of the way on hands and knees.'

Since the day that Mary Queen of Scots supposedly brought down a stag with her crossbow in Glen Shira, – which Victoria and Albert saw in 1847 when visiting the Duke of Argyll at Inverary Castle – there has been a long royal tradition of shooting deer in the Highlands, in spite of the harsh climate. 'The weather is awful, rain and wind every day and on top of it no luck at all – I haven't killed a stag yet,' complained Tsar Nicholas II on a visit to Balmoral in September 1896.

'The exertion and difficulty of stalking was immense,' Albert announced on his first excursion in the Highlands in 1842, although he and an enthusiastic young Queen Victoria came to enjoy the expeditions even before they settled at Balmoral Castle. 'We scrambled up an almost perpendicular place to where there was a little *box*, made of hurdles and interwoven with branches of fir and heather, about five feet in height,' Victoria recorded in her *Journal* in 1848. After a quiet hour of waiting and sketching the deer appeared and 'Albert did not look over the box, but through it, and fired through the branches, and then again over the box.'

Prince Charles, out painting in 1989, was startled by a stag rounding up a party of hinds. 'They had no idea I was in the vicinity because of the slope and because the wind was in my favour,' he explained. 'Amidst a great deal of roaring and grunting, the stag suddenly chased a hind right up to where I was sitting with a brush poised in my hand and a surprised look on my face.'

Even without binoculars, the deer are visible now, across the peat stream. But the problem, Philip whispers to his wife, is that the only way to take aim is from above, which requires climbing up on hands and knees.

The Queen fell in love with stalking in 1945 when she was taken out by her father. She breeds the Haflinger and fell ponies that bring the dead stags down from The Hill.

OPPOSITE: *The red deer stag does enormous damage if numbers are not kept down through culling. Stalking requires hours of patient trekking across difficult terrain before a shot is fired.*

Inch by inch, they squirm upwards, three mottled grey figures against a stony backdrop. In the eerie silence of the empty glen, the Queen's kingdom of familiar sounds – whispers of anticipation, the roar of an excited crowd, the clatter of applause – is reduced to the single sound of a thumping heart. Instead of the sea of upturned expectant faces, the eyes are focused on myriad bits of scree that scrape against knees and dig through gloves into the heel of the hand.

The cover is in sight, nearly in touch. One last heave and on to the ridge; a slithering forward movement until the chin rests on a boulder and there is a clear view to where, 50 yards below, the herd grazes quietly. Philip's heaving breaths die down to a quiet pant as the three stalkers gaze at the stags feeding among the deer. The ghillie loads quietly and passes the rifle. The trio wait absolutely still as the larger stag turns its angle, moving by degrees like the hands of a clock to present broadside on in the gun's sights.

A rifle shot. Like an unexpected clap of thunder, the sound echoes and crackles through the corrie; the herd scatters with deft speed, up the ravine, over the brow, haunches up, heads back in spiky silhouettes. Gone, quite gone – except for the stag lying where it fell, its antlers an upturned arc to the empty sky.

'Her Majesty is a dead shot,' said a former head stalker. 'I have never known her fail to kill a stag clean.'

The relief at having scored a hit after four – nearly five – hours is out of all proportion to the stag itself – a relatively small eight-pointer. There is a sense of mission accomplished, rather than the rage that Philip felt when, after an entire day out, his shot was thwarted at the very last moment by a couple of hikers in fluorescent waterproofs who disturbed his quarry.

'I'm awfully sorry, sir, we're on the Duke of Edinburgh's Award Scheme,' the hikers told the apopleptic Prince.

Right through her widowhood, Queen Victoria retained a keen interest in sporting prowess. 'No one was really kinder to bad shots as a rule than she was,' says Fritz Ponsonby. 'Although the head stalker came in every night to tell her exactly what each person out stalking or fishing had done.'

The ghillies were more outspoken when their skill and guidance was wasted at the final moment. 'Ye blithering idiot, you've ruined the whole thing,' exclaimed head ghillie Arthur Grant when Edward VII's brother the Duke of Connaught missed two easy stags at Balmoral in 1915.

Later, George V rounded on Grant when he missed a stag. 'Take this damn rifle away. Never let me see it again,' he said.

'Your Majesty, dinna waste yer breath damning the rifle,' replied Grant. 'It was a verra bad shot.'

The ghillie is working quickly and deftly to gralloch (or gut) the stag. In silhouette, on the pony's back on the way down the hill, the beast looks like one of Landseer's sketches come to life. But there will be no triumphant return to Balmoral; and no antlers mounted on the wall.

THE PAINTER PRINCE

In the early mornings, long before anyone awoke, little Gorm Heathercraft could
be seen flying to and fro over the hills spraying out the purple liquid. If they didn't
do that, the heather wouldn't be as beautiful and purple as it is.

The Old Man of Lochnagar

VIEWED from the park at Invercauld, Lochnagar, under a sullen sky, is a
heavy, elephant-grey mass. Prince Charles washes a black ridge
across the white paper, above where he has sketched in a fringe of
pines and clumps of larches. 'Definitely sited by someone with an artist's eye,'
Charles says. The dark wooded hill framing the right of the picture is balanced
by the snowy whiteness dabbing the mountain at the top. The light is now so
low that the paper itself stands out in bright relief. Charles looks up anxiously,
ready to protect his afternoon's work from the first splatters of rain.

'All my sketches have been made outside, in all weathers (hence some of
them have been affected by rain!)' he says. 'And as a result I find it easier and
simpler to paint on fairly small pieces of paper.'

His painting has become an aspect of life in the country – a record of
changing landscapes and seasons and a reflection of his interest in his surroundings.

'Ever since he was a small boy Prince Charles has taken an interest in his
surroundings,' said his grandmother in the foreword she wrote for the book
of water-colours he published in 1991. 'Painting became a necessary and vital
expression of that interest.'

The Queen Mother's good friend, the cherubic-faced Sir Hugh Casson, a
former President of the Royal Academy, has encouraged the Prince – as well
as illustrating Charles's best-selling children's story *The Old Man of Lochnagar*.

'The Prince of Wales, like every serious artist, paints not just what he sees
but what he is . . . a man happiest in the open air,' Sir Hugh says. The small
Winsor & Newton paintbox, the soft lead pencils, the Kleenex tissues for
mopping up and the precious sketchbook are all stacked away into Charles's
brown canvas fishing bag ('invariably in a dreadful mess!' he says) before the
first drops start to plop onto the path and Lochnagar disappears behind a
curtain of rain.

Charles took up water-colour painting in his early 20s 'when I found
photography less than satisfying'. It became a private relaxation and a record
of his life. 'These sketches are very much part of myself,' he says. 'And I am
sure those who paint themselves will understand how hard it is to part with
something into which, when inspired, you have poured your heart and soul.'

He was first encouraged to paint as a child by his governess Miss 'Mipsy'
Peebles. The canny Scottish woman (who had taught the Kent children,
Princess Alexandra and Prince Michael) recognized Charles's sensitive nature
compared to the outgoing and boisterous Princess Anne. Charles was also
influenced by his father, himself an amateur oil painter in a bold, modern
style. Prince Philip's artist friend, the Norfolk painter Edward 'Ted' Seago,
helped Prince Charles in the early stages.

'I'd tried to paint when I was about seven or eight when my father had
shown me how to do it with oils,' says Charles. 'Then, about two years before
Ted died, I suddenly had a yearning to try with water-colours – firstly because
it was something different and, secondly, because I thought it was somehow
more expressive than oils and such painting was more alive and had more

178

texture and depth than a photograph,' he explains.

In 1987, Charles's private hobby went public when his water-colour of a Norfolk farm scene submitted under the name of Arthur George Carrick (one of his many pseudonyms) was selected for the Royal Academy Summer Exhibition.

Charles admitted that he was pleased with the 'pale rather transluscent colours which you do find in Norfolk', but he felt that he had 'made a bit of a mess of this sketch. The paint had run all over the place in a thoroughly uncontrolled fashion and the buildings hadn't been drawn very well.'

In the summer of 1990, he put his favourite paintings on display in aid of the British Institute in Florence. They were almost all landscapes recorded out in the open: tidy farms and flat windswept scenes at Sandringham; the grey-green olive groves and pink-roofed villas of Tuscany; the wild, wooded hills of Balmoral.

'He draws inspiration from ordinary scenes and simple places that he knows and loves,' says Hugh Casson, who claims that the Prince is 'preoccupied (like all English men) with our landscape and our weather'.

Charles's view from Invercauld Park, looking east down the Dee Valley towards Balmoral, is indeed focused on the weather – the low cloud veiling the mountainside. But this Scottish vista will also become, on paper, a fragment of memory, recording a tranquil moment during the Balmoral break.

Prince Charles sketching with his Winsor & Newton paintbox and painting paraphernalia stored in an old fishing bag that he describes as 'a dreadful mess'.

Queen Victoria sketching by the water in Tuscany with her faithful Indian servant and courtiers at her side. Professional artists were summoned to Balmoral to teach her to paint, and she recorded her life in her sketchbooks.

'They represent, more than anything else, *my* particular form of 'photograph album' and, as such, mean a great deal to me,' says Charles. 'The great thing about painting is that it is your *own* individual interpretation of whatever view you have chosen. Because it obliges you to sit down and make a careful observation of the chosen subject you discover so much more than by just pointing a camera.'

Royal photographers have recorded faithfully the Balmoral holidays: happy snaps of picnics and boating parties, as well as more serious studies. Prince Andrew, Duke of York, caught on film the rugged, grandiose beauty of Loch Muick – its still waters as grey as the leaden sky. In 1855, Prince Albert had summoned the landscape painter George Washington Wilson to Balmoral to make a photographic record that included the first photograph of the glassy lake and sheer cliffs of Lochnagar. Queen Victoria, who frequently found herself blurred in early photographs, hoped that Lochnagar would be in focus.

'If not, you must not blame your sitter,' she told the artist tartly. 'As Lochnagar keeps very still and does not fidget.'

Prince Charles, who intends to see 'a worthwhile record' left for posterity, has taken painters Martin Yeoman, Peter Kühfeld and Derek Hill with him on official tours – just as Ted Seago joined Prince Philip on a trip on *Britannia* to Australia in 1956.

'One of the things I feel strongly about is the need to keep the Royal Collection alive through the commissioning of works of art,' the Prince says.

The ancestry of Prince Charles as a landscape artist goes back in a bloodline to Queen Victoria, whose sketchbooks of Scotland – left to the Crown on her death in 1901 – were both a physical record of the place and an emotional response to the beauty and tranquillity of the area.

'What is there more beautiful than Nature, "the autograph work of God",' she wrote. In Queen Victoria's many sketches, she recorded with equal enthusiasm her children, the fine upstanding Scottish people and the scenery. But she responded mainly to the surroundings.

In August 1849 she sketched the sturdy shiel – used as a royal retreat – surrounded by conifers at Allt-na-guibhsaich at the northern end of Loch Muick. In 1985 and again the following year, Charles captured the austere charm of the same stone cluster. John Ward was tactful about another of the Prince's efforts in 1988. 'How well is the character of Allt-na-guibhsaich Lodge at Balmoral grasped despite wobbly perspective,' he said.

Sir Edwin Landseer, the artist whose paintings did for the Highlands what Sir Walter Scott's romantic novels accomplished in prose, painted Queen Victoria, sketchbook at her side, on a family outing to Loch Laggan.

William Leighton Leitch, who gave Queen Victoria painting and drawing lessons from 1846, described 'Her Majesty sitting in the middle of a country road, with a great rough stone out of the river to put her paint box on; Lady Churchill holding an umbrella over the Queen's head.' Three of Queen Victoria's ladies-in-waiting – Lady Canning, the Hon. Eleanor Stanley and the Hon. Georgiana Liddell – shared her enthusiasm for amateur painting and drawing.

'I am afraid I am very bad at mountains; I never have half the trouble with my buildings, and they always succeed,' said Eleanor Stanley in 1854 of her attempts to paint Lochnagar.

'My particular form of photograph album,' says Prince Charles of his painting. He took time out on a tour of Japan to sketch in the gardens of the Omiya Sento Palace in Kyoto.

In 1844, Lady Canning was stranded when her pony, startled by pencils and paintboxes rattling in the saddlebag, took off across the Highlands.

The tradition of royal painting continued with Victoria's daughters and with her daughter-in-law Queen Alexandra, whose immaculately tidy 'painting room' at Windsor had her framed water-colours on the walls and clean brushes upstanding in a jar.

Prince Charles has his skinny Roberson paintbrush in his hand, his cousin Sarah Armstrong-Jones a soft lead pencil, as both sketch an abandoned croft against a background of dappled mountain. Beside Charles on his camping stool, Sarah sits cross-legged on the ground, her long hair falling to her waist. Harvey the labrador and the royal detective sprawl on the far side of the royal artists.

Sarah, trained at Camberwell College of Art and at the Royal Academy of Arts (where she had two paintings selected for the Summer Exhibition in 1988), is an artistic companion for Charles. In 1986, she joined him on a painting trip to Italy, a country that inspires him as a painter because, he says, 'the light is so marvellous there and the scenery. It is quite breathtaking.'

On his first trip to Italy – an official visit with Diana in 1985 – he decided to take with him artist John Ward, who had painted the royal wedding and Prince William's christening.

'If my grandmother can take Sir Hugh Casson to Venice, can I take you?' Charles asked Ward. The Queen Mother says that Charles is fortunate in being able to 'bask in the beauties of Tuscany'.

Diana defended her husband when he went back to Italy to paint yet again after a visit to Spain in May 1987. 'My husband is going to do something he has wanted to do for years – tour the Italian countryside and paint,' she said. 'He takes his painting really seriously, although it is just a hobby,' a house guest who has seen Charles in Italy says. 'The Prince and John Ward would go off every day and work together.'

'I have a passion for Italy, her people and her countryside,' Charles admits in the introduction to his book. 'The way in which art quite naturally seems to invade every aspect of life produces, for me, an atmosphere that it totally irresistible and utterly unique.'

Queen Victoria's passion for self-improvement was first served by Edward Lear, who fired her enthusiasm for landscape painting. Then, on 15 July 1846, she received her first lesson from Leitch, progressing 'really, I must own, very nicely, considering that I only started sketching in July.'

Once Balmoral holidays were established, Victoria and Albert would invite a professional artist to Scotland each year to record royal life in the Highlands. In 1850, Queen Victoria told the Duchess of Sutherland that Landseer had 'made a beautiful Sketch and some very fine Studies for a picture he is to paint for us illustrative of our life & pursuits in these <u>dear</u>, beautiful Highlands.'

Landseer, also there to teach, introduced Queen Victoria to chalk pastels. 'But I never could manage that well,' she said.

Sketching became a recreation that the royal couple shared. In 1848 Victoria recorded a day out with Albert and the ghillie Macdonald. 'We sat quite still, and sketched a little; I doing the landscape and some trees, Albert drawing Macdonald as he lay there.' she said.

'Every turn you have a picture,' she said of Scotland.

To their own sketched souvenirs were added, after Albert's death, the heroic paintings she commissioned from Landseer of her husband deerstalking, or more domestic scenes of family outings and picnics by the German painter Carl Haag. 'Landseer's pastel pictures are justly famous,' Prince Charles says. 'But Carl Haag is, I think, less well-known.' Haag's mirror of

Lady Sarah Armstrong-Jones, who has studied at art school, has been on painting trips abroad with her cousin Charles.

'Morning in the Highlands', painted by Carl Haag in 1853, conveys the romance of the Highlands in vivid water-colours. The German painter was as popular with Queen Victoria as Landseer.

happier days, all painted after Albert's death, include the royal party wading on horseback through a ford and a family picnic at Carn Lochan, both painted in heather-soft Scottish colourings in 1865. These contrasted with the more dramatic, colourful and formal 'Morning in the Highlands' of 1853, in which Prince Albert on horseback and Queen Victoria on a dappled grey pony start the rocky ascent to Lochnagar that stands like a beacon in the background, rising from a pool of blue shadow.

Haag's 'richness of colour and lucidity' were praised by contemporary critics. 'His exquisite water-colour records of Queen Victoria's expeditions through the Highlands are amongst my favourite pictures in the Royal Collection,' says Charles.

Prince Charles's pale wash of brown and grey with the stippled outline of trees and hills is the opposite of detailed Victorian painting.

'The shortage of personal time which compels him to catch his subjects on the wing led him early on to choose water colour as his medium,' Sir Hugh Casson says. 'Its fleeting immediate quality gives no time for second thoughts.'

Charles is frustrated by his lack of time, claiming that when he can paint for five consecutive days, he can see an immediate improvement. 'You become increasingly more aware of the quality of light and shade, of tone and texture and of the shape of the buildings,' he claims.

But he says of water-colour, 'I very quickly discovered how incredibly difficult it is to paint well in such a medium, and the feeling of frustration at not being able to achieve on paper the image that your eye has presented you with is overwhelming!'

Yet Prince Charles shares with Queen Victoria a sense of the romance of the Highlands and the poetic beauty of the landscapes he tries to record. 'The dear Highlands which I feel I *love* – I fear more than matter-of-fact unpoetical England,' admitted Victoria.

Allt-na-guibhsaich, sketched by Queen Victoria, was her private hideaway with Prince Albert. Prince Charles has made many drawings and paintings of the crofters' cottage looking over Loch Muick.

Lord Byron, who spent the first ten years of his life in Aberdeen during the late eighteenth century, expressed in his juvenile collection *Hours of Idleness* the soaring excitement of the Scottish Highlands and of Lochnagar which dominates the view from Balmoral to the south:

> England! thy beauties are tame & domestic
> To one who has roved o'er the Mountains afar;
> Oh for the Crags that are wild & majestic!
> The steep frowning glories of dark Loch na Gar!

Charles and Sarah are looking up at the mountain, silhouetted against a sky woolly with thick black clouds fringed blood red by the setting sun.

'As the sun went down the scenery became more and more beautiful, the sky crimson, golden-red and blue, and the hills becoming purple and lilac, most exquisite, till at length it set, and the hues grew softer in the sky and the outline of the hills sharper. I never saw anything so fine,' said Queen Victoria of a Balmoral sunset.

The sketchbooks, pencils and paints are put away, and the royal cousins start downhill, the deep colours and the savage beauty absorbed in the mind as well as in marks on drawing paper.

'It has revolutionized my life,' Charles say of his painting. 'And through the requirement of intense concentration, it is one of the most relaxing and therapeutic exercises I know.'

Sarah's brother, Lord Linley, was once asked his idea of perfect happiness. 'Sitting on a hill in Scotland, sketching the view,' he said.

In his paint bag, Charles carries a piece of his paradise. Or, as he puts it: 'When I am feeling decidedly gloomy and claustrophobic in London, it reminds me of where my heart is . . .'

FISHY WATERS

The old man gave them their instructions and they rose up far above the loch to look for some trout. When they spied some they plummeted down together and disappeared with two great splashes, to reappear a second later clutching two fine trout.

The Old Man of Lochnagar

GAUZY WHITE wings fluttering against gin-clear spray, and the swallows swooping low, signal that the mayfly is up. To the Queen Mother watching from the river bank, the peaty water, in the sun, looks like neat whisky.

'As brown as brown ale' her good friend Lady Salisbury says of the frothy waters of the River Muick as it runs down to the Dee.

'Queen Elizabeth loves her fishing,' says Lady Salisbury. 'All her life she has been a keen and highly skilful fisherman.'

'At Balmoral, all the royal family would lead an outdoor life, but of all the ladies it was the Queen Mother who was the most energetic,' wrote Mrs McKee. 'Her great passion was for salmon fishing, and this she did with intense concentration for hours on end. She would put on waders and old clothes and attempt to catch the biggest salmon she could find. She liked no interruption and took with her only the simplest of cold picnics.'

Alas, no more! Bowing to pressure from the family – and especially from Charles – Queen Elizabeth no longer stands up to her waist casting across the Dee in spate, hoping the fast waters will give a slithering silver salmon.

On this spring visit to Birkhall, the Queen Mother stands instead in shallow water, her ghillie beside her.

'I just go along to please Pearl,' she would say of days out on the Dee with the faithful ghillie Jimmy Pearl who died in 1980.

Now, under the pork pie tweed cap, is the beaming face of Charles Knight, who improved Lady Diana Spencer's rudimentary casting in May 1980, when Charles was courting her and they stayed with the Queen Mother at Birkhall.

'I always used to say that the ones who survived Scotland, Craigowan and the fishing had a chance of surviving the course to becoming the Princess of Wales,' commented Barry. But although her mother Frances Shand Kydd is an eager angler, taking a beat on the Spey each season, Diana is rarely seen nowadays even on the river bank.

The Queen Mother's fluffy green feather wafts in the green felt hat outlined against the green trees, where a log cabin – an 80th birthday present from close friends – serves as a spanking new fishing lodge.

'She always wears that hat,' says a friend. 'When we stay at Mey, she takes a boat out on the estuary and spends hours – four or five – on the river fishing for salmon. It can get just a teeny bit boring for the rest of us.'

Those hours spent on the Thurso – one of the best known salmon rivers in Scotland – are a real test of the Queen Mother's enthusiasm and of her prowess.

'The Queen Mother throws a beautiful line. She is a keen angler and fished four hours continuously, enjoying every minute of it,' said Donald Murray, an angling expert, of a day out from Mey.

The ghillie is sitting among the lush green vegetation threading a spread-eagled dragonfly. An old toffee tin full of flies is beside him and a swarm of mayflies dances in wild arcs above his head. As Lady Elizabeth Bowes Lyon, the Queen Mother was first hooked as a child when she went coarse fishing

The deep waters of the River Dee, which flows through the Balmoral estate, are a favourite fishing ground with all the royal family, from Prince Philip and Charles, to the Queen Mother and Princess Alexandra of Kent.

INSET: The Queen watches Philip, who once landed 15 salmon when fishing at the Queen Mother's home, Birkhall.

with bent pins and worms with her brothers at St Pauls Waldenbury in Hertfordshire, or when they pulled brown trout out of the Scottish lochs. She learned fly fishing in the River Dean that runs through the grounds of Glamis Castle. Now she is quite content to wait in the shallows, contemplating the fleeting passages of sun on water and the crystalline spray as the trout rise.

'I can pray when I'm fishing but I can't fish in church,' says Prince Charles, who shares with his grandmother the peace and pleasure of fishing, but will rarely be seen by the Reverend Angus at Crathie Parish Church, rebuilt in 1893 on the slope facing the Balmoral bridge.

Charles was shown how to cast a fly by Uncle Dickie Mountbatten, but his fishing memories are of the ghillies at Balmoral and of escapades with his childhood friend Anthony Tryon, who is still a favourite angling companion, along with his ebullient Australian-born wife Dale.

'I find it highly therapeutic to stand on a river bank with the water flowing by and nobody else in sight. All worries seem to disappear because you have to concentrate entirely on the fly and the speed of the line,' Lady Tryon has said. She would host an annual August party to Iceland where her husband and a group of friends had built a fishing lodge on the River Hofsa near Vopnaf-jördhur. Prince Charles was there when news came of the assassination of Lord Mountbatten – on a fishing trip in Ireland – in 1979.

Charles is trying to teach his own boys to fish, but mostly he spends hours fishing alone, especially at Balmoral, but also in the trout stream at Windsor that he persuaded his father to stock.

'If anyone asks you what I want for a present, tell them something to do with fishing,' Charles would tell his valet. In Scotland he buys his own fishing tackle from Countrywear in Bridge Street, Ballater, where wooden drawers pull out to display every colour and variety of fly. Alas for the royal family, Colonel Clifton Jefferies, who ran Countrywear for years and held the Royal Warrant, decided to retire in 1991 to indulge his own enthusiasm for fishing and stalking. 'Prince Charles always used to drop in for a chat when he was up here,' a Ballater resident says. 'It was a very friendly shop and the Colonel's leaving is a great loss.'

The tangle of ancient cane rods and new carbon fibre ones by the garden entrance at Balmoral proves that fishing is a royal family tradition. 'I love a gun; but I am never so happy as when I am fishing the pools of the Dee, with a long day before me,' said George V.

George VI learned trout fishing as a boy on Loch Muick, when put in quarantine by whooping cough.

Prince Philip, like his son, is a keen angler. 'One of his wedding presents was a handsome set of fishing tackle, and the Duke delighted in using this while we were staying in Scotland,' Dean said.

It was on this very stretch of river at Birkhall, that Philip made a dramatic catch. 'The Duke burst in with the news that he had caught fifteen salmon,' Dean reported. 'A kitchen maid rushed to fill one of the sinks with water, and we all helped to immerse the catch.' The staff were then each given a fish 'to send home'.

The Queen Mother is equally generous. 'Once, after two whole days of concentrated fishing, the Queen Mother presented me with two salmon, one of which must have weighed about twenty pounds,' says Mrs McKee. 'Do what you like with them,' the Queen Mother said to her cook. 'Why not give the staff a treat?' Mrs McKee cooked the smaller of the two salmon in a *court bouillon* and served it cold with a lemon and mustard sauce.

In spite of the auspicious signals, it is not proving to be a bumper day. The line drifts across the water and occasionally goes taut, but there are none of the

Lady Diana Spencer fishing on the Dee with the help of ghillie Charles Wright in May 1980. Although her mother Frances Shand Kydd is a keen angler, Diana has never taken to fishing.

The Queen Mother as young Duchess of York fishing for rainbow trout during an expedition to the Torgariro River at Tokaanu, New Zealand.

And, below, with the faithful royal ghillie. In spite of her robust energy, the family now discourages the Queen Mother from wading into deep water.

fierce slashing rises that can make the arms jump and quiver, and the heart leap with the fish.

'There is nothing more exciting than when the line goes tight, the reel screams, and there is that split second of mind-blowing excitement when you don't know what you've got, or how big it is. Absolutely fantastic,' Dale Tryon says.

The Queen Mother has her own fishing memories – of the April day when she waited all day for the pools of the Dee to fill up, started fishing as the light fell and returned hours late for dinner to meet the hurricane lamps of an anxious search party. 'This is what kept me late!' she said, holding up a 20-pound salmon.

Charles takes Prince Harry out fishing, passing on his skill and enthusiasm to the next generation. Prince Charles was taught to cast a line by his grandmother in the River Muick below Birkhall.

There was another excitement in the summer of 1976, when the river was running too low for most anglers to bother, yet Charles landed seven salmon.

Today his grandmother returns empty-handed, but in good spirits, to Birkhall, looking up from the river to the bank of lawn where Charles first practised casting down the slope. He learned from her the lie of the river, the habits of its salmon, and the importance of counting the hours of enjoyment rather than the catch.

'He's a good fisherman and doesn't get upset if he comes home empty-handed,' Barry said of Prince Charles. 'I've known him go two days without a catch and still stay cheerful. I think a lot of the appeal of fishing for him is because with a rod in his hand and his feet in the water, he doesn't have to talk to anyone.'

The steep garden, set among pines and a green meadow on the bank of the Muick, is crowned by the white-walled Queen Anne house which has played honeymoon host to the Queen, to Princess Margaret, to the Duchess of Kent and her sister-in-law Princess Alexandra – as well as being a retreat for Charles and Diana.

'It was made for a honeymoon,' the Duchess of Kent said.

'It is the nicest place in the whole world,' announced 12-year-old Princess Elizabeth, who knew Birkhall first as a childhood retreat.

Her words were an unconscious echo of Queen Victoria's granddaughter, Princess Alice of Athlone. 'Here we spent some of the happiest days of our lives,' she said. 'It was a small place in those days. We loved the sloping gardens full of fruit and sweet peas, and at the bottom, a chain bridge, heavenly to jump upon, which spanned the rushing little Muick, where we loved to play.'

Princess Elizabeth and Margaret Rose stayed in the tranquillity of Birkhall through the autumn of 1939. 'The River Muick rippled merrily through the gardens just as usual in those lovely autumn days, while Poland was being overrun and "lights were going out all over Europe",' Crawfie wrote.

Although the Queen Mother added an L-shaped extension with four new bedrooms, bathrooms, a modern kitchen and central heating to the original structure in 1952, Birkhall retains the homely charm of a small manor house.

'The staircases are lined with Spy's caricatures. Some of these caricatures have personal letters attached to the backs of them, and we spent many wet days reading them,' says Crawfie of the time when Birkhall was still lit by oil lamps 'and very smelly oil stoves were carried up to the bedrooms in bitter weather.' 'Spy' (the *nom de plume* of Sir Leslie Ward) was famous for the caricatures he drew for *Vanity Fair* from 1873 to 1909.

'Big log fires kept the house cosy,' says Dean. In October 1980, Lady Diana Spencer, working on her needlepoint, would sit by Birkhall's fire with her grandmother Lady Fermoy, while she waited for Charles to come in. Nowadays the Princess of Wales is impatient about her husband's dedication to field sports – as was a former girlfriend: 'I think she thought the week would be rather glamorous – a romantic interlude in the Highlands with the Prince,' says Barry of one of Charles's breaks in Scotland. 'Nothing of the kind. He was standing with his feet in the water all day while she was bored out of her mind.'

The royal mistress Lillie Langtry devised a game for ladies to play while their men were out all day in Scotland: they tobogganed on tea trays down the stairs until the butler felt obliged to lock up the silver. William tried the same trick when staying at Althorp before his grandfather's death.

Prince Albert bought Birkhall – literally 'birch hall' after the surrounding silver birches – in 1849 for the Prince of Wales, who in fact preferred to rent the grander Abergeldie Castle. But Queen Alexandra, a keen angler, would send her three daughters to fish in the River Dee and visit Birkhall when it was leased to her comptroller and friend Sir Dighton Probyn in the 1890s.

Upstream, there is the lure of the loch and its wild brown trout. Generations of royal fishing parties have trawled the still waters since Queen Victoria described 'various scrambles in and out of the boat'. 'I wish an artist could have been there to sketch the scene,' she said. 'It was so picturesque – the boat,

The Queen Mother's timber fishing lodge – a log cabin on the river bank. Her friends clubbed together to give it as an 80th birthday present.

LEFT: *Prince Philip fishing at Balmoral. Friendly competition among anglers has been a feature of royal summer holidays since George VI took guests to Loch Muick to catch brown trout. He had learned to fish there as a child when quarantined with whooping cough.*

Birkhall on the Balmoral estate, used by the Queen Mother when staying on Deeside. At the bottom of the sloping gardens is the River Muick which flows from the loch.

the net, and all those people in their kilts in the water and on the shore.'

A few days later, Victoria had her wish, as Landseer came with her and Albert out on Loch Muick on 17 September 1850.

'The Lake was like a mirror & the extreme calmness, with the bright sunshine, hazy blue tints on the fine bold outline of hills coming down into our sweet Loch, quite enchanted Landseer,' she wrote. 'We landed at the usual landing place, where there was a haul of fish, and upward of 20 trout were caught.'

In her widowhood, Queen Victoria kept up her interest in fishing – and kept the score. She castigated Fritz Ponsonby for his lack of skill. 'Not a very good fisherman, I fear,' she said.

Friendly competition among anglers was a feature of Balmoral holidays under George VI. 'Expeditions on Sunday afternoons either to the far end of the Loch Muick, for tea in the Glassalt or some light-hearted trout-fishing in the Loch – or to the Queen's charming little cottage,' said a summer visitor. 'There a more serious and less reputable form of fishing often produced some salmon, bearing mysterious marks almost suggestive of foul-hooking.'

'I was given the task of getting as many varieties of fish and anything else that I could find,' said Jack Eldon of a sportsman's day out with his shooting chum George VI. 'One of the ladies rowed me up and down the loch for about two hours, but I only succeeded in catching a few small brown trout.'

Today, the locals complain vociferously that they are not allowed to fish Loch Muick 'for security reasons'.

'Security! The best security they have is not that policeman standing in the sentry box down by the Dee at Balmoral, nor all that fancy electronic equipment they have installed,' says a Ballater resident. 'It's us, with our sharp eyes and our knowing what is going on.'

Down the glen flow the unfathomable waters of the loch to become the merry little stream at Birkhall, with its fringes of rhododendrons and narcissus, and banks of bright laburnum.

A stop at Birkhall for 'a vast tea of scones and cakes and jam' is now, as for previous generations, a ritual for Balmoral guests. 'We saw many of the relations at these teas,' said Princess Alice of Athlone, 'including bearded Uncle Louis of Hesse, Aunt Alice's husband, his son Ernie and daughter Alix [later the Tsarina] and cousin Eddie of Wales . . . No one was in a hurry in those days and Balmoral was ten miles off.'

As an unhappy schoolboy at Gordonstoun, near the Morayshire coast, Prince Charles would escape to see his grandmother, taking a friend to Birkhall for Sunday lunch and staying on for the day.

'I'm very sorry to have got them back late, but you know what grannies can be like,' the Queen Mother would tell the school in an apologetic phone call.

'She lives in a unique haven of cosiness and character,' says Charles of the 'fun, laughter, warmth, infinite security' of his grandmother's home. He stays at Birkhall, rather than with his parents at Balmoral, for fishing – and for preference.

PLAYING HOUSE

He had made his house in a cave by the Loch of Lochnagar and it was a surprisingly comfortable cave.

The Old Man of Lochnagar

THE LAND-ROVER is driving fast and steadily up the track, the dogs in the back swaying to the rhythm of the ruts. It stops in front of a pair of square stone cottages and the Queen fishes in her pocket for the door key. 'She likes being on her own, that is one of the first things you notice about her,' says a house guest. 'At Balmoral she is always off on her own, and she even makes tea for herself. There is never anyone fussing round her.'

Today, she and Princess Margaret are at Allt-na-guibhsaich – 'goo-shich'

ABOVE: Prince Charles is a keen angler. 'Tell them something to do with fishing,' he says, when asked about a present.

The Queen exercises and feeds the corgis herself. When they die, they are buried in the grounds of whichever residence she is living in at the time.

the locals pronounce it, like water washing ashore. It means in Gaelic 'burn of the Scots pine'.

'Our wild little place near Loch Muick' Queen Victoria called the cluster of buildings she made into a rural retreat. It was here at Allt-na-guibhsaich that the future George VI spent a month in isolation with whooping cough as a boy in 1909, a visit that planted in him the enthusiasm for Scotland that he passed on to his elder daughter.

The house – two cottages linked by a connecting passage – stands on an incline, screened at the front by pines and with mountains behind. The slope, with wind-blown rhododendron bushes as the remains of a garden, is filled with scrawny deer grazing right down to the edge of Loch Muick in the right-hand distance.

'Somebody must have laid out a rather nice garden in the foreground,' says Charles of his great-great-great-grandmother's retreat. 'The garden has long since ceased to exist, the rhododendrons have gone wild and multiplied and the rabbits have taken over the job as lawn-mowers.'

The front porch is supported on the same gnarled and knotted tree-trunk pillars used for Garden Cottage at Balmoral. The grey door opens, a sharp left down the corridor, into the dining room and then through to the modern kitchen, where the kettle is put on to boil, the brown earthenware teapot beside it, cups, saucers and plates stacked on the yellow Formica-topped table.

There is a long family tradition of expeditions to one or other of the empty houses dotting the estate or 'an abandoned little house up on the moor' that Crawfie described from holidays at Balmoral when Lilibet and Margaret Rose were children. 'The kitchen had a big fireplace, and there were handy cupboards for pots and pans where we could put our picnic gear,' she said.

Now the Queen, presiding over the pine table in the dining room, is playing house as Queen Victoria did before her, when she laid out a cold lunch for Albert at Allt-na-guibhsaich in 1848. Victoria described the rooms as 'delight-fully papered, ceiling as well as walls, and very nicely furnished'.

Today, apart from the kitchen with its mock-wood wipe-down cupboards and shiny brown gas cooker, the house has gone to seed; the dining room curtains are in shreds and the sitting room a jumble of faded brocade chaise-longue and chairs round a tartan rug in front of the Victorian tiled fireplace and a lamp of carved wooden storks picked up on some royal tour. Only a large framed photograph of a corgi hanging on the wall, a tartan sausage dog draught-excluder and children's books on the shelves provide homely touches.

In the summer holidays after the Great Exhibition of 1851, the ghillie would build a fire and Victoria lay 'snug and warm' on her sofa while Albert played Chopin's nocturnes on the piano that had been hauled up the hill. And here too at Allt-na-guibhsaich, in the last summer of her life, the frail and fading Queen Victoria took 'tea' – just a few sips of arrowroot and milk.

The Queen has tranquil memories of visits to the secluded Garbh-allt-Shiel that she lent to freed hostage Terry Waite and his family in December 1991. There are more boisterous memories of summer evenings at the Danzig Shiel in the middle of the Ballochbuie Forest, and of shrieks of hysteria over singed sausages after Philip's trailer had disgorged food for a barbecue at a lonely croft.

'Invariably one's without electricity,' said Barry, who joined in the staff barbecue at the end of Charles and Diana's Scottish honeymoon, the young royal hostess dispensing 'lethal cocktails quite unaware of their strength'. 'There was just a rough table and long benches in the cabin, and the Princess set the table and we all sat around,' he said.

The Queen and Margaret are making a tour of the house which has a dank chill in spite of the sunshine and the Dimplex heaters. It is sometimes loaned out as a holiday cottage to Palace staff and is surprisingly roomy, with its five bedrooms on the ground floor, including one with engravings of the young Victoria and Albert above twin beds.

'We are all well, and live a somewhat primitive, yet romantic life, that acts as a tonic to the nerves,' Albert claimed.

After the Prince Consort's death, when she could hardly bear to visit a place that was 'speaking of happy days in the past', Queen Victoria abandoned Allt-na-guibhsaich, and instead extended the Glas-allt-Shiel to make another country cottage idyll of flower-sprigged paper and chintzy furnishings. She returned to Balmoral 'much the better and livelier', said Fritz Ponsonby.

The royal family has a deep-seated instinct to leave the vast grandeur of palaces and live on a human scale. The Princess Royal will take her children out from Sandringham to the Queen's beach hut. Charles and Diana have spent a holiday on the Isles of Scilly – part of the Duchy of Cornwall – living like an 'ordinary' family in the royal bungalow 'Tamarisk'. Even Queen Mary and a convalescing George V went to stay in a house in Bognor in 1929, where their granddaughter Princess Elizabeth, nearly three years old, came to visit them. 'Played with Lilibet in the garden making sand pies!' Queen Mary recorded of her stay.

The Queen is drying each cup and replacing it carefully in the cupboard, defying Barry's claim that the royals 'don't mind serving themselves. They don't even mind cooking. But clearing up is out.'

'The royal family always enjoy "picnicking" as they call it – as long as it doesn't go on for too long – and they don't have to do the washing up,' Barry claimed.

'I remember seeing Lilibet standing and looking ruefully at a large cauldron full of greasy dishes into which she had to plunge her arms to do the washing-up,' said Crawfie when the princesses formed a Girl Guide company at Windsor.

The kitchen is tidied, the stainless steel sink wiped, the dog bowls picked up, the corgis marshalled, the door carefully locked. The detective emerges discreetly from the broken down gazebo and primitive outbuildings round the back.

For Princess Margaret and her elder sister, this private tea is a grown-up version of the games of their childhood, for just as William and Harry have their own Wendy House (in modular plastic, with a green roof, yellow window and red door) in the play area at Highgrove, so the two princesses had their own miniature homes. A half-timbered thatched cottage bought at the Inverness Highland Show survives in the gardens at Birkhall, a bumpy ride from here across the deer track, through the gate and by the rushing falls of Muick.

'It is made of "rustic" wooden planks with the bark left on the outside, its roof thatched with heather . . . One of the summerhouses in which they played and held tea parties,' says Lady Salisbury.

The three summerhouses – by the apple trees, down by the river and in the woods – were the big attraction of Birkhall to the two princesses. 'We used to have our tea one day here and another there, and it was quite fun deciding where we would give a little tea party, or have a little tea party, said Princess Elizabeth. 'Sometimes Princess Margaret would do the honours, and sometimes I would.'

The grey stone of Allt-na-guibhsaich recedes, shrinking in size in the driving mirror until it looks in outline like the Little House indelibly stamped on royal childhood memory.

Prince Harry playing in the modern-day plastic Wendy House in the garden at Highgrove.

ABOVE RIGHT: *Princess Elizabeth and Margaret Rose with their parents and the dogs at the Little House just before the Abdication brought George VI to the throne.*

FACING PAGE: *The Welsh Cottage in the grounds of Royal Lodge, Windsor, was given to Princess Elizabeth on her sixth birthday in 1932 by the people of Wales. The perfect replica of a 1930s cottage, designed by E. C. Morgan Willmott of Cardiff, is now used by the Queen's grandchildren.*

In the grounds of Royal Lodge, Lilibet and Margaret's childhood home at Windsor, stands a thatched 1930s house in its neat suburban garden of low clipped hedge, lawn and beds filled with polyanthus, tulips and forget-me-nots.

Y Bwthyn Bach To Gwellt (The Little House with the Straw Roof) was presented to Princess Elizabeth by the people of Wales on her sixth birthday in 1932. 'Not a doll's house, but a real habitable miniature house with thatched roof, whitewashed walls, flowering garden, four rooms, a staircase and *real* water laid on – both hot and cold,' said Lady Cynthia Asquith, when the Little House was first installed. It went on to become 'An endless source of pleasure to the Queen Mother's grandchildren and great-grandchildren,' says Lady Salisbury.

The photographer Lisa Sheridan was shown over the scaled-down house designed by the Cardiff architect E. C. Morgan Willmott. She saw the parlour, complete with polished oak dresser, table and grandfather clock and with a miniature portrait of Queen Elizabeth over the mantelpiece; the bathroom with tiny rolls of Bronco toilet paper; the sturdy enamel cooker in

ABOVE RIGHT: *From inside the Little House, a bay window with checked curtains, in the dining alcove, looks out on the rose garden.*

ABOVE: *Prince Charles looking out of the window when he played in the house as a child in 1954.*

the kitchen where blue and white check curtains hang at casement windows.

'We've got everything except a telephone,' said Princess Margaret.

Three generations of royal children have now played in the house, where the Queen remembers two-year-old Peter Phillips making a cup of tea 'for granny' and shutting the rolling pin in the oven; and Prince Charles at the same age knocking over the sundial in the garden.

The fun was keeping house, and there still exists, in careful joined-up writing, an assessment of housewife's chores by one of the first royal occupants: 'Sitting room – floor bad'; 'bedroom – good but untidy', as well as an index card of meter readings from the Southern Electricity Board.

Lady Peacock, who wrote about Prince Charles and Princess Anne in 1955, described how 'the children love dusting, tidying up, making the beds and playing at tea parties and also enjoy themselves turning the electric lights on and off.'

'Not a speck of dust anywhere!' Lisa Sheridan had claimed, when she photographed George VI romping with his family and their dogs by the Little House.

Balmoral comes into view, with its gothic turrets, towers and spires, all the trappings of a fairytale castle. Yet in comparison with big, businesslike Buckingham Palace or the grandeur of Windsor Castle, the Highland retreat still seems like a real home.

The royal family 'live there without any state whatever', wrote Charles Greville in his memoirs of Victoria and Albert's Scottish hideaway. 'They live not merely like private gentlefolks, but like very small gentlefolks, small house, small rooms, small establishment.'

WINGED MAGIC ON THE MOOR

Soon there was a noise of wings beating and twelve huge cock capercaillie came
up the valley in perfect formation and settled beside the old man.

The Old Man of Lochnagar

PRINCE CHARLES is king of a miniature castle. His head in a flat tweed cap
crowns the stone ramparts – a semi-circular stone fortress upstanding in
a sea of heather. From this imperious height he looks out on nothing
but a barren incline; to his right, three more drystone butts pierce the
moorland that rolls on down to a peat-brown stream. There is no sound in the
absolute stillness but the gurgling of the burn or the gusts and eddies of a stiff
wind. Then up goes the white flag of a flanker. Let battle commence!

A shot rattles out downhill. There is a warning whistle from beyond the
horizon as the grouse burst over the ridge, the pack flying in one long line like
a dark jetstream.

'What I call "a river of grouse",' said Sir Joseph Nickerson.

A sudden squall and the pack breaks line, a few bulbous silhouettes blowing
away downwind, others beating up, three curling high up and away, some
angling across on a side wind, banking and dropping against the contours of
the moorland. Nickerson called it, 'winged magic on the wild moor!'

Prince Charles finds the same satisfaction in downing a crossing bird as his
grandfather and great-grandfather would have had before him. 'The King was
a most beautiful shot,' remembers a shooting companion of George VI. 'I
have seen him kill high grouse coming downwind, one after another and all as
dead as doornails, with a skill that could stand any comparison.'

Although George V preferred to shoot pheasants at Sandringham and stags
at Balmoral, he too was an extraordinarily fine shot on the grouse moors. The
writer Eric Linklater, who worked as a beater at Balmoral with fellow
students in 1921, remembered the King's unerring aim, and that 'every bird
that fell to the King's gun was dead in the air before it dropped. It was the very
summit of marksmanship, the nonpareil of shooting,' Linklater recalled.
'While we watched – and we knew what to look for – not a bird came
fluttering down, but every one was a meteor falling or a plummet dropping
straight.'

Up here on The Brown Cow, as the hill is quaintly named, the grouse
shooting is a monument to George VI, who bought part of the Glen Muick
estate and planned the drives and butts, just as his own grandfather, Edward
VII, had created the shoots at Sandringham.

'There he was in some respects content to follow precedent: here he was the
originator,' says a habitué of Balmoral who watched the development of
George VI's meticulous programme of drainage and heather-burning, and his
early experiments with planned drives and placing butts. The grouse became
the focus of the royal holiday.

'The King, as the most enthusiastic shot of them all, would sometimes
arrive for the daily shooting parties on the moors long before the other guns,'
says John Dean.

Prince Charles now has access to another moor of 6,700 acres (2,711
hectares), part of Delnadamph hill land on Upper Deeside, 16 miles north of
Balmoral, acquired by the Queen in 1977. It has added a further dimension to
the Balmoral shoots, which are oases of well-keepered and managed moorland among the general degeneration of the heatherlands in Scotland.

The red grouse finds its natural habitat on the moors and feeds on shoots of heather. Other species on the Scottish estate include blackcock, ptarmigan and capercaillie.

'It is likely that capercaillie, snipe and even grouse would have disappeared entirely from some areas, had it not been for the care and interest shown by those with a personal interest in their survival as quarry species,' says Prince Charles.

Prince Philip, out of sight in a distant butt, insists that the shooting fraternity are the best conservationists, because they look after the wildlife habitats by muirburn – setting fire to strips of old heather to encourage the vigorous young shoots on which the grouse feed – or by looking after the forests of Scots pine which provide needles, shoots and buds for the grouse's hefty cousin the capercaillie. 'The grouse are in absolutely no danger from the people who shoot grouse,' he claims.

'I know what he meant,' said Nickerson. 'But the literal interpretation would also be true of some of the people I have watched.'

Prince Philip has just effortlessly downed two grouse flying high across wind. But he was not always a fine shot. He was introduced to shooting by his royal father-in-law and his valet remembers his early efforts on the grouse moors.

'In the beginning, he made all the mistakes a novice does make, missed his birds, and he often aired his frank opinion of the whole operation to a sympathetic audience in the butt consisting – fortunately – only of a gun dog and me,' says John Dean. Later, Philip instructed the fatherless young Duke of Kent as to how to use the set of guns the King had given him, and introduced his own sons to shooting.

The long wait while the 40 beaters, keepers and flankers beat up to the butts is often a time of contemplation for Prince Charles. But today he itches to exchange the formal driven shoot for walking-up the grouse, tramping over the miles of moorland in the exhilarating openness of the tops, the slopes a pretty patchwork from the effect of planned muirburn, the sweeping panorama to the far hills and the sudden shock as the birds hurtle out from behind a tall clump of heather grating out 'cok-ok-ok'.

'The grouse raised its familiar old cry "go back, go back", unharried for once by the guns which were all employed elsewhere,' Crawfie said of the first autumn season of the Second World War.

Before the war, and the advent of the Land-Rover, a Balmoral visitor remembers how a picturesque post-prandial procession 'would wind diagonally up the hillside to the next drive'. But in these mechanized days, shooting has become an army manoeuvre of four-wheel drive vehicles, and the signal for lunch is likely to be the Queen bumping across the moor at the wheel of the old 1971 gun Land-Rover with the picnic on the back seats, and parking it high up on The Hill beside the royal fleet. That includes a newer 1983 Range-Rover, two Land-Rover station wagons and a 1983 Sherpa four-wheel-drive minibus, as well as the estate vehicles.

'I have a vivid picture of shooting mornings, with the guns assembled in the hall, waiting for their host to join them,' says a fellow shot, who remembers George VI appearing punctually from a conference with his ghillie Gillan and clambering in his Balmoral tweeds onto the waiting bus. 'In one hand would be a long walking stick, in the other, very often, some special article of apparel of his own planning for combating the possible trick of the weather: a cap, a scarf, or some ingenious kind of coat, for he was always a great contriver.'

Such visions of how shooting used to be put a romantic gloss on a sport that not all the participants enjoyed. 'Frankly I loathed all these shooting parties, at which I had to load for Prince Philip,' admits Dean. 'The long walks over the moors made no appeal to me. At Balmoral, I used to leave in the shooting brake with the rest of the loaders around eight-thirty in the morning, and the King and his party would start at nine. From the start we might have to walk a couple of miles over the moors to the line of butts. The King would place the guns, and invariably it would be Philip's misfortune – as I see it – to be sent to the top of the line, with perhaps a hillside climb to make.'

The forty-odd soldiers from the Highland Regiment, dragooned from guarding Balmoral to act as beaters, were in no position to complain to their King, any more than visitors to Victoria and Albert's Balmoral could escape the bracing walks. 'There are no signs of a thaw yet, but the Queen sets us a good example, and we trudge through the snow valiantly,' said Queen Victoria's Home Secretary Lord Aberdare, who reported that on one occasion 'a great golden eagle flapped by us, close to the ground'.

Even in those days of shooting at anything that moved, Prince Albert did

The future Edward VII, in a kilt, shooting grouse in August 1881. He called Balmoral 'a Highland barn of a thousand draughts'.

Prince Edward, like the rest of the family, takes pleasure not just in shooting but in a day out with his dog in the open air.

not have much luck with grouse. 'The birds were shy, but we suspect the "shyness" was on the part of the Prince's sportsmanship,' claimed *Punch* in 1844.

George VI, by contrast, was renowned for his prowess. 'Grouse were plentiful, and the King was such an excellent shot that he seldom missed,' says Dean. 'When he did he would throw his hands in the air in a gesture of annoyance.'

Those post-war shoots were halcyon days, before the royal family was forced to go on the defensive about shooting and explain, with the help of the Game Conservancy, that shooting grouse to keep down numbers is essential to the survival of the species.

'There is no doubt whatsoever that when grouse stocks are high it is absolutely essential to shoot them hard in the interests of the years to come,' said Nickerson, who worked ceaselessly at moor-management, setting up the Joseph Nickerson Heather Improvement Foundation in 1985.

'I happen to believe that man has had such an immense impact on the natural world, and assumed a position of such power, that he now has to manage the situation which he himself has created,' says Charles. 'Some people would no doubt characterize this as interference. Personally, I see it as stewardship – an important duty to be carried out with an eye to both this and future generations.'

Both Charles and his father believe in 'conservation through wise use', as the Game Conservancy's motto puts it. In Scotland, that means looking after the habitat, to ensure the fresh growth of heather and blaeberries; dipping sheep, so that the sheep tick (a problem round Balmoral) does not get passed on to the grouse as the debilitating louping ill virus; and, to keep down the tiny threadworm that affects grouse when the population over-expands, culling especially the older grouse that fly first in the covey. Grouse cannot be reared, like pheasants, and they and the other wild species – some in danger of extinction – need to be controlled to ensure the survival of all.

'Which will generally mean favouring the specialized and the scarce, at the expense of the adaptable and plentiful,' explains Charles.

Controlling the grouse population cannot be left to nature, especially since the grouse are affected not so much by predators, but by decline in habitat. They tend to become diseased when heatherlands are not looked after or are over-grazed by sheep.

'The so-called "balance of nature" is, of course, a great deal more complex than a simple one-to-one relationship between predator and prey,' Prince Philip says.

There has been a wait of half an hour for the next drive. Charles has brought a book, but he finds that he prefers to drink in the stillness, to watch for the sudden erratic movement of sheep in the distance that warns that the beaters are on their way and heralds a grouse covey coming over. There is the occasional buzzard, wings like outspread fingers as it hovers over the peat hags before making an abrupt retreat from the line of butts.

He hopes to spot the more unexpected species: the blackcock with its glossy plumage and striking, fluted tail; the lumbering cock capercaillie ('caper-cailzie' the locals call it), all yellow beak, black head, blue-green breast and black and white barred tail; or the elusive ptarmigan in its full snow-white winter camouflage with just a black stripe behind the eyes.

'Ptarmigan are curiously unreliable and shifting birds,' said John Elphinstone who went on a high climb across Lochnagar with George VI, scrambling over rocks and crags. 'Then at last far below me I saw a single ptarmigan rise very far out in front of the King, who, with an amazingly good shot, hit it very hard indeed, and the bird fell a long way down the steep slope beyond him.' To the King's chagrin, the Master of Elphinstone then spotted more birds camouflaged against a rock, and brought them down.

'Really! I do all the climbing up and down, and all the hard work, and *you* just sit on a rock and shoot five ptarmigan in two shots without moving a yard,' teased King George VI.

The birds have appeared from nowhere. Charles lifts his gun, pointing forward on the parapet of the butt as he picks out one single bird, flying low; a smooth mount onto the shoulder, weight swaying onto the front foot, a brief track, then through and shoot; a surge of adrenalin, a half-turn to the loader, and a second steady aim to take out two birds in the covey behind, angled and streaking fast in the wind across an angry sky. Two down! And the second was a difficult crossing bird, yet it fell straight into the scree, an easy retrieve for the pickers-up.

'The grouse is the most exciting bird,' said Nickerson, citing the bird's speed downwind, its soaring and dipping movements that make it 'the greatest sporting bird in the world'.

Prince Charles has been on memorable shoots with Joe Nickerson, and seen his balletic performance in the butts, dancing about as the grouse fly fast and fall all round him to his graceful, accurate aim.

'You are under test now!' Prince Charles said to Nickerson, when his host had rested one beat for a month in preparation for the royal visit – and then promised a bag of 300 brace.

Nickerson remembers one exceptional grouse shoot in September 1978. 'The Prince of Wales, who shot like a tiger, killed 380 brace in a day,' he says.

On the moors, the quality of the bag has always been more the issue than its size. There is the possibility of counting in rare species beside the red and black grouse – dotterel, snow bunting, ptarmigan and capercaillie, soon to be prohibited for shooting under a Government proposal.

On 3 September 1945, a bad year for grouse, George VI decided to take a Balmoral shooting party out for one day to fill a game card with as many

ABOVE: 'Winged magic' of the grouse whirring above the moor.

RIGHT: The heather-covered moors and open skies offer peace and solitude, as well as recreation for the royal family. Looking after the habitat ensures a fresh growth of blaeberries and heather.

species as possible, fish as well as fowl. This extraordinary obstacle course took his distinguished guests out on the loch in search of sea trout, salmon and mallard, up hill after stag, roe deer and ptarmigan; down dale and through the woods for rabbit and hare, woodcock, partridge, pheasant, pigeon and, finally, a capercaillie.

'While I paused to talk to the policeman who was on duty at the crossroads, I suddenly saw a hen capercaillie sitting on top of a fir tree above us,' said Jack Eldon. 'I shot it and it almost landed on his head, and I have never seen a policeman so surprised as he was, particularly as he had never seen a "caper" before in his life.'

'A lovely day,' wrote George VI in his game book of the Boy Scout adventures which ended at dusk when a woodcock was driven from Balmoral's fir wood and dropped, 'slap into the River Dee', where the keeper's dog finally retrieved it.

A silver platter engraved with the names of the guns and the 19 various species was presented to the King on his next birthday as a memento.

Princess Anne recalls the cornucopia of wildlife at Balmoral in her childhood. 'We would come across red squirrels, roe deer, red deer, black game, capercaillie, buzzards and any number of small birds and wild flowers,' she says.

Prince Charles out on the moors for a day's shoot.

A flurry of larks through the line signifies the end of the final drive. The beaters appear on the horizon, still marching in a straight line, the white flags of the flankers standing out in the fading light.

The guns are climbing down from the butts, grouping together while the dogs finish picking up. Rheumy-eyed spaniels sit wedged between the flankers' knees as Prince Charles and his father thank the keepers and analyse the day's drives.

'The ghillies were grand people and the King, who loved them, addressed them all by their Christian names,' said Dean of the days when the redoubtable Gillan marshalled his team of keepers.

As the shooting party moves away towards the Land-Rovers, Charles lingers behind, looking at the empty butts standing sentinel on the silent moor.

'It was wonderful not seeing a human being, nor hearing a sound, excepting that of the wind, or the call of blackcock or grouse,' Queen Victoria recorded in her *Journal* in September 1848.

The silence is awesome, absolute. There is a grandiose emptiness of landscape as far as the eye can pick out brush-stiff tufts of heather etched against a horizon of light.

'Whenever I am shooting I feel remote from the mundane, but a grouse moor is truly out of this world,' said Joe Nickerson.

EPILOGUE

THE ROYAL year is as fixed as the stars in what Prince Charles calls 'these sweeping East Anglian skies'. January means Sandringham, for the shooting and the stud farm, the season brought to a close by the big cock shoot, the birth of the first foals and the wheezing flu that decimates the household after the damp Norfolk weeks.

Then it is on duty until Easter. February is the month for a royal tour: to New Zealand for the Commonwealth Games in 1990; to Australasia and the Pacific in Jubilee Year 1977; to South East Asia and the Indian Ocean in 1972; to the Caribbean in 1966. Forty years ago, there was the Commonwealth tour when, during a visit to Kenya, Princess Elizabeth was called to the throne by her father's death in February 1952.

Just as the Queen continues to uphold the ideals of the Commonwealth out of a sense of duty and in deference to her father's memory, so she sticks to a rigid royal timetable. She is apparently determined for 'everything to continue exactly as it did under my father', as she told a page on her accession.

This applies as much to private life as public, for the weekends at Windsor, the visit to the Sandringham stud in April, the June Derby and Royal Ascot race meetings all bear sweet family memories, as well as nourishing the Queen's countrified interests which she shares lock, stock and gun barrel with her late father.

The long summer holiday at Balmoral is the most deeply-felt family tradition. It stretches from early August – these days from just after the Queen Mother's 4 August birthday which is celebrated in London – well into the frosty side of October. Then it is back to London for the State Opening of Parliament, for the November Investitures and the reception for the Diplomatic Corps. Late October/early November is also prime time for State Visits, as are April/May, and these months may be used for royal overseas travels. Recently, because of major works at Windsor Castle, the year has ended as it has traditionally begun at Sandringham; otherwise, the move to Norfolk comes after Christmas for the New Year holiday which lasts until the end of January.

The royal year thus pivots on the Queen's personal and public commitments, and the calendar has to be fixed in advance because of the peripatetic nature of her household. It is generally assumed that the royal residences are staffed with posses of servants who have nothing to do for weeks on end until a royal arrival. The reverse is true: each house – Sandringham, Balmoral and Holyroodhouse, Edinburgh (where the Queen holds an official Scottish court each July) – has a nucleus of live-in staff and regular locals who are called in to help when necessary. But the main staff is the permanent one brought from Buckingham Palace to Norfolk or Deeside, as in the Royal Progress of the past.

In keeping up various homes and living between them, the Queen is protecting an endangered way of life which existed as the norm among the nobility in the eighteenth century yet has been gradually eroded by the industrialization and urbanization of England, and by the growth of a more egalitarian society.

The traditional upper-crust weekend, running from Friday or Saturday to Monday, survives more generally, especially in the winter sporting season. The country weekend, as the Duke of Windsor pointed out, was a phenomenon introduced to the landed classes only after the First World War. 'I can recall older people pitying poor So-and-so because he had to go to the City to work, and couldn't hunt for six days a week any more,' he said. 'All he had now was a weekend.'

Those weekends in the country are more or less sacred to the royal family, and both the Queen and Prince Charles are 'off-duty' and on a far-flung estate rather more often than the Queen's subjects realize. Charles will stay (although seldom with his wife) at Chatsworth with the Devonshires, at Broadlands with the Romseys, or at Belvoir Castle with the Duke of Rutland. These visits are mostly for specific hunting or shooting days when the hosts know not to make a royal fuss. The Duke of Marlborough once carried that to extremes by retiring early to bed when Prince Charles was late arriving at Blenheim – leaving only his deaf Spanish housekeeper who failed to hear the royal knock.

Although the Queen and Prince Philip send out invitations to 'dine and sleep' at Windsor, and ask friends to Sandringham and Balmoral, their own stay-away options have been reduced since Lord Mountbatten's murder and the death of 'Master' (the old Duke of Beaufort) have changed the respective regimes at Broadlands and Badminton; and now tragedy has come to Luton Hoo, where Philip's godson Nicky Phillips died in his fume-filled BMW in 1991. The Queen and Philip traditionally spent their wedding anniversary in November at a shooting weekend at Luton Hoo in Bedfordshire, which Nicholas Phillips inherited from his mother Lady Zia Wernher, a cousin and good friend of the Queen.

The Queen Mother's weekend invitations to Royal Lodge, Windsor are legendary, but even she finds it harder these days to get aristocratic bed and board. For her annual visit to France, potential hosts are increasingly reluctant or unable to entertain her and an entourage of fourteen, so that in 1991, she was obliged to follow in Queen Victoria's carriage-wheel tracks by staying at a Grand Hotel. The Queen's private visits abroad are focused on the studs in Kentucky (staying with the Farishes) or Normandy, where she can stay with the trainer Alec Head. Charles lodges abroad in Italy with noble families in Florence, or in France in Provence. Both he and his mother prefer to scale down the grandeur, which is why the Queen demolished a wing of 90 rooms at Sandringham and why both often stay at Wood Farm on the Norfolk Estate, rather than in the big house.

Will the number and scale of royal retreats be reduced by the next generation? The Queen Mother is said to have destined Birkhall (which belongs to the Queen) for Charles. Yet this would leave Princess Margaret (who was born in Scotland and loves the place more than the public realize) out in the cold; her children Lady Sarah Armstrong-Jones and Viscount Linley (also Scottish devotees) could perhaps have the use of Craigowan Lodge where Charles and Diana often stay. But the extended royal family of the next generation – William and Harry, the Yorks' girls (and perhaps Prince Edward's family yet to come) – will make the logistics increasingly difficult. Already the Christmas move from Windsor to smaller Sandringham House has meant excluding some royal relations.

Queen Victoria's children mostly left home for the palaces of Europe. Even in more recent times, royal progeny would set up their own grand establishments. Now, although the Queen bought Gatcombe Park for Anne, neither the Kents nor the Gloucesters have the means to invest in new estates. Unless they marry into the landed aristocracy, most of the Queen's grandchildren are going to find themselves living in relatively modest circumstances.

The traditional pattern of country weekends is also changing with a new generation, now that all the royal children go to regular school. Whereas the Kensington Palace staff on weekend rota duty at Highgrove load up the estate car on Friday morning, somebody (usually Diana) waits until Harry finishes school or to arrange William's brief weekends out from prep school. And, as Anne, the Princess Royal says, the lengthy Sandringham New Year holiday of her childhood (when she and Charles had a private governess) is now curtailed by the start of the new school term.

However, the psychological importance of the country as an escape from the royal goldfish bowl into an ocean of solitude is likely to continue. Charles expresses a fierce love for Scotland, which suggests that the Balmoral bloodline has descended directly from his mother and grandfather.

Of the many vivid vignettes given to me about the Queen, the most arresting is the description of *Britannia* berthing in some inaccessible inlet on its way north at the start of the Scottish holiday: a determined figure scrambles up the cliff, strides through a waist-high undergrowth of ferns, to reach a distant hilltop. It is an image of the Queen contrary to how her subjects see her, always surrounded by crowds; and a symbol of her insistence on getting away from royal duty and separating public and private lives.

'From the time that the Western Isles cruise is set, a portcullis comes down,' says a member of the household. 'Nothing disturbs the privacy, barely even the visit from the Prime Minister.'

The Queen's absolute refusal to break into 'private time', and a rigid adherence to unwritten rules about when she is on and off-duty, is beginning to be questioned by the public, which failed to see why the Queen could not respond to national tragedies such as the Lockerbie plane crash or the Clapham rail disaster.

If the Queen were to retreat behind castle walls into a life of cosseted luxury, she might risk the public opprobrium that came after Queen Victoria's long indulgence in mourning. Yet although the Queen is an enormously wealthy landowner, her pleasure in the great estates obviously lies very close to the soil. Her subjects can see that written on her face – so solemn when undertaking public duties and so illuminated with enthusiasm among gun dogs and muddy fields. It is not an affectation to suggest that the Queen would happily turn her back on pomp and palaces and retire to a sprawling house in the country – had she not resolved in 1952 to follow her father's 'shining example of service and devotion'.

Likewise Prince Charles, who is so anxious about the world, but so relaxed in the saddle or with a gun or rod in his hand. Working on this book has made me see that Charles is more like his mother than is generally realized. His ecological and environmental causes are taken up not from a romantic urban perspective, but from deep conviction. He is a countryman through and through, even if he happens to live in one palace and be destined for another. He himself puts his public and private lives in perspective when he says 'I have a house in London – at Highgrove I have a home.'

ROYAL PATRONAGE OF 'GREEN' INTERESTS

HM The Queen

AGRICULTURAL

Agricultural Benevolent Institution, Royal (Patron)
Agricultural College, Royal (Patron)
Agricultural Society of England, Royal (Patron)
Association of British Dairy Farmers, Royal (Patron)
Ayrshire Cattle Society of Great Britain and Ireland (Patron)
Bath and West of England Society, Royal (Patron)
Birmingham Agricultural Exhibition Society (Patron)
British Goat Society (Patron)
Cornwall Agricultural Association, Royal (Patron)
Council for the Protection of Rural England (Patron)
Devon County Agricultural Association (Patron)
East Berks Agricultural Association, Royal (Patron)
Farmers' Club (Patron)
Guernsey Agricultural and Horticultural Society, Royal (Patron)
Highland and Agricultural Society of Scotland, Royal (Patron)
Highland Cattle Society (Patron)
Jersey Agricultural and Horticultural Society, Royal (Patron)
Jersey Cattle Society of the United Kingdom (Patron, and President 1992/93)
Lancashire Agricultural Society, Royal (Patron)
National Dairymen's Benevolent Institution Inc (Patron)
National Federation of Young Farmers' Clubs (Patron)
National Institute of Agricultural Botany (Patron)
National Pig Breeders' Association (Patron)
Norfolk Agricultural Association, Royal (Patron)
Norfolk Island Agricultural and Horticultural Society (Patron)
Northern Agricultural Society, Royal (Patron)
Red Poll Cattle Society (Patron)
Scottish Agricultural Benevolent Institution, Royal (Patron)
Scottish Forestry Society, Royal (Patron)
Scottish National Fat Stock Club (Patron)
Shorthorn Society of the United Kingdom of Great Britain and Ireland (Patron)
Smithfield Club, Royal (Patron)
South Bucks Agricultural Association, Royal (Patron)
South of England Agricultural Society (Patron)
Welsh Agricultural Society, Royal (Patron)
Yorkshire Agricultural Society (Patron)

HORTICULTURAL

Ballater Royal Horticultural Society (Patron)
Botanical and Horticultural Society of Manchester and the Northern Counties, Royal (Patron)
Guernsey Agricultural and Horticultural Society, Royal (Patron)
Horticultural Society, Royal (Patron)
Horticultural Society of Aberdeen, Royal (Patron)
Horticultural Society of Perthshire, Royal (Patron)
Jersey Agricultural and Horticultural Society, Royal (Patron)
King's Lynn Horticultural Society (Patron)
Norfolk and Norwich Horticultural Society (Patron)
Norfolk Island Agricultural and Horticultural Society (Patron)
Sandringham Estate Cottage Horticultural Society (Patron)

Windsor Rose and Horticultural Society, Royal (Patron)
Windsor and Slough Chrysanthemum, Fuchsia and Pelargonium Society (Patron)

FORESTRY

Commonwealth Forestry Association (Patron)
Forestry Society of England, Wales and Northern Ireland, Royal (Patron)
Scottish Forestry Society, Royal (Patron)

ORNITHOLOGICAL

Pigeon Racing Association (Patron)
Society for the Protection of Birds, Royal (Patron)
Wildfowl and Wetlands Trust (Patron)

CANINE

Dogs' Home Battersea (Patron)
Garth and South Berks Hunt Club (Patron)
Kennel Club (Patron)
Labrador Retriever Club (Patron)
National Canine Defence League (Patron)
Peterborough Royal Foxhound Show Society (Patron)
Two Bridges Hunt Club (Patron)
Windsor Championship Dog Show (Patron)
Yellow Labrador Club (Patron)

EQUESTRIAN

Ashbourne Shire Horse Society (Patron)
British Horse Society (Patron)
British Show Jumping Association (Patron)
Caledonian Hunt, Royal (Patron)
Cleveland Bay Horse Society (Patron)
Epsom Club Stand (Honorary Member)
Fakenham Races (Patron)
Fell Pony Society (Patron)
Garth and South Berks Hunt Club (Patron)
Highland Pony Society (Patron)
Hunt Servants' Benefit Society (Patron)
Jockey Club (Patron)
National Horseracing Museum (Patron)
National Light Horse Breeding Society (Patron)
Naval Equestrian Association, Royal (Patron)
New Zealand Thoroughbred Breeders' Assocation (Inc) (Patron)
Pegasus Club (Patron)
Rotten Row 300 (Patron)
Shire Horse Society (Patron)
Thoroughbred Breeders' Association (Patron)
Two Bridges Hunt Club (Patron)
Victorian Racing Museum (Patron)
Welsh Pony and Cob Society (Patron)
Windsor Horse Show, Royal (Patron)

HRH The Duke of Edinburgh

AGRICULTURAL

Agricultural Society of the Commonwealth, Royal (President)
Agricultural Society of England, Royal (Trustee)
Asda Festival of British Food and Farming (Patron)
Association of British Dairy Farmers, Royal (Honorary Life Member)
Bath and West of England Society, Royal (Vice President)
Commanderie du Bontemps de Médoc et des Graves (Commander of Honour)
Egham and Thorpe Royal Agricultural and Horticultural Association (Patron)
Forest Agricultural Association, Royal (Patron)
Highland and Agricultural Society of Scotland, Royal (Honorary Member)
Highland Fund (Patron)
Scottish Forestry Society, Royal (Honorary Member)
Smithfield Club, Royal (Vice President)
Society of Dairy Technology (Patron)
Welsh Beekeepers' Association (Honorary Member)
Windsor Great Park (Ranger)

ENVIRONMENTAL

1001: A Nature Trust (Member)
Anglers' Co-operative Association (Patron)
British Association for Shooting and Conservation (Patron)
Cumbria Wildlife Trust (Life Member)
Fondation de la Faune du Quebec (Honorary Life Member)
Friends of the Serengeti (Friend)
Game Conservancy Trust (Patron and Life Member)
International Union for Conservation of Nature and Natural Resources (Vice President)
South Saskatchewan Wildlife Association (Honorary Life Member)
World Wide Fund for Nature International (President)
Yosemite Natural History Association (Honorary Life Member)

ORNITHOLOGICAL

Australasian Ornithologists Union, Royal (Patron)
British Association for Shooting and Conservation (Patron)
British Falconers' Club (Honorary Member)
British Trust for Ornithology (Patron)
Cornell University Laboratory of Ornithology (Member)
20th International Ornithological Congress (Patron)
International Council for Bird Preservation Rare Bird Club (Honorary Member)

Naval Bird Watching Society, Royal (Patron)
Pensthorpe Waterfowl Trust (Founder Patron)

EQUESTRIAN

American Horse Shows Association (Honorary Life Member)
Australian Driving Society (Patron)
Bibury Club (Member)
British Driving Society (Patron)
British Equestrian Centre (Founder Member)
British Horse Society (Honorary Member)
Calcutta Polo Club (Honorary Life Member)
Canadian Cutting Horse Association (Patron)
Canberra Polo Club (Honorary Life Member)
Circolo della Caccia (Honorary Member)
Coaching Club (Member)
Coachmakers Driving Awards Committee (Member)
Cowdray Park Polo Club (Honorary Member)
Epsom Club Stand (Honorary Member)
Guards Polo Club (President)
Ham Polo Club (Honorary Member)
Hawaii Polo Club at Mokuleia (Honorary Member)
Household Division Saddle Club (Member)
Hurlingham Polo Association (Patron)
Jockey Club (Honorary Member)
Jockey Club of France (Membre Permanent)
Ligue Française pour la Protection du Cheval (Honorary Member)
Marines Saddle Club, Royal (Honorary Life Member)
Modern Pentathlon Association of Great Britain (Patron)
National Horse Driving Championships (President)
Naval Equestrian Association, Royal (Life Member)
Newbury Race Club (Member)
Northern Country Fair and Horse Show (Patron)
Pittsford Carriage Association (Life Member)
Sandringham Driving Trials (President)
Scottish Horse Driving Trials (President)
Singapore Polo Club (Honorary Life Member)
Società Milanese Redini Lunghe (Honorary Member)
Société d'Encouragement pour l'Amélioration des Race de Chevaux en France (Honorary Member of Committee)
South African Polo Association (Patron)
Stoke Mandeville Finmere Show (Patron)
Turf Club (Honorary Member)
Windsor Driving Championships (President)
Windsor Park Equestrian Club (President)
Worshipful Company of Coachmakers and Coach Harness Makers (Liveryman)

HRH *The Prince of Wales*

AGRICULTURAL

Agricultural College, Royal (President)
Agricultural Society of England, Royal (President)
Bath and West of England Society, Royal (Vice President)
College of Estate Management (President)
Launceston Agricultural Association (Patron)
Mid-Somerset Agricultural Society (Patron)
Norfolk Club (Honorary Member)
Worshipful Company of Farmers (Honorary Liveryman)

HORTICULTURAL

Botanic Gardens Conservation Secretariat (Patron)
Chelsea Physic Garden (Honorary Fellow)
Cornwall Garden Society (Patron)
Garden Festival Wales (Joint Patron)
Garden Society (Honorary Member)
Gloucestershire Root, Fruit and Grain Society (Patron)
Incorporation of Gardeners of Glasgow (Honorary Member)
Museum of Garden History: The Tradescant Trust (Patron)
National Council for the Conservation of Plants and Gardens (National Collection Holder)
National Trust 1990 Trees and Gardens Storm Disaster Appeal (Patron)
Oxford Botanic Garden (Patron)
Worshipful Company of Fruiterers (Honorary Liveryman)
Worshipful Company of Gardeners (Liveryman)

ENVIRONMENTAL

Blue Seal Club (Member)
British Association for Shooting and Conservation (Honorary Member)
British Deer Society (Patron)
Brunei Rainforest Project (Patron)
Conservation Trust (Honorary Member)
Cornwall Crafts Association (President)
Country Gentlemen's Association (Member)
Forestry Society of England, Wales and Northern Ireland, Royal (Honorary Member)
Friends of Conservation (Patron)
Game Conservancy Trust (Member)
Geographical Society, Royal (Honorary Member)
Institute of Water and Environmental Management (Honorary Fellow)

Isles of Scilly Environmental Trust (Patron)
London Cornish Association (Vice Patron)
Maraca Rainforest Project (Patron)
Marine Conservation Society (President)
Men of the Trees (Patron)
Meteorological Society (Fellow)
National Rifle Association (President)
National Trust's Wales Coastline Appeal (Patron)
National Waterways Museum (President)
Painshill Park Trust (Patron)
Rare Breeds Survival Trust (Patron)
Scottish Wildlife Trust (Patron)
Society for Nature Conservation, Royal (Patron)
Water Aid (President)

ORNITHOLOGICAL AND ANGLING

Atlantic Salmon Trust (Patron)
Exeter and District Angling Association (Life Member)
Flyfishers' Club (Patron)
National Anglers' Council (Patron)
Naval Bird Watching Society, Royal (President and Life Member)
Taupo International Fishermen's Club (Member)

EQUESTRIAN

Amateur Riders Association of Great Britain (Honorary Member)
Australian Stock Horse Society (Patron)
British Equestrian Centre (Honorary Founder Member)
British Horse Society (Founder Member)
Dartmoor Pony Society (Honorary Member)
High Peak Hunt (Honorary Member)
Hunt Servants' Benefit Society (Governor)
Jockey Club (Honorary Member)
National Steeplechase and Hunt Association (Honorary Member)
Tarporley Hunt Club (Patron)
Turf Club (Honorary Member)

GENERAL

Institute of Painters in Watercolours, Royal (Honorary Member)
Society of Painters in Water-Colours, Royal (Honorary Member)
Turner Society (Patron)
Zoological Society of London (Associate Member)

DUCHY OF CORNWALL ESTATES

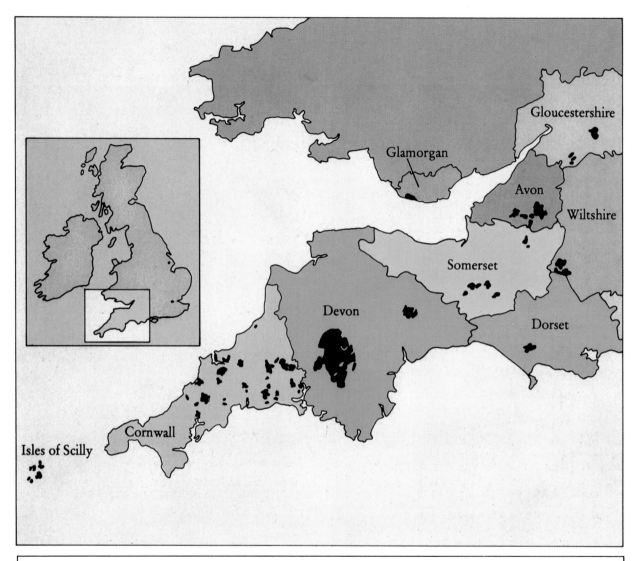

The Duchy of Cornwall is a landed estate of approximately
128,000 acres spread over twenty-two counties. The extent and distribution
of the major holdings at 31 December 1990 were as follows:

County	Acreage
Devon	72,492
Cornwall: Mainland	21,253
Isles of Scilly	3,978
Avon	8,903
Somerset	7,718
Wiltshire	3,763
Dorset	3,460
Gloucestershire	2,025
Lincolnshire	1,936
Hereford & Worcester	1,927
Cambridgeshire	1,185
South Glamorgan	712
Nottinghamshire	714
London	35

BIBLIOGRAPHY

ALICE, Princess, Countess of Athlone: *For My Grandchildren*, Evans Brothers, 1966

AMIES, Hardy: *Still Here, An Autobiography*, Weidenfeld & Nicolson, 1984

ASQUITH, Lady Cynthia: *The Family Life of Queen Elizabeth*, Hutchinson, 1937

ASQUITH, Lady Cynthia: *The King's Daughters*, Hutchinson, 1937

ASQUITH, Lady Cynthia: *The Queen*, Hutchinson

ASQUITH, Lady Cynthia: *Queen Elizabeth*, Hutchinson

BARRY, Stephen P.: *Royal Service*, Avon Books, New York, 1983

BELLAMY, David and LYON, Marjorie: *The Queen's Hidden Garden*, David & Charles, 1984

BENNETT, Daphne: *King Without a Crown*, William Heinemann, 1977

BRADFORD, Sarah: *King George VI*, Weidenfeld & Nicolson, 1989

BURNET, Alistair: *In Person, The Prince and Princess of Wales*, Independent Television News Ltd, 1985

BURNET, Alastair: *In Private in Public, The Prince and Princess of Wales*, Guild Publishing, 1986

BUXTON, Aubrey: *The King in His Country*, Longmans, Green & Co, 1955

CAESAR: *Where's Master?*, Hodder & Stoughton, 1910

CATHCART, Helen: *Sandringham*, W. H. Allen, 1964

CATHCART, Helen: *The Royal Lodge, Windsor*, W. H. Allen, 1966

CATHCART, Helen: *The Royal Bedside Book*, W. H. Allen, 1969

CATHCART, Helen: *The Married Life of the Queen*, W. H. Allen, 1970

CAYZER, Beatrice: *The Royal World of Animals*, Sidgwick & Jackson, 1989

CHANCE, Michael: *Our Princesses and Their Dogs*, John Murray, 1936

CLARK, Ronald W.: *Balmoral, Queen Victoria's Highland Home*, Thames & Hudson, 1981

COATS, Peter: *The Gardens of Buckingham Palace*, Michael Joseph, 1978

COATS, Peter: *Of Kings and Cabbages*, Weidenfeld & Nicolson, 1984

COOPER, Lady Diana: *The Light of Common Day*, Rupert Hart-Davis, 1959

COURTNEY, Nicholas: *Sporting Royals*, Stanley Paul, 1983

CRAWFORD, Marion: *The Little Princesses*, Cassell, 1950

CRAWFORD, Marion: *The Queen Mother*, George Newnes, 1951

CRAWFORD, Marion: *Princess Margaret*, George Newnes, 1953

CRAWFORD, Marion: *Happy and Glorious!*, George Newnes

DALY, Macdonald: *Royal Dogs*, W. H. Allen

DEAN, John: *HRH Prince Philip Duke of Edinburgh*, Robert Hale, 1963

DEVONSHIRE, The Duchess of: *The Estate, A View from Chatsworth*, Macmillan, 1990

DONALDSON, Frances: *Edward VIII*, Weidenfeld & Nicolson, 1974

DUFF, David: *Whisper Louise*, Frederick Muller, 1974

EDGAR, Donald: *Happy and Glorious, The Silver Jubilee 1977*, Arthur Barker, 1977

EDGAR, Donald: *The Royal Parks*, W. H. Allen, 1986

EDINBURGH, HRH The Duke of: *Living Off the Land*, BBC Books, 1989

EVERINGHAM, Barry: *MC, The Adventures of a Maverick Princess*, Bantam Press, 1985

FAUCIGNY-LUCINGE, Jean-Louis: *Un Gentilhomme Cosmopolite*, Perrin (Paris), 1990

FISHER, Graham and Heather: *Bertie and Alix*, Robert Hale, 1974

FISHER, Graham and Heather: *The Queen's Life*, Robert Hale, 1976

FULFORD, Roger: *The Prince Consort*, Macmillan, 1966

GILL, Crispin (Ed): *The Duchy of Cornwall*, David & Charles, 1987

GLENTON, Robert and KING, Stella: *Once Upon a Time, The Story of Antony Armstrong-Jones*, Anthony Blond, 1960

HALL, Unity and SEWARD, Ingrid: *By Royal Invitation*, Sidgwick & Jackson, 1988

HAMILTON, Alan: *The Real Charles*, Collins, 1988

HARRIS, Paul: *By Appointment, The Story in Pictures of Royal Deeside and Balmoral*, Archive Publications, 1988

HARTNELL, Norman: *Silver and Gold*, Evans Brothers, 1955

HASTINGS, Max: *Outside Days*, Michael Joseph, 1989

HEALD, Tim: *The Duke*, Hodder & Stoughton, 1991

HOEY, Brian: *Invitation to the Palace*, Grafton Books, 1989

HOEY, Brian: *The New Royal Court*, Sidgwick & Jackson, 1990

HOEY, Brian: *Anne, The Princess Royal*, Grafton Books, 1990

HOLDEN, Anthony: *Charles*, Weidenfeld & Nicolson, 1979

JAMES, Paul: *Anne, The Working Princess*, Pan Books, 1988

JENCKS, Charles: *The Prince, the Architects and New Wave Monarchy*, Academy Editions, 1988

JUNOR, Penny, *Charles*, Sidgwick & Jackson, 1987

LACEY, Robert: *Majesty*, Hutchinson, 1977

LACEY, Robert: *God Bless Her!*, Century, 1987

LEMOINE, Serge and FORBES, Grania: *The Sporting Royal Family*, Queen Anne Press, 1982

LICHFIELD, Patrick: *A Royal Album*, Elm Tree Books, 1982

LONGFORD, Elizabeth: *Victoria RI*, Weidenfeld & Nicolson, 1964

LONGFORD, Elizabeth: *Elizabeth R*, Weidenfeld & Nicolson, 1983

McKEE, Mrs: *The Royal Cookery Book*, Arlington Books, 1964

MACKENZIE, Compton: *The Queen's House*, Hutchinson, 1953

MARIE-LOUISE, HH Princess: *My Memories of Six Reigns*, Evans Brothers, 1956

MARTIN, Ralph G.: *Charles and Diana*, Grafton Books, 1986

MATHESON, Anne and DAVIS, Reginald: *Princess Anne*, Frederick Muller, 1973

MILLAR, Delia: *Queen Victoria's Life in the Scottish Highlands*, Philip Wilson Publishers, 1985

MORRAH, Dermot: *Princess Elizabeth, Duchess of Edinburgh*, Odhams Press, 1950

MORROW, Ann: *The Queen*, Granada, 1983

MORROW, Ann: *The Queen Mother*, Granada, 1984

MORTON, Andrew: *Inside Kensington Palace*, Michael O'Mara Books, 1987

MORTON, Andrew: *Theirs is the Kingdom*, Michael O'Mara Books, 1989

MORTON, Andrew: *Diana's Diary*, Michael O'Mara Books, 1990

NICKOLLS, L. A.: *Our Sovereign Lady*, Macdonald, 1956

NICOLSON, Harold: *King George the Fifth*, Constable, 1952

NICOLSON, Harold: *Diaries and Letters, 1930–1939*, Collins, 1966

PAGE, Robin: *The Wildlife of the Royal Estates*, Hodder & Stoughton, 1984

PARKER, John: *Prince Philip, A Critical Biography*, Sidgwick & Jackson, 1990

PEACOCK, Lady: *The Queen and Her Children*, Hutchinson, 1955

PEACOCK, Lady: *TRH Prince Charles and Princess Anne*, Hutchinson, 1955

PHILIP, HRH Prince: *Down to Earth*, Collins, 1988

PLUMPTRE, George: *Royal Gardens*, Collins, 1981

PONSONBY, Sir Frederick: *Recollections of Three Reigns*, Eyre & Spottiswoode, 1951

POPE-HENNESSY, James: *Queen Mary*, George Allen & Unwin, 1959

PRANCE, Ghillean: *The Rainforest, A Celebration*, Barrie & Jenkins, 1989

RHODES-JAMES, Robert: *Albert, Prince Consort*, Hamish Hamilton, 1983
RICHARDS, Clive: *The Queen Mother and Family at Home in Caithness*, North of Scotland Newspapers Ltd, 1990
RING, Anne: *The Story of Princess Elizabeth and Princess Margaret*, John Murray, 1930
ROBERTS, Jane: *Royal Artists*, Grafton Books, 1987
ROBYNS, Gwen: *Royal Sporting Lives*, Elm Tree Books, 1971
ROPER, Lanning: *Royal Gardens*, W. H. & L. Collingridge Ltd, 1953
ROPER, Lanning: *The Gardens in the Royal Park at Windsor*, Chatto & Windus, 1959
ROSE, Kenneth: *King George V*, Weidenfeld & Nicolson, 1983
SALISBURY, The Marchioness of: *The Gardens of Queen Elizabeth the Queen Mother*, Viking, 1988
SAVILLE, Margaret: *HM Queen Elizabeth the Queen Mother*, Pitkin
SEWARD, Ingrid: *Diana*, Weidenfeld & Nicolson, 1988
SHERIDAN, Lisa: *The Queen and Her Children*, John Murray, 1953
SHERIDAN, Lisa: *From Cabbages to Kings*, Odhams Press, 1955
SHERIDAN, Lisa: *A Day with Prince Andrew*, Hodder & Stoughton, 1962
SHEWELL-COOPER, W. E.: *The Royal Gardeners*, Cassell, 1952
SUTHERLAND, Douglas and PURDY, Anthony: *The Royal Homes and Gardens*, Leslie Frewin, 1966
TALBOT, Godfrey: *Queen Elizabeth the Queen Mother*, Country Life Books, 1989
TOWERS, Frances: *The Two Princesses*, The Pilgrim Press
VEREY, Rosemary: *A Countrywoman's Notes*, Gryffon Publications, 1989
WAKEFORD, Geoffrey: *His Royal Highness Charles Prince of Wales*, Associated Newspapers Ltd, 1962
WALES, HRH The Prince of: *The Old Man of Lochnagar*, Hamish Hamilton, 1980
WALES, HRH The Prince of: *A Vision of Britain*, Doubleday, 1989
WALES, HRH The Prince of: *An Exhibition of Watercolour Sketches By*, Anna Hunter and Guy Thompson Art Publishers, 1991
WALES, HRH The Prince of: *Watercolours*, Little, Brown & Co, 1991
WARD, Cyril: *Royal Gardens*, Longmans, Green & Co, 1912
WARNER, Marina: *Queen Victoria's Sketchbook*, Crown Publishers, 1979
WENTWORTH-DAY, J.: *HRH Princess Marina Duchess of Kent*, Robert Hale, 1962
WHEELER-BENNETT, John W.: *King George VI*, Macmillan, 1958
WHITLOCK, Ralph: *Royal Farmers*, Michael Joseph, 1980
WINDSOR, The Duchess of: *The Heart has its Reasons*, Michael Joseph, 1956
WINDSOR, The Duke of: *A King's Story*, G. P. Putnam & Sons, 1947
WINDSOR, The Duke of: *A Family Album*, Cassell, 1960
WINN, Godfrey: *HRH Princess Margaret, The Younger Sister*, Hutchinson, 1951
WINN, Godfrey: *The Young Queen*, Hutchinson, 1952
WULFF, Louis: *Queen of To-morrow*, Sampson Low, Marston & Co, 1946

HORSES: BREEDING, DRIVING, HUNTING, RACING, RIDING

BEAUFORT, The Duke of: *Fox Hunting*, David & Charles, 1980
CAMPBELL, Judith: *The Queen Rides*, Lutterworth Press, 1965
CAMPBELL, Judith: *Royal Horses*, New English Library, 1983
CLAYTON, Michael: *The Chase*, Stanley Paul, 1987
CLAYTON, Michael: *Prince Charles, Horseman*, Stanley Paul, 1987
CRANHAM, Gerry and PITMAN, Richard: *The Guinness Book of Steeplechasing*, Guinness Publishing Ltd, 1988
EDINBURGH, HRH The Duke of: *Competition Carriage Driving*, Horse Drawn Carriages Ltd, 1982
FITZGERALD, Arthur: *Royal Thoroughbreds*, Sidgwick & Jackson, 1990
MEADS, Jim: *They Will Always Meet at Eleven*, Quiller Press, 1991
MITCHELL, Charles: *The Queen's Horses*, Macdonald, 1955
MORRIS, Tony and RANDALL, John: *Horse Racing*, Guinness Publishing Ltd, 1990
MURPHY, Genevieve: *Princess Anne and Mark Phillips – Talking About Horses*, Stanley Paul, 1976
MURRAY SMITH, Ulrica: *Magic of the Quorn*, J. A. Allen & Company Ltd, 1980
PRINCESS ROYAL, The (with Ivor Herbert): *Riding Through My Life*, Pelham Books, 1991
STEWART-WILSON, Mary: *The Royal Mews*, The Bodley Head, 1991
TANNER, Michael: *The Major*, Pelham Books, 1991
YUILL WALKER, Alan: *Thoroughbred Studs of Great Britain*, Weidenfeld & Nicolson, 1991

SHOOTING/FISHING

BARNES, Mike: *The Game Shot*, The Crowood Press, 1988
COLES, Charles (Ed): *Shooting and Stalking*, Stanley Paul, 1983
HEATH, Veronica: *A Dog at Heel*, The Boydell Press, 1987
JACKSON, Tony: *Classic Game Shooting*, Ashford Southampton, 1990
LITTLE, Crawford: *Pheasant Shooting*, Unwin Hyman Ltd, 1989
LITTLE, Crawford: *The Great Salmon Beats*, David & Charles, 1989
MARTIN, Brian P.: *The Great Shots*, David & Charles, 1987
MARTIN, Brian P.: *Tales of the Old Gamekeepers*, David & Charles, 1989
NICKERSON, Joseph: *A Shooting Man's Creed*, Sidgwick & Jackson, 1989
RUFFER, Jonathan: *The Big Shots*, Quiller Press, 1977
SMITH, Guy N.: *Gamekeeping and Shooting for Amateurs*, The Boydell Press, 1976
SWAN, Mike: *Fowling for Duck*, The Crowood Press, 1988

PHOTO CREDITS

SOURCES AND NOTES

Hunting

I am indebted to Michael Clayton, Editor of *Horse and Hound*, for generous permission to ferret in the *H & H* bound volumes and photographic archives. This chapter also draws on Clayton's excellent books *The Chase* and *Prince Charles, Horseman*. Grateful thanks also to Brian Toon of the MFH Association, and for much off-the-record help, especially from members of the Beaufort, the Quorn and the VWH.

Page 3

'It was ironic . . .': Barry, Stephen, *Royal Service*, p.125
'It was my impulse . . .': Windsor, Duke of, *A Family Album*, p.105
'string of hunters': Windsor, Duke of, *A King's Story*, p.194
'Since the beginning . . .': Oaksey, Lord, *Horse and Hound*, 24 July 1981
'Pronounced "Beaver"': Windsor, *A King's Story*, p.195
'The magic of Leicestershire . . .': Prince of Wales, Foreword to *Magic of the Quorn*

Page 4

'Dominant Passion': Barry, *Royal Service*, p.260

Page 5

'His Royal Highness . . .': Beaufort, Duke of, *Horse and Hound*, 28 February 1975
'Princess Anne is a very good judge . . .': Clayton, Michael, *Prince Charles, Horseman*, p.77
'I really like hunting for the view . . .': Princess Anne in *Country Living*, July 1991
luxurious white carpets: Murray Smith, Ulrica, *Magic of the Quorn*, p.4
'Intermixed with the local . . .': Windsor, *A King's Story*, p.195
'Craven Lodge had been madly gay . . .': Murray Smith, *Magic of the Quorn*, p.2

Page 6

'The night air . . .': Clayton, Michael, *The Chase*, p.28
'You don't think it will . . .': Clayton, *Prince Charles, Horseman*, p.104
'She doesn't like horses . . .': Barry, *Royal Service*, p.260
'Sarah's as keen as mustard . . .': to author, 13 November 1991
'Horses, horses! . . .': Cayzer, Beatrice, *The Royal World of Animals*, p.134
'Derbyshire is wonderful . . .': Duchess of Devonshire to author, 13 July 1990
'In the early days . . .': Barry, *Royal Service*, p.58
'Gentlemen wore scarlet . . .': Murray Smith, *Magic of the Quorn*, p.3

Page 7

'Nowadays there are new materials . . .': Beaufort, Duke of, *Fox-Hunting*, p.199
'Princess Anne was the first . . .': ibid, p.196
'She adores hunting . . .': to author, 3 May 1990
'Very picturesque': Fulford, Roger, *The Prince Consort*, p.92
'Like some foreign tenor': Windsor, *A Family Album*, p.31
'Riding like an old hand': Bennett, Daphne, *King Without a Crown*, p.32

Page 8

'My riding boots . . .': Windsor, *A Family Album*, p.125
'The light blue watered-silk . . .': ibid, p.117
'Please, not "pink" . . .': Beaufort, *Fox-Hunting*, p.201
'There are paintings of the King . . .': Windsor, *A Family Album*, p.16

Page 9

'I selected some of my . . .': ibid, p.125
'He has no hunting clothes . . .': Beaufort, *Horse and Hound*, 28 February 1975
'Hello, been rat-catching?': Windsor, *A Family Album*, p.57
'Clothes are part of the ritual': to the author, 3 May 1990

Page 10

'The Prince of Wales always wore . . .': Murray-Smith, *Magic of the Quorn*, p5
'Prince Charles was . . .': Clayton, *Prince Charles, Horseman*, p.85
'What is dangerous? . . .': Prince Philip, *Competition Carriage Driving*, p.109
'He won't hurt himself . . .': Courtney, Nicholas, *Sporting Royals*, p.22
'We were all taught to ride . . .': Windsor, *A King's Story*, p.45
'She rides and goes well . . .': Cayzer, *The Royal World of Animals*, p.61
'I must tell you the tragic news . . .': Clayton, *Prince Charles, Horseman*, p.16
'The Princess Elizabeth . . .': Courtney, *Sporting Royals*, p.23

Page 11

'Hounds had not been long . . .': Clayton, *Prince Charles, Horseman*, p.16
village decked out: Cathcart, Helen, *Sandringham*, p.77
'A characteristic reception . . .': Duff, David, *Whisper Louise*, p.72
'I hoped the poor fox . . .': Cayzer, *The Royal World of Animals*, p.23

'I was taken to a meet there . . .': Clayton, *Prince Charles, Horseman*, p.72
'Harry's the one . . .': to the author, 11 June 1991
'T'ain't the red coat . . .': Beaufort, *Fox-Hunting*, p.200

Page 12

'The Prince of Wales gate': Clayton, *Prince Charles, Horseman*, p.104
'two hundred carriages . . .': Cathcart, *Sandringham*, p.77

Page 13

'I have met more farmers . . .': Prince of Wales, speech to MFA 1981
'He has a friendly word . . .': Murray Smith, *Magic of the Quorn*, p.87
'Because my official life . . .': Windsor, *A King's Story*, p.194

Page 14

'Not as though I were a prince . . .': Windsor, *A Family Album*, p.92
'Like most of the Prince's friends . . .': Barry, *Royal Service*, p.211
'I can still hear Harold . . .': Murray Smith, *Magic of the Quorn*, p.93
'no one seems happier . . .': ibid, p.86
'How many recollections . . .': Rhodes-James, Robert, *Albert, Prince Consort*, p.149

Page 15

'One of the most intelligent . . .': Cayzer, *The Royal World of Animals*, pp.129–30
'Made or marred': Beaufort, *Fox-Hunting*, p.68
'The late Duke of Gloucester . . .': Murray Smith, *Magic of the Quorn*, p.18
'It really thrilled me . . .': Oaksey, *Horse and Hound*, 24 July 1981
'When you first visit . . .': Prince of Wales, Foreword to *Magic of the Quorn*
'The only difficulty . . .': ibid
'I have been one of six . . .': Windsor, *A King's Story*, p.195

Page 16

'It is like the start of . . .': Clayton, *Prince Charles, Horseman*, p.87
'Push on . . . barge': ibid, p.87
'My view is that . . .': Prince of Wales, Foreword to *Magic of the Quorn*

Page 17

'Why doesn't my son . . .': Cayzer, *The Royal World of Animals*, p.46

215

'Strong workmanlike hands . . .': Hoey, Brian, *Anne, The Princess Royal*, p.16
'To be able to go . . .': Courtney, *Sporting Royals*, p.22
'You wouldn't mind . . .': Clayton, *Prince Charles, Horseman*, p.125
'Had I been of a studious . . .': Windsor, *A King's Story*, p.196

Page 18

'That flying descent . . .': ibid, p.22
'NOW, vere are all your sorrows . . .': Clayton, *The Chase*, p.64
'Like a swallow . . .': Fulford, *The Prince Consort*, p.94

Page 19

'Albert's riding so boldly . . .': Cayzer, *The Royal World of Animals*, p.14
'Come back, young feller . . .': Windsor, *A King's Story*, p.195
'He went like a bomb . . .': Murray Smith, *Magic of the Quorn*, p.5
'Bloody Hell!': Clayton, *Prince Charles, Horseman*, p.110

Page 20

'The whole idea of taking off . . .': Oaksey, *Horse and Hound*, 24 July 1981
'Not being nearly as brave . . .': Clayton, *Prince Charles, Horseman*, p.26
'Loving horses, she rode better . . .': Windsor, *A King's Story*, p.44
'My sister was always . . .': Oaksey, *Horse and Hound*, 24 July 1981

Page 21

'My nerves are a mixture . . .': Princess Anne and Mark Phillips, *Talking About Horses*, p.32
'There is little doubt . . .': Beaufort, *Fox-Hunting*, p.117
'There is this feeling . . .': to author, 3 May 1990

'In a small way . . .': Clayton, *Prince Charles, Horseman*, p.85
'My love of the chase . . .': ibid, p.81
'The Prince is a remarkable person . . .': *Daily Mail*, 12 September 1990
'I went into the mud . . .': Oaksey, *Horse and Hound*, 24 July 1981
'Most of the bad falls . . .': Murray Smith, *Magic of the Quorn*, p.71
trapped under her mount: *Daily Mail*, 15 March 1989

Page 22

flask to lips: Clayton, *Prince Charles, Horseman*, p.116
'Just kiss me': ibid, p.102
'Jokes about the Prince of Wales . . .': Windsor, *A King's Story*, p.196
'There was always so much fuss . . .': *She* Magazine, December 1960, interview with Nancy Spain
'I disappeared over his head . . .': Princess Anne and Mark Phillips, *Talking About Horses*, p.36
'It always amazes me . . .': Beaufort, *Fox-Hunting*, p.117
special stirrup: Murray Smith, *Magic of the Quorn*, p.71
'the dull crack of breaking bones . . .': ibid
'I hope, Sir . . .': Windsor, *A King's Story*, p.164
'Predictably there has been . . .': *Horse and Hound*, 5 July 1990
'To refrain from taking chances . . .': Windsor, *A King's Story*, p.197
'The Duke loved horses . . .': Laura, Duchess of Marlborough, to author, 18 March 1987

Page 23

'Those of us who knew . . .': to author, 8 January 1991
'Like most men . . .': *Daily Mail*, 13 October 1990

Page 24

'At least in matters . . .': Windsor, *A King's Story*, p.196
'When I am approaching . . .': Cayzer, *The Royal World of Animals*, p.121

'Princes learn no art truly . . .': Clayton, *Prince Charles, Horseman*, p.26
'You throw yourself over . . .': ibid, p.100
'There is no thrill . . .': Windsor, *A King's Story*, p.196
'A marvellous-looking girl . . .': Barry, *Royal Service*, p.194
'I drove her to Gloucestershire . . .': ibid, p.219
'a screaming scent . . .': Cayzer, *The Royal World of Animals*, p.23
'a beautiful figure . . .': Longford, Elizabeth, *Victoria, R.I.*, p.165
'We embraced each other . . .': Rhodes-James, *Albert, Prince Consort*, p.82
'Rosy and wind-swept . . .': Longford, *Victoria, R.I.*, p.180

Page 26

'I can't help thinking . . .': Mrs McKee, *The Royal Cookery Book*, p.193. Swedish-born Mrs McKee married a Scot, became cook for Princess Elizabeth at Clarence House in 1951, and stayed on to cook for Queen Elizabeth the Queen Mother.
'I would like to grow up . . .': Cayzer, *The Royal World of Animals*, p.149
'I'm missing my riding . . .': Windsor, *A Family Album*, p.96
'It has come as a great shock . . .': Courtney, *Sporting Royals*, p.23
'He just could not cope . . .': to author, 13 November 1991
'I do not enjoy . . .': Oaksey, *Horse and Hound*, 24 July 1981
'I caused a major row . . .': Princess Anne, *Country Living*, July 1991
Oscar Wilde: Morton, Andrew, *Diana's Diary*, p.69
'I try to look at things . . .': Clayton, *Prince Charles, Horseman*, p.97
'Everyone has views on hunting . . .': Prince Philip, *Down to Earth*, p.16

Page 27

'On a good day . . .': Oaksey, *Horse and Hound*, 24 July 1981

Shooting

I have drawn on accounts of Edward VII's shooting parties from contemporary sources, and was much helped by Aubrey Buxton's memoirs of George VI as countryman. Now that shooting is a controversial subject, those who have provided me with information about Sandringham today inevitably wish to remain anonymous.

Page 31

'If a sportsman . . .': Windsor, *A King's Story*, p.87
'The quintessence . . .': Windsor, *A Family Album*, p.43
'We'd be dressed in tweeds . . .': Barry, *Royal Service*, p.213
'Faded photographs of portly groups . . .': Buxton, Aubrey, *The King in His Country*

Page 32

'A thick brown suit . . .': Ruffer, Jonathan, *The Big Shots*, p.38
'The bright tweeded opulence . . .': Windsor, *A Family Album*, p.41
'Plus 20s with vivid . . .': Cooper, Diana, *The Light of Common Day*, p.161
'My short stalking trousers . . .': Windsor, *A Family Album*, pp.136–7
'Sherlock Holmes!': ibid, p.41
'a trim figure . . .': Buxton, *The King in His Country*, p.84

'The Duke of Edinburgh . . .': Martin, Brian P., *Tales of the Old Gamekeepers*, p.47

Page 33

'A very jolly . . . gun.': Morton, *Diana's Diary*, p.99

Page 34

'He is an excellent and stylish shot . . .': Nickerson, Sir Joseph, *A Shooting Man's Creed*, p.202
'A legend in his own . . .': ibid, p.219
mighty birthday bag: Ruffer, *The Big Shots*, p.37
'The reporters turned up . . .': Barry, *Royal Service*, p.226
'You are despicable': private information to author, 12 November 1991
'I think it is a sad . . .': Princess Anne, *Riding Through My Life*, p.12
'I also discovered . . .': Dean, John, *HRH Prince Philip*, p.53
'Philip, don't get so annoyed': ibid, p.54
'I can't hit a feather . . .': Windsor, *A Family Album*, p.60
'perhaps the best shot . . .': Martin, *Tales of the Old Gamekeepers*, p.47

Page 35

'To me it has become . . .': Junor, Penny, *Charles*, p.103

'I was so shocked . . . do that again.': Martin, *Tales of the Old Gamekeepers*, p.70
'My father's favourite . . .': Windsor, *A Family Album*, p.8
'My two eldest sons . . .': Rose, Kenneth, *King George V*, p.49
'a pair of Purdey guns . . .': documented in royal wedding presents

Page 36

'Everything about him . . .': Windsor, *A King's Story*, p.185

Page 37

'I'll tell the office . . .': Barry, *Royal Service*, p.16
'These days I tend to use . . .': *Shooting Times*, 2–8 August 1990
'One cold and clammy day . . .': Dean, *HRH Prince Philip*, p.54
'Years ago . . .': Devonshire, The Duchess of, *The Estate: A View from Chatsworth*, p.97
'My left arm arched . . .': Windsor, *A King's Story*, p.88
'Take the damned lot!': Buxton, *The King in His Country*, p.27
'Your Royal Hugeness': private information to author, 18 February 1991

Page 38

'The Queen never shoots . . .': Martin, *Tales of the Old Gamekeepers*, p.47
'The dogs are part of . . .': Devonshire, *The Estate*, p.95
'I reckon that about . . .': Nickerson, *A Shooting Man's Creed*, p.175
'She really has marvellous control . . .': to author
'soda water . . . I've been trying . . .': Barry, *Royal Service*, pp.68–9

Page 39

'People keep writing . . .': ibid

Page 40

'He knows the likely . . .': Devonshire, *The Estate*, p.95
'most accomplished retriever . . .': Courtney, *Sporting Royals*, p.105
'The Princess Royal . . .': Nickerson, *A Shooting Man's Creed*, p.202
'She gets everybody organized . . .': Hoey, *Anne, The Princess Royal*, p.135
'He really enjoys . . .': Nickerson, *A Shooting Man's Creed*, p.202
'My feet haven't recovered . . .': Hoey, *Anne, The Princess Royal*, p.164
clumber puppies: *Daily Mail*, 4 January 1991
'This is the shooting . . .': letter from Duchess of Windsor, September 1958
'My mother . . .': Windsor, *A Family Album*, p.7

Page 42

'Philip gets bad arthritis . . .': Martin, *Tales of the Old Gamekeepers*, p.47
'A "Norfolk liar" . . .': to author, 27 November 1991
'Anyone who has the interests . . .': Hastings, Max, *Outside Days*, p.160
'I watched the King . . .': Rose, *King George V*, p.99

Page 43

'Can this terrific slaughter . . .': ibid, p.100
'When I took over . . .': Martin, Brian P., *The Great Shoots*, p.149
'On a shooting day . . .': ibid, p.240
'I don't think . . .': *Shooting Times*, 2–8 August 1990
'There is still a tendency . . .': to author, 18 November 1991
'What they appear to find . . .': Prince Philip, *Down to Earth*, p.8
'Conservation and shooting . . .': Martin, *The Great Shoots*, p.123

Page 44

'The Conservancy was . . .': Prince of Wales, Foreword to *The Big Shots*
'There was no going back . . .': Martin, *Tales of the Old Gamekeepers*, p.44
'The place is literally crawling . . .': Rose, *King George V*, p.293
'There were so many birds . . .': Martin, *Tales of the Old Gamekeepers*, p.45
Lady Fellowes: ibid, p.43
'golden pheasants . . .': Princess Anne, *Riding Through My Life*, p.13
'Some people treat game . . .': Prince of Wales, Foreword to *The Big Shots*
'Judging from your letters . . .': Windsor, *A Family Album*, p.61

Page 46

'Rather wild-looking . . .': Cathcart, Helen, *Sandringham*, p.97

Page 47

'Hurrah! Hurrah! . . .': Duff, *Whisper Louise*, p.74
'A swarm of little brown ears . . .': ibid, p.87
'Wait until your mount . . .': Princess Anne, *Riding Through My Life*, p.13
'I always suspected . . .': Windsor, *A King's Story*, p.88
Duchess of Beaufort: Rose, *King George V*, p.100
bird trays: Robyns, Gwynneth, *Royal Sporting Lives*, p.12

Page 48

'HRH Prince Philip . . .': Nickerson, *A Shooting Man's Creed*, p.202
'It must be very difficult . . .': Prince of Wales, Foreword to *The Big Shots*

Page 49

'A band of gamekeepers . . .': Duff, *Whisper Louise*, p.76
'They wore bowler hats . . .': Windsor, *A Family Album*, p.42
'Always a-spying . . .': Duff, *Whisper Louise*, p.75
'A dark green loden . . .': Windsor, *A Family Album*, p.33
'Father had a lighter suit . . .': Martin, *Tales of the Old Gamekeepers*, p.45
'The King is having good sport . . .': Rose, *King George V*, p.293
'Only just more mobile . . .': Duff, *Whisper Louise*, p.76
'The coverts which he planted . . .': ibid

Page 50

'Sandringham is not really . . .': private information to author, December 1990
'Prince Charles is known . . .': ibid, February 1991
'Sandringham and all it stands for . . .': ibid
'It was in the Glamis pattern . . .': Buxton, *The King in His Country*, p.29

Page 51

'He's a much better . . .': to author, 12 June 1991
'It is part of keeping . . .': to author, Norfolk, 12 November 1991
'When I first went . . .': Barry, *Royal Service*, p.72
'The guns would go out . . .': ibid, p.213

Page 52

'Luncheon out shooting . . .': Ponsonby, Sir Frederick, *Recollections of Three Reigns*, p.201
'Heaven defend my stomach . . .': Fulford, *The Prince Consort*, p.91
'He stops shooting . . .': ibid
'Sometimes when I am sitting . . .': Buxton, *The King in His Country*, p.5
'great chunk of bread . . .': Martin, *Tales of the Old Gamekeepers*, p.45
'We were out from . . .': Dean, *HRH Prince Philip*, p.55
'Mother did our big . . .': Martin, *Tales of the Old Gamekeepers*, p.45
'As solemn and grave . . .': Cayzer, *The Royal World of Animals*, p.40
'This may have been . . .': Ponsonby, *Recollections*, p.201

Page 53

'The great function . . .': Cathcart, *Sandringham*, p.78

Page 54

'It is quite wrong . . .': Prince Philip, *Down to Earth*, p.172
'Today it was a harsh . . .': Buxton, *The King in His Country*, p.103
'There are plenty of duck . . .': ibid, p.52

Page 55

'There is poignancy . . .': ibid, p.68
'It is not customary . . .': Cathcart, *Sandringham*, p.145
'He came into the Palace . . .': Crawford, Marion, *The Little Princesses*, p.99

Page 56

'I think there is a special . . .': *Observer*, 19 August 1980
'Simple access in wetland . . .': *Sunday Express Magazine*, 10 June 1990
'A little beach chalet . . .': Faucigny-Lucinge, *Un Gentilhomme cosmopolite*, p.230, author's translation
'They got up from their nest . . .': ibid

Page 57

'The royals love anything . . .': Barry, *Royal Service*, p.72
'But what's controversial . . .': *The Times*, 17 May 1988
'We must protect the land . . .': Prince of Wales, *A Vision of Britain*, p.79
'Very long and handsome . . .': Faucigny-Lucinge, *Un Gentilhomme cosmopolite*, p.229
'Edwardian and cosy': ibid, p.119

Page 58

'It's a wicked lie!': Cathcart, *Sandringham*, p.123
'A little boy was born . . .': Crawford, Marion, *The Queen Mother*, p.65
'I'll fix those bloody clocks.': Donaldson, Frances, *Edward VIII*, p.177

Page 59

'He really is the greatest . . .': Daly, Macdonald, *Royal Dogs*, p.14
'I am Caesar . . .': Caesar, *Where's Master?*
'Horrible, yapping, snapping . . .': to author, 14 November 1991

Page 60

'All of us who . . .': *The Times*, 26 December 1964
'A deuce of a way . . .': Cathcart, *Sandringham*, p.142
'very prettily decorated': ibid, p.123
'Our journeys to Wolferton . . .': Windsor, *A Family Album*, p.66
'It's an inherited place . . .': *Elizabeth R*, 40th anniversary film, 1992
'The five o'clock family . . .': Cathcart, *Sandringham*, p.111
'I arrived just as . . .': Duff, *Whisper Louise*, p.112
'We are not very interested . . .': Morrow, Anne, *The Queen*, p.211
'I too depend . . .': Windsor, *A Family Album*, p.9
'Family tea . . .': McKee, *Royal Cookery Book*, p.163
'an enormous table . . .': to author, 13 February 1991
'her Scotch skill . . .': Asquith, Lady Cynthia, *The Family Life of the Queen Mother*, p.42

Page 62

'The average . . .': Martin, *Tales of the Old Gamekeepers*, pp.71–2

Page 47 [column 2 header]

'How anyone can say . . .': *Elizabeth R*, 40th anniversary film, 1992
'"The Sporting" has determined . . .': Devonshire, *The Estate*, p.90
'I think this is absolutely . . .': Clayton, *Prince Charles, Horseman*, p.99
'Why would you add . . .': ibid

'It was my job at . . .': McKee, *Royal Cookery Book*, p.122

'The Queen so liked . . .': to author, France, 27 November 1990

'We gave him a golden . . .': Nickerson, *A Shooting Man's Creed*, p.107

'In one corner ducks . . .': Cathcart, *Sandringham*, p.153

'I realized that . . .': Nickerson, *A Shooting Man's Creed*, p.202

Page 63

'Is it *raining* . . .': Windsor, *A King's Story*, p.83

'I had this altered . . .': Windsor, *A Family Album*, p.59

'In the entrance hall . . .': Cathcart, *Sandringham*, p.203

'I have seen an equerry . . .': Crawford, *The Little Princesses*, p.97

'Just as we topped . . .': Windsor, *A King's Story*, p.269

Farming

For this section I owe a debt of gratitude to Peter Jones and his studies of royal farms in *Farmer's Weekly*. He was also generous enough to allow me to research his photographic archives. Dr Graham Haslam, then Archivist at the Duchy of Cornwall, helped me to understand Prince Albert's major contribution. Ralph Whitlock's 1980 book *Royal Farmers* provided useful background information. I also studied twenty-five years of Prince Philip's work for the environment, including his 1987 Dimbleby Lecture 'Living off the Land'. Prince Charles has also given many speeches on agriculture and the environment. The rest was gleaned with wellington boots on.

Page 67

Sparkling Natalie/Pretty Polly: Whitlock, Ralph, *Royal Farmers*, p.243

'Her Majesty is very interested . . .': *Farmer's Weekly*, 18 December 1987

'We agriculturalists of England': Fulford, *The Prince Consort*, p.88

'That damned farmer': Rhodes-James, Robert, *Albert, Prince Consort*, p.142

'Who identifies with agriculture . . .': Prince Philip, *Down to Earth*, p.47

Page 68

rotary milking parlour: Whitlock, *Royal Farmers*, p.124

'The appearance of a Turkey carpet . . .': ibid, p.79

'Untreated milk . . .': ibid, p.126

'The Jersey herd produces . . .': *Farmer's Weekly*, 18 December 1987

'There is a lot more . . .': Prince Philip, 'Living off the Land', p.12

Page 69

'She has never lost her interest . . .': Whitlock, *Royal Farmers*, p.13

Duchy of Lancaster: information from Chancellor of Duchy of Lancaster, 26 November 1991

'Responsibility for Sandringham . . .': Whitlock, *Royal Farmers*, p.14

Page 70

'I am never out of the field . . .': ibid, p.61

'from paintings to machines . . .': Bennett, *King Without a Crown*, p.199

'Prince Albert was clearly . . .': Prince of Wales, *Watercolours*, p.20

'People came to wonder . . .': Devonshire, Duchess of, *The Estate*, p.39

'Poor cow': Prince of Wales at model farm, Institut National d'Agriculture, Grignon-Thiverval, France, 9 November 1988

'because it is a traditional British breed . . .': *Farmer's Weekly*, 21 September 1990

'The milking parlour is nowhere . . .': to author, May 1991

Records for Prince Consort's dairy: Whitlock, *Royal Farmers*, p.80

Page 71

'The decision to retain the Jersey . . .': ibid, p.14

'The plague of one's life . . .': Fulford, *The Prince Consort*, p.89

'A place of one's own . . .': Rhodes-James, *Albert, Prince Consort*, p.140

'That ambivalent relationship . . .': Whitlock, *Royal Farmers*, p.14

'I call them the "Hoover" herd': *Farmer's Weekly*, 6 November 1987

Page 72

'We can't grow enough good grass . . .': *Farmer's Weekly*, 4 December 1987

'I swapped architecture for agriculture . . .': ibid

'partly forester . . .': Fulford, *The Prince Consort*, p.89

'Although not strictly speaking . . .': Whitlock, *Royal Farmers*, p.15

Page 73

'People can afford the cattle . . .': *Farmer's Weekly*, 18 December 1987

'These have created their own problems . . .': Prince Philip, 'Living off the Land', p.11

'There are too many chickens . . .': *Daily Mail*, 8 November 1988

'If they are about . . .': *Farmer's Weekly*, 18 December 1987

Page 74

'The Prince turning somersaults . . .': Fulford, *The Prince Consort*, p.95

'Something I don't encourage . . .': Princess Anne, *Riding Through My Life*, p.14

Page 75

'The Princess does not like riding . . .': to author, Chantilly, France, June 1991

Wintered at Broadfield Farm: *Farmer's Weekly*, 21 September 1990

'So that's what hay . . .': Pope-Hennessey, James, *Queen Mary*, p.598

'My mother loathed the country . . .': Pope-Hennessey, James, *A Lonely Business*, p.213

'Prince Charles with crab-apple-red . . .': Beaton, Cecil, *The Parting Years*, p.108

'We've still got a few tonnes left . . .': *Farmer's Weekly*, 21 September 1990

'Many other farmers . . .': *Daily Telegraph*, 15 March 1990

'There is no doubt that . . .': speech to organic farming conference, Gloucestershire, reported in *Daily Mail*, 7 January 1989

'It may well be technically possible . . .': Prince Philip, 'Living off the Land', p.10

Page 76

'We burn no straw here . . .': *Farmer's Weekly*, 21 September 1990

'Stubble burning after the harvest . . .': Prince Philip, 'Living off the Land', p.13

Highgrove house farm details: *Farmer's Weekly*, 21 September 1990

Page 77

'When Zara and William . . .': Morton, Andrew, *Diana's Diary*, p.71

'That's knotgrass . . .': *The Times*, 3 August 1990

'alpine meadow . . . yellow rattle': *Country Living*, January 1991

'We are wholly given up . . .': Fulford, *The Prince Consort*, p.80

Page 78

'If you look around . . .': *The Times*, 3 August 1990

'Large-scale soil erosion . . .': *Daily Telegraph*, 7 January 1989

'It is now that farmers . . .': *Daily Mail*, 7 January 1989

'It needs a hard . . .': *Farmer's Weekly*, 21 September 1990

'It is no secret . . .': *Daily Telegraph*, 17 November 1988

'The greatest difficulties . . .': *The Times*, 3 August 1990

'The conversion period . . .': *Daily Telegraph*, 15 March 1991

'We always start with . . .': *The Times*, 3 August 1990

'There is definitely . . .': *Farmer's Weekly*, 21 September 1990

Page 80

'It is going to become . . .': Prince Philip, 'Living off the Land', p.11

'An East Anglian farmer . . .': *The Times*, 3 August 1990

'It's all down to . . .': *Farmer's Weekly*, 21 September 1990

Page 81

'When you looked at . . .': *The Times*, 3 August 1990

'Highgrove Stoneground wholemeal . . .': information from Tesco, 23 July 1990

'It makes excellent bread . . .': *Farmer's Weekly*, 21 September 1990

'Consumers are increasingly showing . . .': *Daily Mail*, 7 January 1989

'What you are doing . . .': *The Times*, 3 August 1990

'We are learning as we go . . .': *Farmer's Weekly*, 21 September 1990

'The Prince's vision . . .': ibid

'Farming is not like . . .': *Daily Telegraph*, 15 March 1991

Page 84

Material for the Duchy of Cornwall section came from studying archives at the Duchy of Cornwall, Buckingham Gate; through reading the *Duchy Review*, the internal publication; from a visit to the farm of John and Rosemary Berry; and from the book celebrating 650 years of the Duchy of Cornwall in 1987.

Page 85

'The most profitable plan . . .': Whitlock, *Royal Farmers*, p.235

'I must confess . . .': ibid

His reforming zeal: Duchy of Cornwall archives platinum wrist-watch: Cathcart, *Sandringham*, p.219

'threshing the straw . . .': Princess Anne, *Riding Through My Life*, p.13

'We need to get away from . . .': *Daily Telegraph*, 15 March 1991

'Much of the increase . . .': Prince Philip, 'Living off the Land'

Page 86

Sandringham estates details: Sandringham estate guidebook, p.27
'I don't think we can . . .': *Farmer's Weekly*, 6 November 1987
As Duke of Cornwall: information from Duchy, January 1992
'It should provide an example . . .': Gill, *The Duchy of Cornwall*, p.9
'The Duchy is above all . . .': ibid
'Your efforts coincide . . .': letter to Berrys shown to author

Page 87

'The Duchy is fair . . .' (and following quotes): information from John and Rosemary Berry to author, May 1991
'It is much more difficult . . .': *Farmer's Weekly*, 21 September 1990
'He does not expect . . .': *The Times*, 3 August 1990
'It is for you to give . . .': Rhodes-James, *Albert, Prince Consort*, p.115
'Big machines can reshape . . .': Prince Philip, 'Living off the Land', p.13
'The intricacy of hedgerows': Verey, Rosemary, *A Countrywoman's Notes*, p.11
'most self-respecting animals . . .': ibid, p.47
'She makes gardening seem . . .': ibid, p.10

Page 88

'There is no reason . . .': *Farmer's Weekly*, 21 September 1990
'Early in my reign . . .': Windsor, *A King's Story*, p.283
'That umbrella! . . .': ibid, p.284
'This is a period . . .': Gill, *The Duchy of Cornwall*, p.9
'This is where the farming policy . . .': *Farmer's Weekly*, 21 September 1990

Page 89

inspiration was John Higgs: Gill, *The Duchy of Cornwall*, p.75
'The major problem facing all landowners . . .': ibid, p.263

Page 90

'It is the farmer . . .': ibid, p.9
'The Prince welcomes it . . .': *Farmer's Weekly*, 21 September 1990
'His corn was nearly identical . . .': to author, September 1990

Page 91

'How long does it take . . .' (and following quotes): *Farmer's Weekly*, 21 September 1990

Page 92

'It must be saved': Morrow, Ann, *The Queen Mother*, p.145
'This is good strong land . . .': *Farmer's Weekly*, 27 November 1987
'Her Majesty loves walking . . .': ibid
'I always looks at the islands . . .': Richards, Clive, *The Queen Mother and her Family at Home in Caithness*, p.58
'It is either battered by gales . . .': Prince of Wales, *Watercolours*, p.98
'Castle of Mey looks . . .': Richards, *At Home in Caithness*, p.46

Page 94

'The weather rules our lives . . .': *Farmer's Weekly*, 27 November 1987
'The uncertainties of . . .': Richards, *At Home in Caithness*, p.65
emptied the water out: ibid
'They need that almost . . .': *Farmer's Weekly*, 27 November 1987
William M'Combie: Whitlock, *Royal Farmers*, p.167

Page 95

'She takes an active interest . . .': *Farmer's Weekly*, 27 November 1987
'The Prince considers this . . .': *Farmer's Weekly*, 21 September 1990
'That will blow the cobwebs away': to author, December 1990
Balmoral's Soay sheep: Whitlock, *Royal Farmers*, p.172
Spanish merinos: ibid, p.54
'We try to organize the grazing . . .': *Farmer's Weekly*, 27 November 1987
'The peace and tranquillity . . .': Richards, *At Home in Caithness*, p.65
'Stop the car a moment . . .': ibid, p.8

Page 98

'will ye no' come back again': ibid, p.19
The Primrose Lady: ibid, p.8
Dad's Army on the telly . . .': to the author, 18 June 1990
'If you can farm in Caithness . . .': *Farmer's Weekly*, 27 November 1987

Page 99

'It is impossible not to feel awed . . .': Foreword to *The Rainforests, A Celebration*
'The bonniest plaid in Scotland . . .': Clark, Ronald, *Balmoral*, p.86
'The fact that this part . . .': Prince of Wales, *Watercolours*, p.54
'Tough, extremely willing . . .': Prince Philip, *Competition Carriage Driving*, p.16
'Land strung out like this . . .': *Farmer's Weekly*, 20 November 1987

Page 102

Mar Lodge: observation by author, May 1991
'vast and incongruous . . .': Prince of Wales, *Watercolours*, p.86
'like something you'd put . . .': *Daily Mail*, 27 April 1991
'That'll be an absolute ruination . . .': ibid

Page 103

'The planting and replanting . . .': Fulford, *The Prince Consort*, p.89
deer management: Balmoral Castle guidebook, p.27
At Sandringham: Sandringham estate guidebook, pp.27–8
'The massive oak trees . . .': Whitlock, *Royal Farmers*, p.15

Page 104

drystone walls/Norman Haddow: *Daily Telegraph*, 1 January 1992
'Noble, for 15 years . . .': observation by author, May 1991
'Very fine and . . .': Balmoral Castle guidebook, p.2
'neeps': Whitlock, *Royal Farmers*, p.173
'Did you bring the honey . . .': Barry, *Royal Service*, p.50
'had a habit of . . .': *Farmer's Weekly*, 20 November 1987
'It was largely as a . . .': Whitlock, *Royal Farmers*, p.15

Page 105

'Blondes at Balmoral': ibid
'Heinz 57 . . .': ibid, p.186

Page 106

'We are hoping to develop . . .': *Farmer's Weekly*, 20 November 1987
H.M. Sheridan/venison burgers: author's observation, May 1991
'The management of land . . .': Whitlock, *Royal Farmers*, p.16

I soon realized the link between the Queen Mother's horticultural style and that of her grandson. This was reinforced by Prince Charles's discussions of gardening in the ITV film *In Private in Public* of 1986, and by comments made by his gardening 'gurus', Rosemary Verey, Dr Miriam Rothschild and Lady Salisbury, author of a detailed study of the Queen Mother's gardens.

'Our coal production figures . . . Ribena': Whitlock, *Royal Farmers*, p.154
Sandringham's fruit farm: Sandringham estate guidebook, p.27

Page 107

'Gangs of female labour . . .': Whitlock, *Royal Farmers*, p.13
Appleton Farm: Sandringham estate guidebook, pp.23–4
'A square of gladioli . . .': Salisbury, *The Gardens of Queen Elizabeth the Queen Mother*, p.144
'I must have scent here . . .': *Country Living*, January 1991
'The Queen Mother loves . . .': Salisbury, *Gardens of the Queen Mother*, p.124
'They shared a place . . .': ibid, p.123
'We loved the sloping garden . . .': Alice, Princess, Countess of Athlone, *For My Grandchildren*, p.72

Page 108

'I had always rather wanted . . .': *In Private in Public* film
'When I first saw . . .': ibid
'It's rather fun . . .': ibid
'In checked trousers . . .': Salisbury, *Gardens of the Queen Mother*, p.118

Page 109

'Lovage makes interesting soup . . .': *In Private in Public* film
'The layout of the walled vegetable garden . . .': *Country Living*, January 1991
'Two apple tunnels . . .': *In Private in Public* film
experimental fruit station: *Daily Telegraph*, 6 April 1989
'It is virtually impossible . . .': ibid
'I saw Sunset . . .': Shewell-Cooper, W. E., *The Royal Gardeners*, p.38
'No chemical fertilizers . . .': Salisbury, *Gardens of the Queen Mother*, p.166
'Nobody likes them': TV interview with Alastair Burnet

Page 110

'In the midst of . . .': Shewell-Cooper, *The Royal Gardeners*, p.32
'with a barrow of . . .': *Country Living*, January 1991
'It's a disgrace . . .': to author, 18 June 1990
orchard of Cox's orange pippins: Whitlock, *Royal Farmers*, p.112
'We had to go over . . .': Cathcart, *Sandringham*, p.105
glasshouses demolished: Sandringham guidebook, p.29

Page 112

'Our Queen Mother, as Queen . . .': Shewell-Cooper, *The Royal Gardeners*, p.38
'What about growing . . .': ibid, p.25
'cabbages rolling . . .': Salisbury, *Gardens of the Queen Mother*, p.167
'the brilliant emerald . . .': ibid, p.169
'I was also thinking . . .': *In Private in Public* film

Page 113

'I've yet to see . . .': ibid
Charles's first garden: Shewell-Cooper, *Royal Gardeners*, p.51
'The two princesses . . .': Salisbury, *Gardens of the Queen Mother*, p.29

Although I am indebted to those in racing circles who have given me so much time and off-the-record help, the most illuminating material in this section came from the film about the Queen's race horses (shown on TV in 1977) made by Lord Brabourne and narrated by the Queen's racing manager, then Lord Porchester, now Lord Carnarvon. The quotations I have taken from the film show the Queen's knowledge of stud farming and breeding and her boundless enthusiasm for the subject. I am grateful to the office of the Queen's racing manager for help in checking information and for the patience of a former owner in explaining the intricacies of stallion syndication.

Page 119

'My philosophy about racing . . .': Queen's horses film
'one of my earliest memories . . .': Princess Anne, *Riding Through My Life*, p.11
'out of Perdita . . .': Queen's horses film
'Both descendants from Feola . . .': ibid
'A complete expert . . .': Cayzer, *The Royal World of Animals*,, p.80

Page 120

'Genealogies, historical and dynastic . . .': Crawford, *The Little Princesses*, p.28
'Was Arithmetic . . .': ibid
'There was a special building . . .': Windsor, *A King's Story*, p.52
'Nothing ever pleased him so much . . .': Fitzgerald, Arthur, *Royal Thoroughbreds*, p.181
'It seemed that she . . .': Queen's horses film
'The crowd was tremendously friendly . . .': ibid
'the greatest day of our lives . . .': Fitzgerald, *Royal Thoroughbreds*, p.257
'If it were not for . . .': Lacey, *Majesty*, p.332
'If you seat her . . .': to author, Paris, 27 November 1990

Page 122

'While my grandfather . . .': Windsor, *A King's Story*, p.51
horses still lined up: Crawford, *The Little Princesses*, p.17
'Is all well . . .': Longford, *Elizabeth R*, p.191
'I won't put you in the tower . . .': *Sunday Citizen*, 21 March 1965
'One couldn't really be sad . . .': Queen's horses film
'all the horsey books': Crawford, *The Little Princesses*, p.17
'I suppose I first . . .': Queen's horses film
Big Game at Beckhampton: Fitzgerald, *Royal Thoroughbreds*, pp.205–19
'I'd never felt . . .': Queen's horses film
Dr Charles Brook: Fitzgerald, *Royal Thoroughbreds*, p.224
'Well, Aureole was . . .': Queen's horses film

'I noticed the Princess's . . .': Sheridan, *From Cabbages to Kings*, p.104

Page 114

'The Princess showed me how . . .': ibid
own miniature tools: Rhodes-James, *Albert, Prince Consort*, p.142
'What I want to do . . .': *In Private in Public* film
'And while it is growing . . .': Rhodes-James, *Albert, Prince Consort*, p.143
'He was an absolute slave-driver . . .': Crawford, *The Little Princesses*, p.45
'It is a very tranquil place . . .': Windsor, *A Family Album*, p.139
'I now love, it is true . . .': ibid, p.79

Horses

'I shall take a great interest . . .': Fitzgerald, *Royal Thoroughbreds*, p.202
'In my father's time . . .': Queen's horses film

Page 123

'It isn't a profitable venture . . .': *Elizabeth R*, 40th anniversary film, 1992

Page 124

'Our conversations go on . . .': *Sunday Citizen*, 21 March 1965
'Because Prince Andrew . . .': Queen's horses film
'Princess Margaret once showed me . . .': to author, May 1991

Page 125

Dunfermline and Willie Carson: Fitzgerald, *Royal Thoroughbreds*, p.263
'It is always interesting . . .': *Daily Mail*, 25 March 1987
'Being there in January . . .': Princess Anne, *Riding Through My Life*, p.12
'Well, I thought it was . . .': Queen's horses film
'Temperament one has to watch . . .': ibid
'Princess Elizabeth must have a natural eye . . .': Longford, *Elizabeth R*, p.187
'I've quite a good memory . . .': Queen's horses film

Page 126

'For most of the racing period . . .': *The Times*, 18 May 1991
14 brood mares: Lord Carnarvon's office to author, 17 December 1991

Page 127

'The Queen has been unlucky . . .': to author, 3 June 1990
'This is a commercial decision . . .': *The Times*, 18 May 1991
These were bought: *Daily Mail*, 25 March 1983
'Porchester's a bit of a spiv . . .': to author, November 1991

Page 128

Lillie Langtry . . .: Cayzer, *The Royal World of Animals*, p.31
'From my experience of racing . . .': Queen's horses film

Page 129

'Whenever I back one . . .': Lemoine and Forbes, *The Sporting Royal Family*, p.30
'Isn't it a shame . . .': Crawford, Marion, *Happy and Glorious!*, p.48

'Everything has to be done properly . . .': *Country Living*, January 1991
'Very therapeutic, weeding . . .': *In Private in Public* film
'A daffodil!': Hartnell, Norman, *Silver and Gold*, p.124
'I went out to the vegetable garden . . .': ibid

Page 115

'Her pink hands are folded meekly . . .': Beaton, *The Strenuous Years*, p.144
create a phial of oil: Morton, *Diana's Diary*, p.67
'Be thy hands anointed . . .': Lacey, Robert, *Majesty*, p.239
'I put my heart and soul . . .': *In Private in Public* film
'When we were about to leave . . .': Morton, *Diana's Diary*, p.68

Over the Sticks: I am grateful for the information supplied by Sir Martin Gilliat at Clarence House, but the chapter is based mainly on the author's observations at National Hunt meetings, where the Queen Mother's energy and enthusiasm can be witnessed first hand. Michael Clayton was helpful about Prince Charles's jump racing, which is discussed in Clayton's book about the Prince as horseman. I also drew on Lord Oaksey's interview with Prince Charles on the eve of the royal wedding in *Horse and Hound*.

The Argonaut . . .: Grand Military Gold Cup at Sandown Park, 9 March 1990
'Always a great favourite . . .': *Daily Mail*, 25 March 1987
plump, polished Daimler: *Racing Post*, 9 March 1990
'The soldier's Grand National': Clayton, *Prince Charles, Horseman*, p.130
regimental band: author's observation, 9 March 1990

Page 130

left the family christmas, *Daily Express*, 27 December 1950
'I've always loved it . . .': *Daily Mail*, 25 March 1987
'Her real passion . . .': ibid
'Why do you keep . . .': Cayzer, *The Royal World of Animals*, p.78

Page 131

Raymond Glendenning: *Sunday Express*, 3 December 1950
'It's terribly sad . . .': ibid
The two Queens: author's observation, 9 March 1990

Page 132

Queen Mother watched her grandson compete: Clayton, *Prince Charles, Horseman*, p.130
'If people could just understand . . .': ibid, p.127
'the greatest jumping trainer': *Horse and Hound*, 28 February 1991
'I am so pleased . . .': Morrow, *The Queen Mother*, p.206

Page 133

'I suppose there must be . . .': *Daily Mail*, 25 March 1987
'She loves racing so dearly . . .': *Daily Express*, 19 February 1976
'And he bets like smoke': to author, 10 December 1990
'The Blower': *Daily Mail*, 17 March 1965
'My Scottish logic': *Sunday Citizen*, 21 March 1965
'I read *The Sporting Life* . . .': *Daily Mail*, 25 March 1987
'The Queen Mother has an eye': *Daily Mail*, 17 March 1965
'She won't run . . .': ibid

Page 134

'We must get her century up': to author, 16 November
1991
200th and 300th winners: letter from Sir Martin Gilliat
to author, 26 November 1991
'Keep Columbus away . . .': Campbell, *Royal Horses*,
p.104
Sir Martin's detailed reports: *Daily Mail*, 1 February
1967
'I've always loved them . . .': *Daily Mail*, 27 March
1987
'It happens to everyone . . .': *Horse and Hound*, 24 July
1981
'The highly infectious bug . . .': ibid
'the indescribable, tingling . . .': Clayton, *Prince
Charles, Horseman*, p.131
'Talking to people out hunting': ibid, p.128
'They were headline news . . .': *Horse and Hound*, 24
July 1981
'To ride a winner . . .': ibid

Page 135

'He yearns to ride in the Grand National': Barry, *Royal
Service*, p.143
a nervous lady Diana Spencer: Seward, Ingrid, *Diana*,
p.148
Good Prospect . . . misjudged the stride: Cayzer, *The
Royal World of Animals*, p.110
'All he did was . . .': Barry, *Royal Service*, p.144
'For any ordinary amateur rider . . .': *Horse and
Hound*, 24 July 1981
'It is a funny sort of mixture . . .': ibid
'The horse, he insisted . . .': Barry, *Royal Service*,
p.144
'The awful, awful tragedy . . .': Clayton, *Prince
Charles, Horseman*, p.132
'I cried and I cried . . .': Cayzer, *The Royal World of
Animals*, p.126
'has given me as much satisfaction . . .': Princess
Anne, *Riding Through My Life*, p.233
'Nothing quite compares . . .': ibid, p.218

Page 136

'Well. That's racing': *Daily Mail*, 27 March 1987

'She was always the same . . .': *The Times*, 25 March
1987

Page 138

'A nasty, dangerous pastime . . .': Clayton, *Prince
Charles, Horseman*, p.127
'My father's letters . . .': Windsor, *A Family Album*,
p.63
knocked out for half an hour: Windsor, *A King's Story*,
p.197
'The very strong opinion . . .': ibid, p.198
'I enjoyed the whole atmosphere . . .': *Horse and
Hound*, 24 July 1981

Page 139

'Racing is perhaps her favourite . . .': *Daily Express*,
19 February 1976
'It's the one sport that's left . . .': *Daily Mail*, 25
March 1987

Page 140

Four-in-hand: Although I have referred to Prince
Philip's book *Competition Carriage Driving*, the basis of
this chapter was watching Prince Philip in action at the
Windsor Horse Shows in 1990 and 1991. I realized then
that the Queen and Philip, as much as the horses, are
part of a team. They have a close family relationship to
the show in their 'backyard' and to its cast of military
characters, led by Sir John Miller.

'It was easier than last year': *Horse and Hound*, 23 May
1991
'Prince Philip knows I'm a scrap merchant . . .':
Cayzer, *The Royal World of Animals*, p.96
'They are getting better at it!': ibid

Page 141

'I am not sure . . .': to author, 21 May 1991
'A very keen driving man . . .': Prince Philip,
Competition Carriage Driving, p.8
heather-decked landau: Campbell, *Royal Horses*, p.87
'She had tied . . .': Crawford, *The Little Princesses*,
p.11

'a horse fiend': *Sunday Citizen*, 21 March 1965
'Don't ask me, ask Owen': Crawford, *The Little
Princesses*, p.48
'Jock, who taught me more . . .': Campbell, Judith,
The Queen Rides, p.11
'own dear Scottish sociable': ibid, p.83

Page 142

Valkyrie: Cayzer, *The Royal World of Animals*, p.136
'A splendidly old-fashioned . . .': Prince Philip,
Competition Carriage Driving, p.11
'Over we went . . .': ibid, p.107
local agricultural show: Balmoral Castle guidebook,
p.27
give up polo: Courtney, *Sporting Royals*, p.74
'I reckoned that fifty . . .': Prince Philip, *Competition
Carriage Driving*, p.10

Page 143

'As luck and Cupid . . .': Everingham, Barry, *The
Adventures of a Maverick Princess*, p.69
'this driving business': Prince Philip, *Competition
Carriage Driving*, p.10

Page 145

'I am sure they were bulls . . .': ibid, p.108
'People often say . . .': ibid, p.109
'Let no one believe . . .': ibid, p.15

Page 146

converted milk float: Balmoral Castle, May 1991
'She was a lovely lady . . .': *Daily Mail*, 27 April 1991
crisp military titles: Royal Windsor Horse Show
programme

Page 147

'As luck would have it . . .': Prince Philip, *Competition
Carriage Driving*, p.106
'it does not follow . . .': ibid, p.15
'The art of handling horses . . .': ibid, p.102

Balmoral

The passages at the beginning of each chapter come
from Prince Charles's tale of *The Old Man of Lochnagar*,
which expresses, with irony and affection, the Prince's
deep love for the Scottish Highlands. I read widely
from Victorian memoirs and those of more recent
times. I tramped in fair and foul weather round
Balmoral, Ballater and Muick and talked to recent
Balmoral guests. I am grateful to them for entrusting
their observations to me.

Page 151

'Means pigs . . .': Balmoral Castle guidebook, p.10
'The Queen likes . . .': to author, Ballater, 8 May
1991
'It is a marvellous life . . .': Junor, Penny, *Charles*,
p.193
'The whole family . . .': Clark, Ronald, *Balmoral,
Queen Victoria's Highland Home*, p.122
'Come along . . .': Mitchell, Charles, *The Queen's
Horses*, p.110

Page 154

'Picnics to a royal . . .': Barry, *Royal Service*, p.18
'She loves getting dirty . . .': Crawford, *The Little
Princesses*, p.50
'HRH Prince Charles . . . Plain chicken . . .': to
author, 18 January 1991
'Prince Philip designed . . . at lunch the royals . . .':
Barry, *Royal Service*, p.65

'They would find a big boulder . . .': Crawford, *The
Little Princesses*, p.90
'Once when a picnic . . .': Ponsonby, *Recollections*,
p.97
'ate plum pudding . . . he was a countryman . . .':
Crawford, *The Little Princesses*, p.34

Page 155

'Countless feet . . .': Prince of Wales, *Watercolours*,
p.72

Page 156

'great characters in those days . . .': ibid, p.76
archetypal Balmoral picnic: Millar, Delia, *Queen
Victoria's Life in the Scottish Highlands*, p.118
'The luncheon baskets . . .': Buxton, *The King in His
Country*, p.76
'At Balmoral the royals . . .': Dean, *HRH Prince
Philip*, p.90
'Wearing an old friend . . .': Barry, *Royal Service*, p.19
'so decently long . . .': Windsor, *A Family Album*,
p.127
taken on his death: private information to author,
Paris, April 1989
'The Balmoral shooting lunch . . .': Crawford, *The
Little Princesses*, p.91
'Hard-boiled egg . . .': Mrs McKee, *The Royal
Cookery Book*, p.201

Page 157

'The old man . . .': Prince of Wales, *The Old Man of
Lochnagar*, p.2
name means literally: Loch Muick handbook, Scottish
Wildlife Trust, p.36
'Making wild work . . .': Clark, *Balmoral*, p.14

Page 158

'Like all mountains . . .': Prince of Wales,
Watercolours, p.64
'The curse of . . .': *Today*, 9 August 1988
'A busy repacking . . .': Buxton, *The King in His
Country*, p.76
'What astonishes me . . .': Prince Philip, *Down to
Earth*, p.82
'The beauty of . . .': Foreword to Loch Muick
handbook
'When October came . . .': Crawford, *The Little
Princesses*, p.47

Page 159

'People complain about . . .': *Sunday Express
Magazine*, 10 June 1990
'Judging by the . . .': Prince Philip, *Down to Earth*,
p.82
'You spend the . . .': *Sunday Express Magazine*, 10
June 1990
'This is appalling . . . you are my heroine . . .': to
author, May 1991

'All Britain now contends . . .': *The Field*, January 1991
'Scudding clouds . . .': Prince of Wales, *Watercolours*, p.72

Page 160

'There is a lack . . .': ibid
'Modern civilized . . .': Prince Philip, 'Living off the Land', p.14
'Let the Queen of . . .': Longford, Elizabeth, *Victoria, R.I.*, p.265
'It is a hideous . . .': *Sunday Express Magazine*, 10 June 1990
'A *close* time . . .': Clark, *Balmoral*, p.134
'She doesn't even own . . .': Duchess of Devonshire to author, 13 July 1990

Page 161

'Fine pair of hiking . . .': Crawford, *The Little Princesses*, p.50
'The Prince goes up . . .': Barry, *Royal Service*, p.19

Page 162

'I seldom walk . . .': Millar, *Queen Victoria's Life*, p.42
'even her family . . .': Clark, *Balmoral*, p.107
'When Her Majesty . . .': Mitchell, *The Queen's Horses*, p.106
'My God, I was stiff . . .': Barry, *Royal Service*, p.19
'I've only got to . . .': Clark, *Balmoral*, p.132
'chum-up': Bradford, Sarah, *King George VI*, p.82
'an introduction to . . .': Parker, John, *Prince Philip*, p.213
'One thing in . . .': Bradford, *King George VI*, p.302
'Arrived at the Glassalt . . .': Buxton, *The King in His Country*, p.79
set off round the loch: Bennett, *King Without a Crown*, p.158

Page 163

'It seemed to offer . . .': Buxton, *The King in His Country*, p.72
'I'm exhausted . . .': Barry, *Royal Service*, p.96
'countless herds of hills . . . The grandest, wildest . . .': Clark, *Balmoral*, p.74
'The scenery all around . . .': ibid, p.65
'This place is . . .': ibid, p.87
'Like a little squirrel . . .': Rhodes-James, *Albert, Prince Consort*, p.232
'The paradise of . . .': ibid, p.32
'Beautiful wooded hills . . .': Clark, *Balmoral*, p.25
'If I were not . . .': Longford, *Victoria, R.I.*, p.222
'Year of Revolutions': Elizabeth Longford to author, 5 June 1990
'to enter a better . . .': Bennett, *King Without a Crown*, p.158
'She hated leaving . . .': Clark, *Balmoral*, p.136

Page 164

anguish of shared grief: Junor, *Charles*, p.147
George VI was picnicking: Bradford, *King George VI*, p.344
'On foot she made . . .': Crawford, *The Little Princesses*, p.86

Page 165

'As far as I can . . .': Holden, Anthony, *Charles*, p.35
'Then at last . . .': Buxton, *The King and His Country*, p.73

Page 167

'Whether there was . . .': Ponsonby, *Recollections*, p.95
'The people are more . . .': Millar, *Queen Victoria's Life*, p.22
'Scotch air . . .': Harris, Paul, *By Appointment*, p.1
'You can't imagine . . .': to author, May 1991

'in great ecstasy': Fulford, *The Prince Consort*, p.178
'The footmen smell of whisky . . .': Millar, *Queen Victoria's Life*, p.141
'For the staff . . .': Dean, *HRH Prince Philip*, p.89

Page 168

'As I know . . .': *Sunday Express Magazine*, 10 June 1990
'I went to Balmoral . . .': Princess Anne and Mark Phillips, *Talking About Horses*
'The jumbled chaos . . .': Buxton, *The King in His Country*, p.79
'When we had nearly . . .': Clark, *Balmoral*, p.34

Page 169

'I am first . . .': ibid, p.40
'in full Highland dress . . .': Windsor, *A King's Story*, p.315
'patient and slightly martyred . . .': Crawford, *The Little Princesses*, p.47
'My Saxe-Coburg great-grandfather . . .': Windsor, *A King's Story*, p.315
'Bloody hard work': to author, 9 December 1991
'You never really see the Queen . . .': to author, 25 May 1991
'Thistles are in such abundance . . .': Clark, *Balmoral*, p.56
'This tartan has got to go . . .': Bradford, *King George VI*, p.170

Page 170

'I was enchanted . . .': Wentworth-Day, J., *HRH Princess Marina, Duchess of Kent*, p.94
'The amount of whisky consumed . . .': Ponsonby, *Recollections*, p.151
'stalactitic sort of . . .': Clark, *Balmoral*, p.55
'a smell of wood fire . . .': Princess Alice, *For My Grandchildren*, p.77
deers' teeth as a necklace: Bennett, *King Without a Crown*, p.123
'My contribution to the traditional . . .': Windsor, Duchess of, *The Heart has its Reasons*, p.239

Page 171

'large and deep enough . . .': Courtney, *Sporting Royals*, p.107
a couple of Philip's royals: Parker, *Prince Philip*, p.217

Page 172

'The Queen does not wish . . .': Clark, *Balmoral*, p.77
Queen Victoria's 'private memories': Windsor, *A King's Story*, p.16
'promised to become a good shot . . .': Crawford, *The Little Princesses*, p.90
one of the best heads: Courtney, *Sporting Royals*, p.112
'In the evening . . .': Crawford, *The Little Princesses*, p.90
'She was absolutely furious . . .': Barry, *Royal Service*, p.261
'I, naughty man . . .': Courtney, *Sporting Royals*, p.107
'made her shake . . .': Clark, *Balmoral*, p.14
moved by their beauty: Bennett, *King Without a Crown*, p.296

Page 173

'Very clever . . .': Prince Philip, *Competition Carriage Driving*, p.16
Sir Derek Keppel: Ruffer, *The Big Shots*, p.122
'It is such durable . . .': Dean, *HRH Prince Philip*, p.91
'Lilibet wore the plus-four . . .': Crawford, *The Little Princesses*, p.90

Page 174

'Crawling on hands and knees . . .': Clark, *Balmoral*, p.68

'Such sport in the Highlands . . .': ibid, p.70

Page 175

'The weather is awful . . .': ibid, p.112
'The exertion and difficulty . . .': Millar, *Queen Victoria's Life*, p.21
'We scrambled up . . .': CLark, *Balmoral*, p.35
'They had no idea . . .': Prince of Wales, *Watercolours*, p.52

Page 176

'Her Majesty is a dead shot . . .': Mitchell, *The Queen's Horses*, p.102
'No one was really kinder . . .': Ponsonby, *Recollections*, p.59

Page 177

'Ye blithering idiot . . .': Ruffer, *The Big Shots*, p.122

Page 178

'Definitely sited . . .': Prince of Wales, *Watercolours*, p.60
'All my sketches have been made . . .': Prince of Wales, *An Exhibition of Watercolour Sketches*, p.13
'Ever since he was a small boy . . .': Prince of Wales, *Watercolours*, p.6
'like every serious artist . . .': Prince of Wales, *An Exhibition*, p.8
'when I found photography . . .': ibid, pp.12–13
Miss 'Mipsy' Peebles: Holden, Anthony, *Charles*, p.70
'I'd tried to paint . . .': Roberts, Jane, *Royal Artists*, p.205

Page 179

Arthur George Carrick: Hamilton, Alan, *The Real Charles*, p.161
'pale rather translucent colours . . .': Prince of Wales, *Watercolours*, p.28
'He draws inspiration . . .': Prince of Wales, *An Exhibition*, p.9

Page 180

'They represent . . .': ibid, p.12
'If not, you must not blame . . .': Clark, *Balmoral*, p.64
'One of the things . . .': Prince of Wales, *Watercolours*, p.14

Page 181

'What is there more beautiful . . .': Roberts, *Royal Artists*, p.102
'How well is the character . . .': Prince of Wales, *Watercolours*, p.10
Landseer . . . Loch Laggan: Millar, *Queen Victoria's Life*, p.33
'Her Majesty sitting in the middle . . .': Clark, *Balmoral*, p.79
'I am afraid . . .': Millar, *Queen Victoria's Life*, p.35

Page 182

Queen Alexandra's painting room: Roberts, *Royal Artists*, p.167
'the light is so marvellous . . .': Junor, *Charles*, p.234
'bask in the beauties of Tuscany . . .': Prince of Wales, *Watercolours*, p.6
'He takes his painting . . .': private information to author, January 1991
'I have a passion for Italy . . .': Prince of Wales, *An Exhibition*, p.12
'really, I must own . . .': Millar, *Queen Victoria's Life*, p.12
'made a beautiful sketch . . .': ibid, p.47
'We sat quite still . . .': Clark, *Balmoral*, p.35
'Landseer's pastel pictures . . .': Prince of Wales, *Watercolours*, p.64

Page 183

'richness of colour . . .': Millar, *Queen Victoria's Life*, p.109

'The shortage of personal time . . .': Prince of Wales, *An Exhibition*, p.9

'I very quickly discovered . . .': ibid, p.12

'The dear Highlands . . .': Millar, *Queen Victoria's Life*, p.31

Page 184

'It has revolutionized my life . . .': Prince of Wales, *Watercolours*, p.12

'Sitting on a hill in Scotland . . .': *Sunday Correspondent*, 11 November 1990

'When I am feeling decidedly gloomy . . .': Prince of Wales, *Watercolours*, p.74

Page 185

'As brown as brown ale . . .': Salisbury, The Marchioness of, *The Gardens of Queen Elizabeth the Queen Mother*, p.151

'Queen Elizabeth loves her fishing . . .': ibid

'At Balmoral . . .': McKee, *The Royal Cookery Book*, p.49

'I just go along . . .': Morrow, Ann, *The Queen Mother*, p.218

'I always used to say . . .': Barry, *Royal Service*, p.193

'She always wears that hat . . .': to author, Paris, 9 December 1990

'The Queen Mother throws . . .': Richards, Clive, *The Queen Mother and her Family at Home in Caithness*, p.30

Page 188

'I can pray . . .': Barry, *Royal Service*, p.131

Charles shown how to cast: Hamilton, *The Real Charles*, p.121

'I find it highly therapeutic . . .': *Sunday Times*, 7 April 1991

fishing lodge on the River Hofsa: Courtney, *Sporting Royals*, p.115

'If anyone asks you . . .': Barry, *Royal Service*, p.83

'I love a gun . . .': Clark, *Balmoral*, p.124

George VI learned trout fishing: Wheeler-Bennett, John W., *King George VI*, p.43

'One of his wedding presents . . .': Dean, *HRH Prince Philip*, p.90

'The Duke burst in . . .': ibid

'Once, after two whole days . . .': McKee, *Royal Cookery Book*, p.49

Page 189

'There is nothing more exciting . . .': *Daily Express*, 20 April 1989

'This is what kept me late!': Courtney, *Sporting Royals*, p.125

Page 190

'He's a good fisherman . . .': Barry, *Royal Service*, p.131

'It was made for a honeymoon . . .': Sutherland, *Royal Homes and Gardens*, p.115

'It is the nicest place . . .': ibid, p.113

'Here we spent . . .': Princess Alice, *For My Grandchildren*, p.72

Page 191

'The River Muick rippled . . .': Crawford, *The Little Princesses*, p.62

a modern kitchen: Salisbury, *The Gardens of the Queen Mother*, p.154

'The staircases are lined . . .': Crawford, *The Little Princesses*, p.31

'Big log fires . . .': Dean, *HRH Prince Philip*, p.62

Lady Diana Spencer's needlepoint: Barry, *Royal Service*, p.218

'I think she thought . . .': ibid, p.193

Lillie Langtry tobogganing . . . : Harris, Paul, *By Appointment: The Story in Pictures of Royal Deeside and Balmoral*, p.6

'I wish an artist could . . .': Millar, *Queen Victoria's Life*, p.48

Page 192

'The lake was like a mirror . . .': ibid, p.48

'Not a very good fisherman . . .': Ponsonby, *Recollections*, p.59

'Expeditions on Sunday afternoons . . .': Buxton, *The King in His Country*, p.75

'I was given the task . . .': ibid, p.80

'Security! . . .': to author, 5 May 1991

Page 193

'a vast tea . . .': Princess Alice, *For My Grandchildren*, p.72

'We saw many of the relations . . .': ibid

'She lives in a unique haven . . .': Talbot, Godfrey, *Queen Elizabeth the Queen Mother*, Foreword

'She likes being on her own . . .': to author, 9 January 1991

Page 194

'burn of the Scots pine': Loch Muick handbook, p.36

'Somebody must have laid out . . .': Prince of Wales, *Watercolours*, p.58

'an abandoned little house . . .': Crawford, *The Little Princesses*, p.91

'delightfully papered . . .': Millar, *Queen Victoria's Life*, p.132

'snug and warm': Bennett, *King Without a Crown*, p.212

'invariably one's without . . .': Barry, *Royal Service*, p.257

Page 195

'We are all well . . .': Clark, *Balmoral*, p.14

'speaking of happy days . . .': Millar, *Queen Victoria's Life*, p.131

'much the better and livelier': ibid, p.132

royal bungalow 'Tamarisk': Gill, Crispin, (ed), *The Duchy of Cornwall*, p.132

'Played with Lilibet . . .': Pope-Hennessey, James, *Queen Mary*, p.546

'don't mind serving . . .': Barry, *Royal Service*, p.65

'The royal family always enjoy . . .': ibid, p.58

'I remember seeing Lilibet . . .': Crawford, *The Little Princesses*, p.68

'It is made of . . .': Salisbury, *The Gardens of the Queen Mother*, p.166

'We used to have our tea . . .': Shewell-Cooper, W. E., *The Royal Gardeners*, p.30

Page 196

'Not a doll's house . . .': Asquith, Lady Cynthia, *The King's Daughters*, p.48

'An endless source of pleasure . . .': Salisbury, *The Gardens of the Queen Mother*, p.50

Page 198

'We've got everything except . . .': Sheridan, Lisa, *From Cabbages to Kings*, p.62

Peter Phillips and rolling pin: Longford, *Elizabeth, R.I.*, p.298

Prince Charles and sundial: Shewell-Cooper, *The Royal Gardeners*, p.50

'the children love dusting . . .': Lady Peacock, *The Queen and Her Children*, p.26

'Not a speck of dust . . .': Sheridan, *From Cabbages to Kings*, p.62

'live there without . . .': Millar, *Queen Victoria's Life*, p.44

Page 199

'What I call . . .': Nickerson, *A Shooting Man's Creed*, p.87

'winged magic on the wild moor!': ibid, p.84

'The King was a most beautiful shot . . .': Buxton, *The King in His Country*, p.70

'every bird that fell . . .': Rose, *King George V*, p.288

'There he was in some . . .': Buxton, *The King in His Country*, p.74

'The King, as the . . .': Dean, *HRH Prince Philip*, p.90

Page 200

'It is likely that . . .': Prince of Wales, *The Field*, April 1991, p.62

'The grouse are . . .': Nickerson, *A Shooting Man's Creed*, p.144

'In the beginning . . .': Dean, *HRH Prince Philip*, p.75

'The grouse raised its . . .': Crawford, *The Little Princesses*, p.62

Page 201

'would wind diagonally up . . .': Burton, *The King in His Country*, p.76

four-wheel drive vehicles: at Balmoral, May 1991

'I have a vivid picture . . .': Buxton, *The King in His Country*, p.75

'Frankly I loathed . . .': Dean, *HRH Prince Philip*, p.54

'There are no signs . . .': Clark, *Balmoral*, p.89

Page 202

'The birds were shy . . .': Millar, *Queen Victoria's Life*, p.25

'Grouse were plentiful . . .': Dean, *HRH Prince Philip*, p.90

'There is no doubt . . .': Nickerson, *A Shooting Man's Creed*, p.139

'I happen to believe . . .': Prince of Wales, *The Field*, April 1991

'conservation through wise use': Game Conservancy Council

Page 203

'the so-called "balance of nature" . . .': Prince Philip, 'Living off the Land', p.6

'Ptarmigan are curiously unreliable . . .': Buxton, *The King in His Country*, p.79

'Really! I do all the climbing . . .': ibid

'The grouse is the most . . .': Nickerson, *A Shooting Man's Creed*, p.84

'You are under test . . .': ibid, p.136

'The Prince of Wales, who . . .': ibid, p.135

Page 204

'While I paused . . . [and following paragraphs]': Buxton, *The King in His Country*, p.81

Page 205

'The ghillies were grand people . . .': Dean, *HRH Prince Philip*, p.90

'It was wonderful . . .': Millar, *Queen Victoria's Life*, p.42

'Whenever I am shooting . . .': Nickerson, *A Shooting Man's Creed*, p.84

INDEX

(Page numbers in *italic* refer to illustrations.)

224